NEURAL SUITCASE TELLS THE TALES OF MANY MINDS

NEURAL SUITCASE TELLS THE TALES OF MANY MINDS

PURNENDU GHOSH

PARTRIDGE

A Penguin Random House Company

To order additional copies of this book, contact
Partridge India
000 800 10062 62
orders.india@partridgepublishing.com

www.partridgepublishing.com/india

Contents

The most interesting interdisciplinary conversations and the best idea sessions are held inside our mind. Mind, our neural suitcase, tells the tales of so many minds. The tales are beautiful, moral, vulnerable, quiet, chaotic, hungry, obese, real, fictional, memorable, forgetful, creative, curious, humorous, trustworthy, biased, wise, foolish, friendly, hateful, meaningful, and blind. Our mind asks many interesting questions. Mind also builds castles in the air. It is for us to put foundations under these castles. It is for us to pack our neural suitcase sensibly as our mind determines the size of our world.

For

Arun and Namita Ghosh

Arun Kumar Ghosh, my father-in-law met Namita Banerjee, his would be wife when he was 25 and she was 17. They got married and were together for 65 years. One was truly the better half of the other. They understood each other so well. Lately their biggest worry was when one goes what will happen to the other. One went quietly in the wee hours of one fine morning. It happened far from his place, at our place. It was a natural event of life. But it was not 'natural' for the one who remained.

When I told my ma-in-law that he is gone, she did not say much. Not that she was expecting it to happen. Her outwardly emotions were not overwhelming. She did not cry much at that moment. At that moment she did not want to believe that someone so close can go so quietly, never to return. She perhaps understood the reasons of his quietness. If one doesn't know if he is going how he can tell others about his departure. Even if he knows he would not wish for a more painful 'final separation' happen for the one who remains. Even when one knows, one wishes it not to be the final separation. At that moment I could see 'vacuum', not tears, in her eyes. She did not have the courage to touch her companion of so many years. She, instead, touched her daughter, touched me. She did not want to believe that everything was really over. In one sense everything was over. In another sense few things are never over.

Journeys begin. The past remains. The future promises to come. The present shuttles in-between the two. When we think of the future we like to think of it filled with hope. We welcome the new beginning, because in it we see the fruition of our hopes and aspirations. Man goes. His progeny lives to fulfill those hopes and aspirations.

The sun sets in to rise again. The morning sun brings new hopes.

The empires of the future are the empires of the mind.

Winston Churchill

A mind that is stretched by a new experience can never go back to its old dimensions.

Oliver Wendell Holmes, Jr.

The test of a first-rate intelligence is the ability to hold two opposed ideas in mind at the same time and still retain the ability to function.

F. Scott Fitzgerald

You can chain me, you can torture me, you can even destroy this body, but you will never imprison my mind.

Mahatma Gandhi

Any active sportsman has to be very focused; you've got to be in the right frame of mind. Cricket is in the foreground, the rest is in the background.

Sachin Tendulkar

My mind rebels at stagnation.

Arthur Conan Doyle

The face is the mirror of the mind, and eyes without speaking confess the secrets of the heart.

St. Jerome

Minds, like bodies, will often fall into a pimpled, ill-conditioned state from mere excess of comfort.

Charles Dickens

I wonder can our finite minds ever truly understand such things as eternity and infinity.

Jane Goodall

PREFACE

It is difficult to write on a subject that is brilliant and widely liked. Mind is such a subject. So much goes on inside our neural suitcase. Our beautiful mind presents itself in so many facets and in multiple dimensions. It is moral, vulnerable, quiet, chaotic, hungry, obese, real, fictional, memorable, forgetful, creative, curious, humorous, tearful, trustworthy, biased, wise, foolish, friendly, hateful, meaningful, blind, and questioning. We need to keep wide open our mind. We need to pack it sensibly, as the world is overloaded with information and over-burdened mind generates cognitive stress.

In writing this book I have tried to read the mind of others. I have borrowed thoughts of many other beautiful minds. This book is not the outcome of research work, nor it is written in the format of a research paper. This book can only give perspective on few subjects that interest me. I am sure the readers can read much more than what is written in this book.

I could not have written this book had I not received the support of the following individuals.

I am most grateful to my colleague and the first reader Subimal Sinha-Roy for his guidance and constant encouragement. He has helped me to understand the subtleties of mind.

I am most grateful to my wife Indrani for so many things that can't be listed here. I only wish to say that she let me do what my wandering mind wanted to do. She has taken the initiative, as always, to design and paint the cover of this book.

My daughter Paushali is my constant source of strength. She has a beautiful mind; a mind full of VIBGYOR colours, the pristine colours' dreams are made of.

I am appreciative of the efforts made by my son Apalak for planting the writing seed in me and see that the seed gets enough nourishment to grow.

I am most grateful to my 'external mind' Mr Internet (it has almost taken human proportions) for taking me to where my mind wanted to go. I am grateful to all the beautiful minds who shaped and guided my fluid thoughts. I am happy that my thoughts are still fluid.

Purnendu Ghosh
Jaipur, June 2014

-1-

NEURAL SUITCASE

The most interesting interdisciplinary conversations happen inside your mind. Inside your mind, the best ideas are generated. It is your mind where the greatest Adda sessions are held. Mind can't survive without Adda. Adda is talking about anything and everything under the sun at any time of the day. Mind works 24x7, and so our Adda sessions. Adda keeps the mind vibrant as during Adda sessions both idle gossip and cerebral culture are practiced.

Mind, our neural suitcase, determines the size of our world. Our neural suitcase needs repair and maintenance. It appreciates and depreciates. We might lose it if we don't use it. There is nothing like empty mind. So much goes on inside the mind even when it is supposedly 'empty'.

How you conduct your talks with yourself is thus important. Even when you are talking with someone else, you are, in fact, talking to yourself. Mental conversations go on uninterrupted when you are working, studying, reading, watching, walking and eating. You are constantly judging people even when you don't know who that person is and how your judgment matters to you or that person.

My mind wanders. When I told one of my friends that my mind wanders he advised me to let it wander. He said that a wandering mind values others' experiences and allows things to remain as they are. The mind wanders simply because consciousness changes its reference points every moment. It is natural for a wandering mind to experience spontaneous, unfocused, and unconstrained thoughts. Who knows when in those 'unfocussed and unconstrained' moments one may find a gem of a thought?

Science says that in mundane moments of life, our brain shifts to a default mode. This default mode has a role in generating spontaneous internal thoughts. Researchers say that the mind's default network becomes more active during daydreaming. Building castles in the air is thus not a waste of time. "If you have built castles in the air, your work need not be lost; that is where they should be. Now put the foundations under these," advises Henry David Thoreau. There are also many people who are great supporters of focused minds. They say a focused mind is vital for meditation. But my mind wanders during meditation; more so when I think of keeping it focused.

Some people believe that focus has distraction built into it. I would like to believe that imposed restrictions of any kind are not good for meditation. I want to believe that a wandering mind helps me to discover new ways of seeing the reality. Distraction of some kind, perhaps, helps us in finding new ways as we love variety, surprise and adventure of the unknown.

Like mind wandering, daydreaming seems to be a good idea, because it brings in more resources for the mind to work on. T E Lawrence said that people who dream with eyes wide open make their dreams come true for everyone. I also liked the observation of actor Sam Anderson, who said, "The truly wise mind will harness, rather than abandon, the power of distraction. Unwavering focus—the inability to be distracted—can actually be problematic. It suggests that restlessness, in fact, can be advantageous." The message of the wise is that the inability to be distracted can actually be problematic. In other words, restlessness is advantageous. The daydreamers are not necessarily wastrels. John Tierney (1) sees a lot of merit in daydreaming.

Our spiritual and religious traditions tell us that the quieter you become the more you can hear. We are advised to 'watch the thought, feel the emotion, and observe the reaction'. This is exactly what psychologists Mathew Killingworth and Daniel Gilbert experimentally did. They studied people's ongoing thoughts, feelings and actions using smart phones (2). They asked simple questions like 'What are you doing right now?', 'Are you thinking about something other than what you're currently doing?' Their purpose was to understand cognitive and neural bases of mind wandering.

The studies of Killingworth and Gilbert tell us that our mental lives are pervaded, to a remarkable degree, by the 'non-present'. We spend much of our time in the non-present. We spend nearly half of our waking hours on thinking about something other than what is happening in front of us. The conclusion Killingworth and Gilbert have drawn is that a wandering mind is an unhappy mind.

On the other hand, a group of researchers think that a wandering mind can protect you from immediate perils and keep you on course toward long-term goals. They say that a wandering mind keeps the individual's larger agenda fresher in mind. A wandering mind is good for creative activities.

Psychologist Jonathan Schooler (3) rightfully reminds us that just daydreaming is not enough. "Letting your mind drift off is the easy part. The hard part is maintaining enough awareness so that even when you start to daydream you can interrupt yourself and notice a creative thought." Schooler's research shows that mind-wandering can lead people to creative solutions of problems, which could make one happier in the long term.

We all know that we must not pass too much of our time on idle deliberations. It is absolutely understandable that during flow (a feeling of spontaneous joy, while performing a task) one's subjective experience of time is altered. It is also true that being happy makes one more creative. But it is also a fact that it is not easy to control mind wandering. At any given moment so much information about the external world enters our brain. How can we stop them from entering our consciousness?

Going to the Himalayas is one way of experiencing solitude, but it is too bothersome. Moreover, such solitude may not serve the desired purpose. Can one leave his mind elsewhere for the sake of avoiding storms? Keeping a quiet mind amidst storm is not easy, as is remaining an individual in a crowd. The ability to think about what isn't happening is a significant cognitive achievement, but it comes at an emotional cost, say Killingworth and Gilbert.

The extent of mind wandering depends upon the activity we are engaged in at that point of time. Mind wandering is not bad if it wanders during boring tasks. If during a lecture, students are more interested in the opposite sex sitting nearby rather than the lecture, whose fault is it? John Tierney rightly said, it depends on the lecture. If the lecture is interesting, one would not want his brains to miss vital knowledge. Otherwise, the brain would naturally like to be engaged in the more important agenda of finding a mate.

Often we are engaged in useless and futile conversations with ourselves. We often want to send our mind on a brief vacation. Minds that are on short vacation often yield very useful results. You may send your mind on short vacation, but don't let anyone eat your head.

'Don't eat my head' is a very commonly used expression. Interestingly, the usage of the term – 'eating the head' - may very well have been inspired from real instances found in nature. We are talking about sea squirts. These little animals belong to the same group as humans. In this sense sea squirts can be called our ancestors. The sea squirt larvae resemble tadpole larva. It doesn't evolve into fish or amphibian. Instead, this little animal swim to find a good place to rest. Once it finds a good solid surface, it attaches itself there. It wants to take a long rest, and thus remains there permanently.

This distant cousin of our perhaps was too 'smart'. It said to itself, 'What will I do with my head if I don't have to move?' This smart thought made our distant cousin to believe that there is nothing wrong if one eats its own head. In fact, it did so, and started eating its own head. As a result of eating its own head it didn't grow; it remained larva. We have learnt an important lesson from our distant cousin.

Those of us who think that head is a useless organ need remedial measures. Another lesson we have learnt from sea squirt is that if we let someone eat our head, it means we have given the person enough indication that our head has become useless, and one can eat it. So preserve your head with all your might. Don't let anyone eat it. And don't ever forget that your mind is one of your most important assets. If you lose it, you are lost. Your signature is not in your hand but in your mind. Your hand will not work unless your brain allows it to.

Brain works and mind think. Brain is physical. Mind enables one to have awareness and intentionality towards his environment and to have consciousness. Mind does things that enable consciousness, perception, thinking, feeling, judgment, and memory. The brain-mind questions relate the association of the mind with the brain. The brain, the control centre of the central nervous system, is responsible for thought.

Since we can think, we can make sense of things around us. Because we can think, we can generate our own ideas and can also make sense of others' ideas. We can take decisions. We can imagine. We can recognize the patterns and understand their significance. Since we have a mind we can make sense of the world in a meaningful way. Since we have a mind we have the ability of memory. It is because of this ability we can preserve, retain, and subsequently recall, knowledge, information or experience.

Imagination evokes novel situations. Imagination can project possible future. It also can 'see' things from many angles. It is the 'mind's eye' that sees and generates images and ideas.

The brain-mind relationship has been understood from three perspectives. One perspective says that the mind exists independently of the brain. Another perspective holds that mental phenomena are identical to neuronal phenomena. However, another perspective holds that only mental phenomena exist. Philosopher and cognitive scientist Daniel Dennett argues that there is no such thing as 'mind'. There is simply a collection of sensory inputs and outputs. These sensory inputs and outputs are processed through different kinds of 'software' running in parallel.

Whatever are the subtle differences between these concepts, my simple mind doesn't want to get into it at this point of time. I only want to understand if we have mind we need to use it and stretch it. We need to understand, as Ralph Waldo Emerson understood, that little minds have little worries, big minds have no time for worries.

Big or small, we are prisoners of our own mind. Our world is the size of our mind. We only can free our mind. We only can change our mind.

Brain is a physical entity that is there to interpret our senses, initiate our body movements, and control our behavior. Brain has many parts. Each part has a special function. All the parts of the brain work together (4). The three basic units of the brain are the forebrain, the midbrain, and the hindbrain. The hindbrain controls the body's vital functions such as respiration and heart rate. The hindbrain includes the upper part of the spinal cord, the brain stem, and a wrinkled ball of tissue called the cerebellum. The cerebellum coordinates movement and is involved in learned rote movements. The uppermost part of the brainstem is the midbrain, which controls some reflex actions and is part of the circuit involved in the control of eye movements and other voluntary movements. The forebrain is the largest and most highly-developed part of the human brain. It consists primarily of the cerebrum and the structures hidden beneath it. The cerebrum holds our memories, allows us to plan, enables us to imagine and think. It is the source of intellectual activities.

The cerebrum is divided into two halves. The two halves communicate with each other through nerve fibers. These two halves are functionally quite different from each other. For example, the left half possesses the ability to form words, while the right half controls many of our abstract reasoning skills. The right half of the cerebral hemisphere primarily controls the left side of the body, and the left side primarily controls the right side. It means when one side of the brain is damaged, the opposite side of the body is affected; a stroke in the right side of the brain can leave the left arm and leg paralysed.

Each cerebral hemisphere can be divided into sections, or lobes, each of which specializes in different functions. The two frontal lobes, which lie directly behind the forehead, do much of the work when you plan a schedule, imagine the future, or use reasoned arguments. In the rearmost portion of each frontal lobe is a motor area, which helps control voluntary movement. A nearby place on the left frontal lobe called Broca's area allows thoughts to be transformed into words.

The two sections behind the frontal lobes, called the parietal lobes, are at work to enjoy the taste, aroma, and texture of the food. The forward parts of these lobes, just behind the motor areas, are the primary sensory areas that receive information about temperature, taste, touch, and movement from the rest of the body.

The occipital lobes, the two areas at the back of the brain are at work when you look at the words and pictures. These lobes process images from the eyes and link that information with images stored in memory. Damage to the occipital lobes can cause blindness.

Our sense of music is through the activities of the temporal lobes that lie in front of the visual areas and nest under the parietal and frontal lobes. At the top of each temporal lobe is an area responsible for receiving information from the ears. The underside of each temporal lobe plays a crucial role in forming and retrieving memories, including those associated with music. Other parts of this lobe seem to integrate memories and sensations of taste, sound, sight, and touch.

Most of the actual information processing in the brain takes place in the cerebral cortex, commonly known as the 'gray matter'. The structures that lie between the spinal cord and the cerebral hemisphere determine our emotional state and also modify our perceptions and responses depending on that state, and allow us to initiate movements that we make without thinking about them.

A pearl sized part of our brain, hypothalamus, does many important things like waking us up in the morning, controlling our adrenaline flow during an exam or an interview. The thalamus that lies near the hypothalamus is a major information track that goes to and from the spinal cord and the cerebrum. The basal ganglia are clusters of nerve cells surrounding the thalamus. They are responsible for initiating and integrating movements.

Amygdala, an almond-shaped structure in the brain is an indicator of our social networking capability (5). Located deep within the temporal lobe of the brain, amygdala is involved in the processing of emotions such as fear, anger and pleasure. Amygdala is also responsible for determining what memories are stored and where the memories are stored in the brain. Neuroscience researchers have shown that nonhuman primate species with larger social groups tend to have greater amygdala volumes. Animal studies have also shown that damage to the amygdala impairs social functioning.

In one study, researchers wanted to know how the size and complexity of the social network correlate with the size of amygdala. The participants were asked questions like "how many people they kept in regular contact with and how many groups those individuals belonged to." The researchers, on the basis of brain images, found that volunteers who had bigger and more complex social networks had larger amygdala volumes. This observation was found to be independent of the age of the volunteers or their perceived social support or life satisfaction. The results thus ruled out the possibility that happiness is the underlying causal factor that links the size of this brain structure in an individual to their number of friends.

Researchers have pointed that the job of amygdala is to signal to the rest of the brain when something that you're faced with is uncertain. "For example, if you don't know who someone is, and you are trying to identify them, whether it is a friend or a foe, the amygdala is probably playing a role in helping you to perform all of those tasks." Researchers also pointed out that amygdala size was not related to the quality of the relationships or to whether or not people enjoyed socializing.

How the amygdala contributes to social network is still a mystery. It is not clear if a big amygdala is a cause or a consequence of having a large social network. It is not yet clear if certain people are born with larger amygdala and therefore, create bigger social networks, or does the amygdala grow as one gains more friends and foes. Probably, it is both.

The primary functional unit of the brain is a cell called the neuron. All sensations, movements, thoughts, memories, and feelings are the result of signals that pass through the neurons. Neurons consist of three parts. The cell body contains the nucleus, where most of the molecules that the neuron needs to survive and function are manufactured. Dendrites extend out from the cell body like the branches of a tree and receive messages from other nerve cells. Signals then pass from the dendrites through the cell body and may travel away from the cell body down an axon to another neuron, a muscle cell, or cells in some other organ. The neuron is usually surrounded by many support cells. Some types of cells wrap around the axon to form an insulating sheath. This sheath can include a fatty molecule called myelin, which provides insulation for the axon and helps nerve signals travel faster and farther. Axons may be very short, such as those that carry signals from one cell in the cortex to another cell less than a hair's width away. Or axons may be very long, such as those that carry messages from the brain all the way down the spinal cord.

Scientists have learned a great deal about neurons by studying the synapse—the place where a signal passes from the neuron to another cell. When the signal reaches the end of the axon, it stimulates the release of tiny sacs. These sacs release chemicals known as neurotransmitters into the synapse. The neurotransmitters cross the synapse and attach to receptors on the neighbouring cell. These receptors can change the properties of the receiving cell. If the receiving cell is also a neuron, the signal can continue the transmission to the next cell.

Acetylcholine, a key neurotransmitters, makes cells more excitable; it causes glands to secrete hormones. GABA (gamma-aminobutyric acid), a neurotransmitter that tends to make cells less excitable; it is an important part of the visual system. Serotonin is a neurotransmitter that controls sleep, temperature regulation. Dopamine is an inhibitory neurotransmitter involved in mood and the control of complex movements.

To know how the brain works we need to know the map of the brain. The idea of the connectional map is to integrate anatomy, neuronal activity, and function. We need to draw the wiring diagram of the brain to understand how the brain functions. The wiring diagram of the human brain will also shed light on disorders that are presumed to originate from faulty wiring.

The human brain is an intricate network of 100 billion neurons and 100 million synapses. Obviously, the wiring diagram of the brain is not easy to draw. Scientists have been able to draw the invaluable wiring diagram of C. elegans, a microscopic worm containing a mere 302 neurons. It took them more than a decade to draw the diagram of this tiny worm. In spite of the difficulties envisaged, scientists are hopeful of completing the human brain's wiring diagram. The technological advance in neuroscience is one of the reasons of their optimism.

The classical approach to understand the working of a neurological system requires identification and connectivity of neurons that are involved in defined behaviours. The individual neurons are then excited to understand their role in influencing behaviour.

As we move from sponges and anemones to primates and humans, the neurological complexity increases several folds. It is much more difficult to identify neurons and then perturb individual neurons in the human brain. It is also difficult to record neuronal activity with enough spatial and temporal resolution. To address the challenges of spatial and temporal resolution, the development of multi-channel microelectrode recording arrays allows researchers to accurately measure the activity of multiple neurons at a single time.

Brain imaging techniques reveal how specific mental tasks selectively activate particular brain regions. By observing the brain activity one can actually read the mind of the subject. One can tell if one is thinking about a face or a place.

The brain imaging technique started with ventriculography procedure (drilling holes into the patient's skull and injecting air into the lateral ventricles of the brain to obtain accurate x-ray images). Less invasive and more precise methods were then developed. The techniques include electroencephalography (EEG, measuring electrical movement by connecting electrodes to the patient's scalp to read brain activity), computerised axial tomography (CAT, a computer-aided x-ray technology), positron emission tomography (PET, injecting radioactive tracers into the bloodstream and then tracing them into the brain), magnetic resonance imaging (MRI, using magnetic fields and radio waves to create brain maps).

The ability to observe both the structures and specific functions is possible using functional magnetic resonance imaging (fMRI). The technique provides high resolution, noninvasive information of neural activity. It is a tool to understand which region of the brain is working, for how long, and for a particular task. The brain regions that work harder need more oxygen. fMRI measures blood oxygenation levels as it varies with the varying metabolic demands of active neurons. Changes in demand for oxygen by the neural tissues reflect their underlying activity.

Not only, the diagnosis of neurological disorders is possible with fMRI; it can also read the brain's reaction to foreign stimuli, and this forms the basis of drug development to correct certain disorders. fMRI development has also expanded the boundaries of cognitive neuroscience to non-health-related knowledge about human motivation, reasoning, and social attitudes. fMRI can reveal hidden thoughts, such as lies, truths or deep desires, say behavioural neuroscience researchers.

Researchers say that there are areas in the brain which respond to indoor and outdoor scenes depicting the layout of space. These areas, however, do not respond at all to faces. There are also regions that respond strongly when subjects view photographs of faces but weakly to other images. fMRI can tell which particular part of the cortex is used when we see or think about faces, and what cortical region is used during the perception and imagery of places.

In one experiment, subjects were asked by the researcher to look at the photographs of places or faces. Then the same subjects were asked to make mental images (with their eyes closed) of the same faces and scenes (6). The brain scan data revealed, "a striking similarity between regions activated during (mental) imagery and those activated during (visual) perception." Since it is difficult to stop or restrict imagining while seeing, the interpretation of the data seems a challenging exercise.

The human brain is not complete at the time of birth. Much of the brain weight increase is during the first three years after birth. Dynamic changes take place in the human brain throughout life, probably for adaptation to our environment.

The average newborn human brain weighs less than 400 g. A typical human adult brain weighs about 1400 g. After reaching an age of about 20 years, the brain weight starts to decline, slowly but steadily.

The conventional view was that we are born with a set number of neurons, and we are hardwired in a certain way. It was also the view that we lose connections and neurons as we age, and finally, the brain falls apart. But the new understanding about brain functioning is that the human brain can shape, form, eliminate and strengthen new connections throughout life.

Neuroscientists say that neurons can change their connectivity, morphology and strength of the connections in their early as well later stages of life in response to environment and experience. Research has also shown that brain has "use it or lose it" approach to neurological maintenance.

Synapses are essential to neuronal function. They permit a neuron to pass an electrical or chemical signal to another cell. There is substantial rearrangement and pruning of synapses during brain development and growth. Experience influences the rewiring of synapses during brain maturation. This rewiring is not just limited to the young brain.

The young brain is more plastic than the adult brain. Synapses are added as well as lost; the peak is between six and eight months postnatal. The initial synapses formation is independent of stimulation. But if the synapses are not used, the brain eliminates them. Conversely, more often a connection is used, stronger it becomes in a physical sense, with more dendritic spines connecting to one another and a stronger net connection over time.

For the brain to be plastic there must be genes responsible for it. The capacity of the brain to change its connections is dependent on genetic regulation. This new understanding raises a number of interesting questions. For example, "how the brain can be so plastic and yet still retain memories over time." To answer such questions one would have to address the underlying genetics. Fortunately new gene-profiling tools now available can figure how neurons are manifest in the body. Understanding how genes and experience come together to impact the brain could significantly alter how we think about treating neurological diseases.

The advent of high-throughput gene profiling and the growing sophistication of our ability to manipulate genes in animal models have given us an opportunity to explore the role that genes play in both creating and modulating our neural structures. At the same time, new imaging techniques and technologies have made us better equipped to characterise neural systems and their response to the world around us.

It is the interplay of biology and experience that makes us who we are. A person after killing his family kills himself. Those who knew him couldn't believe that he could commit such a heinous crime. They thought he was a normal person, but after the autopsy, doctors found a tumour in his brain, and that affected his emotional regulation. They argued if he had no tumour in the brain he would not have done what he did. Doctors thought the effected amygdala affected his decision-making. Should one blame the killer or his biology? Can biologism — the use of biological explanations in the analysis of social situations — be used to resolve legal questions?

"Perhaps not everyone is equally "free" to make socially appropriate choices," writes David Eagleman (7). Genes don't tell the whole story. Environment is needed to complete the story. Our experience can change the genetic expression and thus the story.

Neuroscience says actions can occur even when the will to act is missing. Some people can't override or control what subconscious parts of their brain have decided to do. Can we hold people who kill without motive responsible for killing? Neurobiologists say that no part in the brain is 'independent' and therefore 'free'. They say even if free will exists it can at best be a small factor riding on top of vast neural networks shaped by genes and environment, writes Eagleman.

Is there nothing 'free' in us? Are 'mind problems' different from 'brain problems? Can we ascribe the cause of psychiatric disorders to neurological disorders? Can the mind be independent of the brain? Is it ok to shift the blame solely to biology? Neuroscientist Robert Sapolsky asks, "Is a child doing poorly at school because he is unmotivated and slow, or because there is a neurobiologically based learning disability?" Can neuroscience do something to control the impulses? These questions can perhaps be resolved once neuroimaging technologies become more credible and trustworthy.

The interpretation of "brainome" seems to be more challenging than "genome". It is needless to state the fact that mapping the brain will require enormous computing capacity than is required for mapping the human genome. Experts feel that additional breakthroughs, particularly in imaging and computer learning, are needed to sufficiently understand how the human brain works.

It is not always necessary to know the purpose or destination before embarking on a journey. Every effect may have a cause, but it is not necessary to know what that cause is. Mackenzie, more than two centuries ago, said that one may not know how to make a good machine, still he can make it. In other words, it is possible to solve new problems independently of previously acquired knowledge. Alan Turing has given us another interesting insight. Turing believed that there is a relationship between formal concept and intuition. He believed it is not necessary to know how the machine carries out its actions. For Turing, machines are simple "abstract computational devices intended to help investigate the extent and limitations of what can be computed." Turing could see the traversable path from absolute ignorance to artificial intelligence.

-2-

EXTENDED MIND

It is a myth that constant exposure to new information makes us more creative. Information overload, in fact, has been found to lessen job satisfaction and damage personal relationships. We are confronted with the explosion of ideas but do not possess enough brains to cover them, says Daniel Dennett. The explosion of ideas and information generates cognitive stress and thus the issues related to information overload are important.

Derek Dean and Caroline Webb (8) have addressed the subject related to information overload. They say that the management of information overload requires enormous self-discipline. One needs time to filter out the unimportant, and also at the same time retain the benefits of connectivity. Research says that multi-tasking is not a productive idea and switching tasks in between, especially the complex ones, makes us less efficient.

One way to deal with information overflow is to keep "alone time", the time during which one does not want to be connected, but wants to get engaged with the self. This is "focused working session." One also doesn't want to be left out. One, therefore, needs to devise his own filtering strategy. One must know what to address and what to delegate. One needs to understand the necessity of prioritising and rationing information. As one CEO advises, "You have to guard against the danger of over-eating at an interesting intellectual buffet."

Infovore is the new kind of 'vore' in the information space. Infovores eat information. When they eat more information than they can digest, they develop infobesity. The major causes of obesity are poor eating habits, both quantitatively and qualitatively, and reduced physical activity. What matters is not only what one eats, but also how one eats it. Similar logic applies for infobesity. Nicholas Carr (9) thinks that thoughts and ideas will need compression if they are to survive in the new environment. "If we're turning into informavores, it's probably because we want to," says Carr. The problem with information is what we are allowing ourselves to be fed with. It is important to know what to remember, what not to remember, which idea is stronger, which idea is weaker, which idea survives, which idea drowns, which idea starves to death. In the Darwinian times, God was an engineer, says Frank Schirrmacher. He is now a computer scientist and a programmer.

Today's generation knows the ways to check infobesity, feels Nick Bolton. Today's generation is aware that a lot of information is available, but they also know what to pick and what to throw. They have the ability to change and share information, and then swiftly move along the path. If one eats smaller portions of information and relishes it, the chances of his developing infobesity are lesser. The Internet, some say, is a paradox. It is making us dumb as well as experts. It is making us socially engaged as well as socially isolated.

Has the Internet changed the way we think? The question Edge (10) posed elicited variety of responses. Some sophisticated minds believe that the Internet has improved our fitness, and is value free. Some believe that the Internet has reduced people's thought process (like calculators have reduced the role of pure computation and simple arithmetic). Some think "speed plus mob" is a scary combination. Some think that Internet gives us the things faster, but not necessarily the right things.

Some believe that "know thyself" requires an internet search. Neuroscientist Sam Harris even relies on the Internet to recall his own thoughts; "the gates of memory swing not from my own medial temporal lobes but from a computer cluster far away, presumably where the rent is lower". A networked computer is designed to scatter our attention, thinks Nicholas Carr. Says Carr, as we adapt to the intellectual environment of the net, our thinking becomes shallower. Kevin Kelly no longer tries to remember facts as these are at his desktop/laptop/ mobile and are available as and when he summons them. But Kelly feels his knowledge has become more fragile and his thinking has become more active, less contemplative.

Internet shifts our cognitive functions from searching for information inside the mind towards searching outside the mind. Gerd Gigerenzer says that in the process, Internet becomes our external memory storage system. Evgeny Morozov sees in the "real-time web" (whereby all new content is instantly indexed, read, and analysed) our inability to look back. What matters is 'now'. Past and future are of little consequence. Scott Sampson tells us about the likely changes due to the internet. The changers include fragmented thinking and shorter attention spans together with a concomitant reduction in reflection, introspection, and in-depth thought. The bigger fear Sampson has is "the extinction of experience." He sees in the internet loss of intimate experience with the natural world.

Neuroscientist Ernst Poppel has beautifully described his feeling of getting lost in the new horizon: "It is like swimming in an ocean with no visible horizon. Sometimes suddenly an island surfaces unexpectedly indicating a direction, but before I reach this island, it has disappeared again. This feeling to be at a loss has become much stronger with the internet." Poppel doesn't want to swim in the ocean of information, unless there is direction, and there is an island. The goal must be to create a personal framework for orientation in the world of too much, he says.

The Internet has now become a large part of our thinking process. May be, the Internet is not sufficient to change the mind, but surely it is necessary. And as Sue Blackmore said, "The words I am writing now are far less 'mine' than they were before."

The Internet has become a primary form of external memory. Betsy Sparrow and her colleagues (11) conducted a series of experiments in relation to the use of the internet. The results suggested that when people are faced with difficult questions, they are likely to think that the Internet will help them find the answers. Internet users are less likely to commit the information to memory. People memorize the answers if they believe that it is the only way they will have access to that information in the future. Sparrow doesn't see much intellectual value in memorizing things. She gives far more importance to understanding information on a conceptual level. She thinks, "More likely, if a person does not think the information will be available later, they will try to memorize it, often at the expense of understanding the concepts." If the internet has made us "lazy, stupid, lonely, or crazy," it has also made us "smarter than we've ever been before." It is fast becoming 'external hard drive' for our brains.

Andy Clark and David Chalmers, who coined the term 'the extended mind', proposed that the modern human mind is a system that transcends the brain to encompass aspects of the outside environment. Now with the extended mind it is possible to remember everything. The technological mind extension holds the promise of freeing our conscious brains to spend more time on higher-order tasks rather than remembering facts and experiences. Some say it is not important to carry such information in mind that are readily available on the Internet.

-3-

BRAIN IS A GOOD SUPERVISOR

Our brain not only thinks, it constantly keeps a tab on how we think. How we think and what we think is due to our metacognitive abilities. This mental ability helps us to reconcile with the fact that we can be biased and, therefore, can go wrong. Metacognition gives us an opportunity to avoid blunders.

Our brain is always eager to check if the progress of our pursuit is satisfactory or not. It takes the path to reach a goal and at the same time also keeps handy another follow-up path, lest the earlier path fails to take us to the destination. Because of this follow-up thought, we can't avoid what we wish to avoid. This follow-up thought is useful in many situations. This act of 'mental eavesdropping' enables us not only to avoid errors, but also to modulate the mind.

Take the case of insomnia or anxiety. The more one wants to avoid anxiety, the deeper one gets entangled in it. The more you try to sleep the further you are from sleep. The insomniac's brain keeps on checking if he has fallen asleep or not.

Viktor Frankl (12) said that the fear of sleeplessness results in a hyper-intention to fall asleep. This hyper intention incapacitates one's ability to sleep. It is a kind of fear. To overcome this particular fear, Frankl advised, the patient should not try to sleep, but rather try to do just the opposite, that is, try to stay awake. In other words, "the hyper-intention to fall asleep, arising from the anticipatory anxiety of not being able to do so, must be replaced by the paradoxical intention not to fall asleep, which will soon be followed by sleep."

Frankl writes about a young boy who stammers. The boy can't get rid of the stammering in spite of his best efforts. One day, the boy was travelling in a bus without a proper ticket. Hoping the conductor would let him off pitying his stammering, the boy tried to stammer, but he couldn't. At that moment, he found himself free of the speech problem. This episode shows that our tendency to behave in undesirable ways increases when we take important decisions.

Decision making is a complex subject. One doesn't expect a universal solution even for similar problems, because, in spite of several similarities, situations can be quite different from each other. Different situations need different kinds of decisions. Some rely on reason and some on emotion.

The 'art of self-overhearing', some psychologists believe, is one way to make good decisions. This 'art' requires one's "willingness to engage in introspection" when one is confronted with an uncertain situation. Such situations don't give enough time for 'doing maths'. Decisions in such situations depend upon one's emotions, instincts, and mental short-cuts. People, who are more rational, don't perceive emotion less, they just regulate it better, believe some psychologists. It is also a fact that acting irrationally in certain situations can also be helpful.

-4-

BALANCED MIND

Women generally understand emotions and thoughts better than men. Women generally are more sensitive and careful. A female brain is predominantly hard-wired for empathy, whereas a male brain is predominantly hard-wired for understanding and building systems. Men understand the underlying behaviour of a system better and have better ability to construct and drive a system.

Even a 12-month-old baby girl, according to the researchers, responds to the distress of others. Picking up non-verbal communications, subtle nuances or judging a person's character is a woman's forte. Males generally show more 'direct aggression', meaning they generally are good at pushing and hitting. Females, on the other hand, show more "indirect aggression", meaning they generally are good at verbal punching and gossiping. The way, a male and a female join a group of strangers is also different. A female will more likely stand and watch for a while, to check out what's going on, and then try to fit in with the on-going activity. A male will more likely have a tendency to direct everyone's attention on him.

Our brains are a mix of both empathy and system. According to the empathising-systemising (E-S) theory, put forward by Simon Baron-Cohen (13), in some individuals empathising (E) is stronger than systemising (S), whereas in some S is stronger than E. In a "balanced brain" both E and S are equally strong.

Cohen says, your sex is not enough to tell you, which type of the brain you have. According to his theory, on an average more males than females have a brain of type S, and more females than males have a brain of type E. His theory, however, doesn't in any way suggest that one sex is better than the other. "The theory is saying that, on average, males and females differ in what they are drawn to and what they find easy, but that both sexes have their strengths and their weaknesses. Neither sex is superior overall."

Some brains may have impaired empathising alongside normal or even talented systemising (extreme male brain). Some brains may have impairments in systemising, alongside normal or even talented empathising (extreme female brain). If brain patterns are known, one can become more tolerant of the differences, says Cohen. He argues that people with autism may have an extreme of the male brain, and that studying autism along with E-S theory, can help increase our understanding of the neurological condition.

A person with autism finds it difficult to develop social relationships, difficulty in communication, and has unusually strong, narrow interests and a strong adherence to routines. Persons with autism often show obsessional interests on a system. Some children can follow their obsessional interests all the way, and this can lead to great achievement or the development of expertise. There could also be a need to interrupt the child's obsessional focus. But the E-S theory "sees individuals with autism spectrum conditions as having a learning style that prefers depth over breadth, and accuracy or exactness over gist," writes Cohen.

Impaired empathising is difficult to handle. Such people are generally misunderstood and mistreated, because they lack empathy. The educators have begun to recognise the existence of this syndrome. It is hoped that this understanding will help the teachers to be more tolerant of the very different learning style such children possess. "If nurtured, systemising is not only a valuable contribution, but can even result in a refreshingly original way of thinking and seeing the world," believes Cohen.

-5-

LOVE AND HATE CIRCUITS

Love and hate are two opposite sentiments. Both often result from irrational thinking. Both represent extreme behaviour, and can lead to heroic or evil deeds. No one loves to hate or hates to love, but love can turn into hate and hate can turn into love. Both love and hate can happen at the first sight, but they don't die with corresponding rapidity. One can love a complete stranger. In the stranger one finds the thrill of the unknown. One can love someone who is well known. In this one finds the delight of knowing.

Hate can be both rational and irrational. Rational hatred is easy to deal with, but irrational hatred is character conditioned. Irrational haters look for an occasion to express hate, although they have no clear idea of rationalising and justifying hatred. They sometimes become so blind that the pleasure in satisfying one's hate desire becomes more important than the practical task of defeating the enemy.

Researchers say that love and hate are intimately linked within the brain. The studies of Semir Zeki and John Romaya (14) reveal that hate circuit has something in common with the love circuit. They say that some of the neural circuits in the brain responsible for hate are also used during romantic love.

The researchers showed volunteers pictures of the hated person, and then they analysed the activity of neural circuits in their brain. The analysis suggested that the putamen (known to be involved in the perception of contempt and disgust) and the insula (involved in responses to distressing stimuli; loved and hated face constitute such a distressing signal) found in the sub-cortex of the brain are part of the hate circuit. The 'hate circuit' has components that are linked to aggression.

The putamen and the insula are also known to be activated by romantic love. Researchers also observed that large parts of the cerebral cortex, associated with judgement and reasoning, become deactivated during love, whereas only a small area is deactivated in hate. This difference was surprising for the researchers because hate, like love, is an all-consuming passion.

In romantic love, the lover is often less critical and judgemental regarding the loved person. Whereas, it is more likely that in the context of hate, the hater may want to exercise judgement to harm, injure or otherwise exact revenge, say the researchers.

Our relationships shape the brain, which in turn shape our relationships. Loving relationships alter the brain most significantly. The imaging studies show that the areas of the brain that register physical pain are active when someone feels socially rejected. That is perhaps the reason of pain all over the body when one gets hurt by the lover. Social pain can trigger the same sort of distress as a stomach ache or a broken bone.

A loving touch can make a big difference. A happy woman in a committed relationship, when given an electric shock, registers less anxiety and pain when holding her partners hand. A lover's touch can significantly lower neural responses throughout the brain. A lover's touch has been shown to subdue blood pressure, ease responses to stress, and soften physical pain. In not-so-loving relationships, this effect was not observed.

When our brains know that we are with someone trustworthy, it allocates precious resources more wisely. Instead of using it for coping with stressors or menace it uses it in learning new things or fine-tuning the process of healing.

-6-

CUDDLE AND EMPATHY CHEMISTRY

Some call it 'the cuddle chemical', because it appears to strengthen the bond between the mother and the child. Some call it 'the moral molecule', because this molecule has possible connection with virtuous behaviours such as generosity, compassion, and resilience. Some call it 'the trust molecule', because this chemical is thought to be involved in the generation of trust. This peptide hormone has even shown the capability of easing shyness and reducing fear. Paul Zak (15) found that empathy is connected to this chemical in our brain. The harmony hormone we are talking about is oxytocin.

Zak and his colleagues studied the generous behaviour of people by inducing their brains (like showing a video to the subject about a terminally ill child) to make oxytocin. The video watchers contributed money to the sick child and his family. Zak's results also indicated that such an induction makes people more likely to share money even with strangers.

Brain imaging studies have shown that oxytocin reduces the activity of brain regions that produce anxiety. Those with autism and other social disorders are often highly anxious and when these patients are given oxytocin, anxiety wanes.

Research suggests that majority of people release oxytocin when they get a feeling of being trusted. Those who didn't release oxytocin when trusted were found to be the people who do not possess the capacity to develop strong attachments with others. The human oxytocin system motivates a desire to interact with others. "In healthy people, oxytocin has a fast on-off switch; it is released a couple of seconds after a stimulus. The release of oxytocin signals that social interactions are safe," says Zak. The oxytocin switch is 'stuck in the on position', means that oxytocin is not providing the brain with a clear signal to guide behaviour. In such a situation, high oxytocin does not result in increased sociality. In other words, social factors that typically cause oxytocin release are behaviourally impotent.

Is oxytocin the cure for shyness, or autism or other psychological disorders (like severe social anxiety)? Cure seems unlikely, say Zak, as oxytocin is only one of the contributing causes, and that simply replacing oxytocin in patients would have only limited effect. He thinks his research is helping him to gain insight into "how the human brain makes us social creatures that we are."

Oxytocin also has a dark side. Research indicates that oxytocin promotes negative emotions, like envy. Andrew Kemp and Adam Guastella (16) think oxytocin plays a role in promoting 'approach-related emotions'. If oxytocin helps to develop "I want what you have" type of emotion, it may give rise to substantial emotional implications. "Oxytocin turns out to be the hormone of the clan, not of universal brotherhood. Psychologists trying to specify its role have now concluded it is the agent of ethnocentrism," writes Nicholas Wade (17). The level of oxytocin goes up when people get together with others who share their values. This observation of Carsten KW De Dreu (18) means that oxytocin promotes human ethnocentrism and thus can play a role in the emergence of intergroup conflict and violence.

Happiness is contagious. We feel happy by participating in others happiness. We feel happy when we increase happiness in the surrounding.

The dedicated neural networks that reflect the world around us reside primarily in the prefrontal cortex. These networks handle many complex-reasoning functions involved in the feelings of empathy. The feeling of empathy makes one understand other person's point of view. It is the ability of the brain to mirror accurately the emotions it perceives in other people. This ability is essential for attachment.

Empathy triggers neurochemicals: dopamine and serotonin. These neurochemicals are associated with the brain's emotion centre. Love, one of the most talked about emotions, involves the brain areas — insula, anterior cingulate, hippocampus and nucleus accumbens. These brain areas are associated with emotional perception, memory and reward.

Romantic love seems to shut off activity in the reasoning part of the brain and the amygdala. Passion, on the other hand, switches off the brain's judgment and fear centres, writes David Cameron. Richard Davidson, a leading happiness researcher, studied 'how much of our joy level is set at birth and how much we can control'. Davidson says that for our happy brain, we should thank our parents and our loving childhood.

Studies have shown that angry or critical parents can actually alter a child's happiness level. Our genes are partly responsible for our temperament. Our genes partly set our 'happiness set point'. The other part of our happiness can be controlled. Sonja Lyubomirsky (19)says that as much as 40 per cent of our happiness is left for the intentional activities that we can choose to engage in. Lyubomirsky found that people can truly become happier if they are engaged in "intentional activities". Intentional activities and thus happiness, can be realised by controlling our thoughts, actions and life circumstances.

Some of the controllable parameters that give happiness include optimism, commitment to goals, ability to nurture relationships, enjoying the present moment, gratitude and forgiveness. Davidson says that our "brains are just waiting to be transformed and they're always being transformed. But we can take responsibility and change the brain in more positive ways."

We do many things even though we know they will not do us good in the long-run. For example, we love to eat the junk food consciously. Enjoyment of eating drowns the harms of the food. George Vaillant says that happiness is a conscious state of mind and is a result of a complex process. Joy is simpler, but more enduring. We don't like to go into the complexity of eating junk food. We like to enjoy the simple joys of life, like following the 'eating way' to happiness. We like to enjoy the pleasures of the present, rather than bother too much about future pains. We like to balance simplicity with complexity. In our pleasures, we leave space for pains, and, as Vaillant points out, "Positive emotions are often associated with tears."

-7-

PRENATAL MIND

Abhimanyu, the son of Arjun and Subhadra, learned the way of entering the 'Chakravyuha' when he was in his mother's womb. This story from Mahabharata suggests that the mysteries of prenatal consciousness are not fantasies.

Researchers have recently confirmed what Arjun knew centuries ago. They say foetus knows and learns much more than we presume they know. Studies have indicated that an infant develops many skills in the prenatal stage. Some believe that something like consciousness exists from the very first moments of conception. This emerging view is giving new insights into the meaning and responsibilities of motherhood.

Babies begin to understand the language of learning and hear the sound of music in the womb. They can recognise what they hear before birth, according to a study. Foeti learn to recognise the native language of their environment, including especially, the language the mother is using. Cognitive scientist Jeff Elman clarifies, "This doesn't mean they understand the language. But if their mother speaks English, for example, they will learn to recognise this as different from other languages." It looks 'foetal learning' can help in shaping a child — like shaping the child's music orientation and ability.

Researchers examined expectant mothers from week 29 until birth. They obtained neural traces of memories from the womb. "Once we learn a sound, if it is repeated to us often enough, we form a memory of it, which is activated when we hear the sound again." The lead researcher Eino Partanena of the University of Helsinki says, "We have known that foeti can learn certain sounds from their environment during pregnancy." They can also detect subtle changes and process complex information.

The Finnish researchers say that foeti can start hearing from the 16th week of pregnancy. In the beginning, they hear only low noises, and slowly they begin to hear higher pitched noises. Also, foeti like soothing music; louder sounds startle them and make them move about. Unexpected noises can also be shocking to the foeti. And what's more, foeti express their dislike for music by kicking, which is also an indication to stop it. The findings of the Finnish researchers indicate, "Prenatal experiences have a remarkable influence on the brain's auditory discrimination accuracy, which may support, for example, language acquisition during infancy." Their studies imply that it might be possible to support early auditory development and potentially compensate for difficulties of genetic nature, such as language impairment or dyslexia.

Exposure to voices is helpful for the baby's brain development. Acoustic stimulation works, but one needs to be careful when using foetal acoustic stimulation devices designed to pipe sounds and music through the uterus, says developmental psychobiologist William Fifer.

Natural sounds are quite effective for brain development. As are familiar music and mother's voice, which help the baby relax.

When we take a look at the chronology of events in foetal development, we find that out of the total gestation period of 40 weeks, the first two weeks go for the egg to fertilise and the remaining 38 weeks are taken by the fertilised egg to develop into a complete baby. Meghan Holohan writes, "All of the foetus's senses will be stimulated naturally during the course of pregnancy, except for vision."

The foetus begins to develop the ability to detect stimuli, such as touch, from as early as 8 weeks. They begin to urinate during the 10th week of pregnancy. The urine thus passed gets mixed in the amniotic fluid surrounding the foetus in the womb. After about 15 weeks, the foetus begins to drink the amniotic fluid, which they like. An expectant mother can feel the baby movement after 16-20 week gestation. Foeti begin to suck their thumb from 20 weeks.

Fetal movements are important for the future development of the child; the movement steadily increases as the pregnancy progresses. Fetal movements help in the development of brain and nervous system. It also allows the joints, bones and muscles to form correctly. Foeti don't breathe (mothers breathe on their behalf; oxygen is passed to the foetus through the umbilical cord), though they do breathing like movements after 9 weeks of pregnancy.

The eye movement begins during the 14th week of pregnancy, and similar complex movements after 24th week. It is said that foeti also dream as in the last third of pregnancy; rapid eye movements have been seen in the foetus.

Foeti also feel pain. How does one know foeti feel pain? Researchers try to find out the status of the brain and from it they interpret if foeti can sense the pain. But to study conscious experience is much more complex. The connections required between brain and body to feel pain are believed to form only after 17 weeks, and they become adequately functional by about 26 weeks.

-8-

TEENAGER'S MIND

We are a product of biology, experience, culture, and relationships. We are born wired for feelings and learning. We begin to explore our environment since childhood. Our development in the early years is both highly robust and highly vulnerable.

Our foundational age (from the time we are born to the age 5) is very important. This is the period when a child's linguistic and cognitive abilities are developed. During this period, they exhibit dramatic progress in their emotional, social, regulatory, and moral capacities. This is the period when one can gauge a child's strengths and weaknesses. This is the period when a child's literacy and numerical skills are developed. This is the period when emotional impairments affect the child quite significantly. This is the period when we should be concerned about our child's emotional, regulatory, and social development. "Indeed, young children are capable of deep and lasting sadness, grief, and disorganization in response to trauma, loss, and early personal rejection (20). Parents are 'active ingredient' of environmental influence during the early-childhood period.

A loving family environment is very important for a child's development. It helps boost a child's vocabulary. It makes them more emotionally secure. The consequences of sour relationship between the parents on a child's development can be severe and long- lasting. Family violence and violent neighbourhood can have demoralizing fallout on the child.

One of the most important things is the role of grandparents for a child's development. Grandparents are the additional source of stability and a big support for a child's development needs. Grandparents-grandchildren relationship is very special. Studies indicate that young children looked after by their grandparents often develop better than those placed in expensive nurseries. The studies found evidence of a positive association between socio-emotional development and being looked after by grandparents among more educated families.

Teenage is one of the most interesting phases of brain development. It is the phase that is developing, yet not fully ready to face the challenges of the complex world. Teenage is not simply the continuation of the childhood. It is the time when teenagers develop their identity and discover things for themselves. It is the time when they are not afraid to take risks. It is the time when all kinds of accidents happen. It is the time peer influence hits its peak. It is the time for heightened self-consciousness. It is the time for the onset of anxiety, depression, addictions, and eating disorders. In short, it is the most paradoxical time of one's lifecycle.

Neuroscientists say that during adolescence, the human cortex undergoes protracted development, both in terms of gray matter and white matter. The gray matter increases during childhood. This process of thickening of the gray matter peaks during 11 to 12 years of age. It peaks in most cortical areas, and then declines during the period of adolescence right into the 20s or even the 30s. After that peak, the gray matter thins as the excess connections between neurons are eliminated or pruned.

It seems our brains follow the principle of "use it or lose it", meaning those cells and connections that are used, survive and flourish, and those cells and connections that are not used, wither and die. During this period, there is an increase in white matter across the brain.

Studies suggest that adolescent social brain is a network of three different regions: the medial prefrontal cortex, the posterior-superior temporal sulcus and the anterior temporal cortex. Adolescents use the same social brain network, writes cognitive neuroscientist Sarah-Jayne Blakemore (21), but what seems to happen is that activity shifts from the anterior region (the medial prefrontal cortex region) to the posterior (the anterior temporal cortex or the superior temple sulcus region), as they go through adolescence. In other words, when thinking about other people, adolescents seem to be using this prefrontal cortex, right at the front region, more than adults do and adults seem to be using the temporal regions more than adolescents do.

It is also possible that at different ages, we use different brain circuitry and cognitive strategy to perform the same task. It is likely that as adults, our decisions to deal with social situations are based more on the prevailing social scenario and norms. It is quite likely that adolescents rely more on their own experiences and gut feeling.

The teenage brain has several advantages. The young brains undergo a massive reorganisation during 12 to 25 years of age, but the brain plasticity also makes adolescent brains more vulnerable to external stressors. Young no doubt have very sharp brains, but they are not quite sure what to do with it. In calm situations, teenagers can rationalise almost as well as adults, but stress can hijack their decision-making.

Our children are often overburdened with all kinds of advises regarding learning atmospheres and good study habits. The parents often don't know where to draw the line between helping and imposing. Studies indicate that when parents guide their teens with a light but steady hand and allow independence, their kids generally do much better in life. The cognitive scientists say that "hurriedly jam-packing a brain is akin to speed-packing a cheap suitcase." Quick learners can hold the load only for a while. A carefully and gradually packed neural suitcase holds its contents much better and prepares it for better recall. We have known and experienced that the harder it is to remember something the more difficult it is to forget later.

-9-

GEOGRAPHY OF THOUGHT

Eastern and western mindsets are quite different from each other. The easterner believes that the world is constantly changing the way one moves along a circle and is thus not so easily controllable, says social psychologist Richard Nisbett (22). Eastern mindset is circular. A westerner's world is linear. By this, Nisbett means that a westerner thinks sequentially and logically, and thus the changes are predictable and controllable, as in a line.

A westerner straight away comes to the point, because his objective is to forge a good deal. An easterner, on the other hand, comes to the point through a long and circuitous route, as his objective is to forge a long-term relationship.

An easterner believes that there is no absolute truth, but still strives to reach it. For an easterner, collective is more important than the individual and, therefore, an easterner is 'relationship focused'. A westerner believes in absolute truth, in the power of individual and his capacity to influence the environment, and is 'object focused'.

For an easterner 'life is a mystery to be unraveled'. For a westerner 'life is a problem to be solved'. The easterner believes in discussions to arrive at a harmonious solution. Westerner's approach is debate.

Biologist T Motokawa's interesting article, Sushi Science and Hamburger Science, has compared the attitudes of eastern and western scientists. Motokowa says that when a westerner reads papers written by Japanese scientists, he often finds it difficult to understand. The reason is the difference in logic. "Western logic is quite clear: it has a structure in which each statement is tightly connected and linearly arranged to reach a conclusion. Japanese logic is not clear.... Japanese people talk about something and, without stating a conclusion, move the discussion to another topic. These two topics often have no logical connection, although they are related in the mind of Japanese people. What the Japanese are trying to do is to describe one fact from various points of view. Each view is connected by imagery to others, not by strict logic."

Bipin Chandra Pal (23) has beautifully described Indian psyche. He writes that Indian psyche is "more transcendental than formal, more metaphysical than scientific, more imaginative than positive, more idealistic than realistic". Indian values are more intellectual than physical, internal not external, emotional and not rational.

When one walks a mile to meet a friend, he feels he has walked only a few steps. If he has to do unpleasant work, he will say he walked a mile, when, in reality, he walked only a few steps. When a friend meeting a friend after a few weeks says, I have not seen you for ages he really, neither exaggerates nor lies, but simply applies his own inner emotional standard to the measurement of our time.

Indians love bright coloured dresses. These dresses may seem loud and flashy to a westerner. Indians are too expressive of the way they talk and display their enjoyment, which a westerner may find too intrusive. An Indian advertising guru nicely sums up the situation with a film analogy: "While both Black and Iqbal are well-made films, Black is India trying to ape the west, while Iqbal is pure Indian creativity."

-10-

WHERE THE MIND IS
WITHOUT FEAR

We all have our own fears. Fear is contagious and needs to be conquered. Rabindranath Tagore rightly said that the head can be held high only if the mind is without fear.

The behaviour of people around us may trigger our responses to threatening situations. Often it is hard to forget threats. The emotional impact of a fearful event often continues for long. Accidents haunt us for a long time; driving at night seems dreadful if the accident had occurred during the night. The fearful memories easily return and are hard to shake off.

Fear is a natural part of the human psyche. Experiencing fear is also a learned activity. Conditioned fear turns out to be one of the most essential techniques that natural selection stumbled across to increase the survival odds of organisms in an unpredictable environment, writes Steven Johnson (24). Fear conditioning prepares an organism to learn about predicting adverse events. The early humans survived as they were quick to respond to dangerous situations. The obstacles to survival prepared our brain to deal with threats.

Fear is frequently related to the escape and avoidance behaviour. When afraid we tend to fight, freeze or flee. Brain researchers say in less than 100 milliseconds sensory information reaches amygdala and in the split seconds our adrenaline surges, eyes widen, heart rate increases, breathing quickens, stomach wrenches, palms moisten, and time slows down. These are the signs of fear.

It is the amygdala, the fear centre of the brain, that contributes to our decision to run when fear grips. fMRI studies indicated hyperactivity in the amygdala when patients were shown threatening faces or confronted with frightening situations. On the other hand, deactivated amygdala has shown to prevent both the learning and expression of fear.

Scientists say that learned fear gets strengthened by reconsolidation after recall. One way to reduce the impact of anxiety producing memory is to guide them to form a new memory that extinguishes fearful memory. Take, for example, a car accident that occurs at a particular intersection, and at that time, a certain song is playing on the radio. For a period whenever you cross the intersection or hear the song, you will re-experience fear. Slowly, this fearful memory will fade, and your fear will extinguish. Ann Marie Menting (25) writes, "This extinction doesn't erase the initial learned fear; instead, it leads to forming a new memory, a 'safety memory'. The learned fear—the neuronal connections that the experience formed within your amygdala and between your amygdala and certain cortical structures—remains."

We experience many kinds of fear: fear of death, fear of the unknown, fear of being alone, fear of the future, fear of failure, and so on. Fear has the key to our survival. If we were not fearful, we wouldn't have survived. Evolution says that only those people survived who feared the right things and at the right time.

Fear is unconscious autonomic responses in some parts of our brain. The thalamus, the key relay station for sensory information, transmits and amplifies only information of particular importance from the mass of signals entering the brain. The incoming sensory data is interpreted at the sensory cortex. The hippocampus stores and retrieves conscious memories. The amygdala decodes emotions, determines possible threats, and stores fear memories. Finally, the hypothalamus activates the fear response in us through two simultaneous roads.

The low road is quick; it first shoots and then asks questions. The high road is more thoughtful; it measures the pros and cons of travelling on the available routes before finally deciding the route. Sooner or later, both the roads lead to hypothalamus, which, in turn, is governed by the sympathetic nervous system and the adrenal-cortical system. The combined effect of these two roads is expressed as a fear response.

Due to the kicking of the sympathetic nervous system, adrenaline flows into the blood stream resulting in an increase in heart rate and blood pressure. At the same time, the hypothalamus in conjunction with the pituitary gland releases certain hormones to prepare the body to deal with the threat.

We have the tendency to anticipate. Anticipating a fearful stimulus can provoke the same response as and when it actually happens and thus can be beneficial for dealing with the threat. Those of us who have a damaged amygdala, perhaps, are not afraid. But, should one sacrifice the amygdala to become brave?

-11-

CHAOTIC MIND

The general belief is that logical operations are made to process information in our brain. Chaos scientists, however, don't subscribe to this view. They say our brain works in unpredictable and random ways, and the secret of the brain function can be found in the chaos theory. They say brain is a chaotic system that is intricately related by internal feedback.

The concept of "self-organised criticality" has been used to understand chaotic brain behaviour. Self-organised critical phenomena are driven by their intrinsic dynamic systems to reach a critical state, independently of the value of any control parameter. The perfect example of a self-organised critical system is a sand pile. As grains build up, the pile grows in a predictable way up to a certain point. Then suddenly the pile collapses. Though unpredictable, the overall individual distribution of sand is regular. The state of self-organised criticality lies right on the boundary between stable, orderly behaviour and the unpredictable chaotic world, writes David Robson (26).

Disorder is essential to the brain's ability to transmit information and solve problems, say the neuroscientists. "Lying at the critical point allows the brain to rapidly adapt to new circumstances." Neuroscientists say that our brains work on 'forest on fire' mode. In forest fire, one burning tree sets alight another one. That is why whole forests don't catch fire all at once.

Experiments have shown that single neuron can trigger fire to the neighbouring neuron, causing an avalanche of activity that can propagate across the network of brain cells. This results in alternating periods of quiescence and activity (much like the build-up and collapse of a sand pile). The brain often synchronises large groups of neurons to fire at the same frequency. This "phase locking" process allows communication of different "task forces" of neurons among themselves without interference from others. During the process there is always a possibility of neurons firing out of sync due to interspersing of the stable periods of phase-locking with unstable periods.

Neurons die if they are not used for long time. To ensure their proper function they must be fired from time to time. Random firing of inactive neurons is a good way to maintain neuron health.

A somewhat chaotic brain is good for our body. They help us to cope up with body's increased demands. Brain's chaotic activity is integral to learning and is believed to create new abilities. Researchers believe that the brain's ability to generate new information internally is critical to our creative processes. It is likely that chaos is essential to create that ability.

Chaotic brains can have ordered thoughts. It means our random thoughts are not really random. Mark Twain thus rightly said, "It usually takes more than three weeks to prepare a good impromptu speech."

-12-

OVERBURDENED MIND

Fatigue sets in when we try to do more than our mind can handle. A fatigued mind's mental energies are in a state that may result in clouded decisions. An overburdened mind often goes wrong. When decision fatigue sets in, either we do nothing, or we take short cuts, and go wrong. Or we try to maintain the status quo. Doing nothing eases the mental strain for the time being, but can create problems, may not be immediately, but in the long run.

Roy Baumeister and John Tierney (27) say that we possess a finite store of mental energy for exerting self-control. Willpower gets exhausted when repeatedly used in a short span of time. It is like a muscle that is fatigued with use.

Making too many choices before actually taking decision saps one's will power, say the researchers. When willpower is depleted, one becomes a "cognitive miser", one becomes one-dimensional, and if you are shopping, it makes you vulnerable and easy target of the sellers and the marketers. Avoid temptations to conserve willpower, the researchers' advice. "When you shop till you drop, your willpower drops, too", is the message of the researchers.

More difficult the choices, quicker the people become fatigued. A fatigued decision maker often tries to avoid his own sense of judgment. A fatigued decision maker tries to take the path of least resistance. Often paths of least resistance don't take us to our desired destinations. One of the least resistances is to follow what the seller or marketer says.

Decision fatigue and willpower are special problems for the poor people. The poor have less buying power. They become satisfied more easily. Choices generally don't matter much to them.

In one study, researchers found that, compared to the rich, the poor are much more likely to eat during the shopping trip. They do more 'impulse purchases'. This they do in spite of their lesser spending capacity. The impulse purchase reflects lesser hold on their self-control.

When you are mentally tired to take decision, one option is to maintain the status quo. It reduces the risks of making wrong decisions, and at the same time keeps your choices open. "Part of the resistance against making decisions comes from our fear of giving up options," say Baumeister and Tierney.

For our older generation, decision fatigue was a lesser problem. Because our older generation had to take fewer decisions, they were under less 'ego-depleting' strain. The present generation, on the other hand, is overwhelmed by too many choices as well as decisions.

We take so many decisions every day; some are small, and some are big. They all add up, and our cumulative decisions affect our willpower. When our willpower becomes weak, our frustrations become more irritating. We develop a "propensity to experience everything more intently." Tierney says, "Ego-depleted humans take illogical shortcuts and tend to favour short-term gains and delayed costs. They become inclined to take the safer, easier option even when that option hurts someone else."

The big problem is that it is not easy to know when we are decision fatigued and when our willpower is low. We think we are always ready to take decisions.

-13-

MIND OF THE CROWD

Is it true that a person is always better off if he has alternatives to choose from. Two microscopes can be used for two different kinds of imaging thus giving a powerful combination of high specificity and detailed structural information. Behavioural economist Richard Thaler, however, doesn't agree with the proposition that two minds are better than one. "I can make myself better off by restricting my future choices and commit myself to a specific course of action", he argues.

What about the crowd behaviour? Being part of the crowd one enjoys the glorious sensation of feeling part of something bigger than oneself. Crowds are known to bring out the best as well as the worst in us. Crowds are known for delivering wise as well as unwise decisions. James Surowiecki (28) says that the diversity of opinion, interdependence, decentralisation, and aggregation are the key criteria that separate wise crowds from irrational ones.

Crowds can also turn individuals into helpless copycats. Gustave Le Bon (29) in his book published in 1896 argued that in a crowd, individuality is lost and rationality is destroyed. This means being part of a crowd can lead one to do things one wouldn't normally do, and might even disprove of in normal circumstances.

It is an acknowledged fact that assembling a perfect crowd is not possible. It is also a fact that all crowds are not bad. All crowds are not necessarily violent. Crowds always don't induce irrational behavior. It is also not true that all individuals lose their sense of self and sense of responsibility simply by being part of the crowd. Crowds are known to have brought changes for the good of society.

Research also says that two people can produce worse judgments, not because together they are not capable of making a good decision, but precisely because they are so confident of togetherness that they can. The researchers have called this the 'cost of collaboration'. Psychologist Julie Minson, the lead researchers of the study, says that people need be aware of the fact that collaboration can lead to overconfidence. Once we are aware of this fact, we can think of the ways to mitigate it.

The important point is how one can remain independent while being a part of the crowd.

-14-

MIND AND MONEY

Only Thakur Ramkrishna could truthfully say that 'taka maati, maati taka'. I am not as truthful as Thakur Ramkrishna was. Money is important to me. As John Armstrong writes (30), money is essential for survival. "Freedom, desire, power, status, work, possession: these huge ideas that rule life are enacted, almost always, in and around money." It is true that money making doesn't appeal to all, but it is also a fact that not everyone can make money. Some of us have greater addiction for money. To make money, it is said, one must have some amount of stupidity and greed. But it is not always greed, which makes us addicted to money. Addiction for money could be for acquiring status or to compensate for social shortcomings.

Thinking about money changes our thinking. To understand money-related worries, Armstrong says, we must first understand why money is important to us, how much money we need to achieve what is important to us, what the best way to acquire that money is, and what our economic responsibilities to others are in the course of acquiring and using that money. Money worries, Armstrong says, are about psychology as much as economics, the soul as much as the bank balance.

A rich man doesn't know what to do with money. A poor man doesn't know what to do without money. We suffer from 'money illusion'. We happily accept 7% rise in a year of 11% inflation, but reject 4% pay cut in a year of zero inflation. We are seized with 'loss aversion'. We react more strongly to losses compared to gains. Psychologists say that money makes one weirder, and less rational.

People get immediate pleasure from obtaining and pain after losing money. The opportunity to make easy money cause a surge of dopamine in our neural machinery. Money makes us more self-centred. Generally money-related decisions are more difficult to take. People value money they have earned compared to the money they are given.

The difficult thing is to resolve the conflict between pursuit of wealth and building and maintaining strong personal relationships. Daniel Ariely (31) says that when we keep social norms and market norms on separate paths, life hums along pretty well, but when they collide, trouble sets in.

The brain imaging studies have indicated that persons preferring instant reward system show brain activity in the areas linked with emotion, especially the limbic system, which is known to be involved in much impulsive behaviour. Those choosing the delayed reward showed activity in the prefrontal cortex, known for rational planning.

Neuroeconomist George Loewenstein (32) observed in one of his studies that the poor spend a disproportionate percentage of their income on lottery tickets. Loewenstein believes that neuroeconomics is going to provide a perspective on human decision that integrates the duality of emotion and deliberation.

We can't ignore money. The important thing to teach the gray matter is to separate the pleasures of purchase from the pains of payment. Those who have zero assets and zero liabilities possibly have such a gray matter. Money can buy many things, but can money buy happiness?

Daniel Gilbert's 'experience-stretching' hypothesis (33) partly explains disconnect between money and happiness. Experience-stretching is described as "an experience that once brought me pleasure no longer does." Money allows us to buy things, but it also deprives us from enjoying the mundane joys of life. Money can be a substitute for social acceptance and can reduce social and physical discomforts, but it also can take us away from the little pleasures of life. If you want to buy material things, you would need a fixed amount of money. But if you want to buy happiness, your money need would be relative, because your level of happiness depends upon the earning levels of your neighbours. This relativity trap is not easy to get by.

Things are not great or small. We make them great or small. This habit of ours has been with us since the beginning, and shall remain till the end. The problem is that we don't realise and accept that we are making comparisons. We make mistakes while making comparisons. We make systematic errors when predicting our future satisfactions, says Gilbert. Because of the wrong predictions, we make wrong decisions. We suffer from blind foresight, like eyesight and hindsight.

The magnitude of expected rewards governs our motivations and efforts. Our motivations are not always conscious. We don't often know what has prompted us to do a certain thing. Neuroscience researchers are trying to understand the connect between expected reward and behavioural activation.

How our brain energises behaviour in proportion to subliminal incentives is the subject of study of one research group (34). In this study, money was used as an incentive. The researchers used research tools to visualise unconscious motivational processes. Besides fMRI to study brain activity, researchers recorded skin conductance response (SCR) and hand-grip force to characterise the effects of monetary stakes. SCR is linked to autonomic sympathetic arousal; the arousal of sympathetic nerves prepares us to deal with fight or flight response. Hand-grip force is a measure of behavioural activation. The studies reveal that a key node (specific basal forebrain region) in the brain circuitry enables rewards to energise behaviour. Interestingly, this doesn't even need the subjects' awareness.

-15-

INTUITIVE MIND

Intuition is sudden flash of insight. It is fast, effortless, associative, and slow-learning. One wouldn't know from where the insight emerged. Intuition is a 'mental matching game', say the psychologists. Intuition is 'just knowing'. It is our 'gut feeling'. Intuition could be due to 'condensed reasoning'. It could be the result of 'unconscious associative processes'. Intuitive decisions are based on understanding rather than on knowledge. Emotions are integral part of intuitions. Intuition often outperforms rational analyses. Intuitions are often wrong because shortcuts sometime lead to bias and sub-optimal decisions. Brain does a quick search of its stored files, finds an analogy with the present situation, and based on the knowledge, its meaning is ascribed.

Logic-based analysis, on the other hand, is slow, controlled, effortful, rule-governed, and emotionally neutral. If you are disturbed by a concurrent activity (like switching on TV while you are reading), you are in the rational mode of thinking.

There is wisdom in lack of knowledge, says Gerd Gigerenzer (35). Intuitive decisions, even when based on pure guesswork, are often right. Nobel Laureate Daniel Kahneman says, "If people can construct a simple and coherent story, they will feel confident regardless of how well grounded it is in reality. But when problems are unique, or fairly unique, then I would be less trusting of intuition. I'd add that the amount of success it takes for leaders to become overconfident isn't terribly large."

Daniel Simons and Christopher Chabris (36) made an interesting observation; people fail to notice unexpected events when their attention is otherwise engaged. There is a mismatch between what we notice and what we think we will notice. While doing a task if our attention is diverted to other tasks (for example, talking on the mobile phone while driving) we may not see the possible dangers, but they are there. "The trouble with intuition is that while intuitive modes of thought are easier to use than analytical modes, they are poorly adapted to many circumstances and decisions we face in the modern world," write Simons and Chabris.

A strong intuition can herald the beginning of a beautiful relationship. Researchers say that in "relationship-threatening situations" happier couples keep their hunches to themselves. They don't bother to test them out as they understand that such thoughts are temporary and not serious.

For a decision, both intuition and reason are necessary. Reason enables us to go beyond mere perception, habit, and instinct. Intuition is an inference that is validated by the thinker's belief systems.

It is generally believed that reason-based decisions are better. We, however, know that many reason-based decisions often go wrong. A study on the psychology of reasoning suggests that we reason rather poorly. Our reasoning-based decision making is subjective. Our decisions fail due to irrational biases. Even decisions of skilled arguers also fail.

Hugo Mercier and Dan Sperber (37) argue that the skilled arguers are not after the truth, but after arguments supporting their views. The result is that bias creeps in our reasoning, and it becomes so motivated that it distorts evaluations and attitudes. Mercier and Sperber say that the arguments used in reasoning are the output of a mechanism of intuitive inference.

Decisions that are taken on the basis of reasons are often not necessarily poor because we are bad decision makers, but because we systematically look for arguments to justify our own beliefs or actions. As a result, we tend to rebut genuine information put forward by others. We are good at 'biased reasoning'. We forget that, in order to pursue truth, the inputs of others are equally essential. We try to be both the judge and the advocate, and that is not the way to pursue truth.

One way to get over biased reasoning is to become more objective. This is possible by developing abilities to distance oneself from one's own opinions, and consider other alternative opinions. We are quite capable of reasoning in an unbiased manner. We need to remember that all arguments are not debates (where the purpose is to win) but also producing arguments that are after the truth.

"I am afraid that the temptation to try to procedurise and checklist everything can get in the way of those kinds of insights and those kinds of social concerns that seem so important," says Gary Klein (38). In order to learn how people make life-and-death decisions under extreme time pressure and uncertainty, Klein talked to some firefighters.

The firefighter told Klein that he couldn't think of a single decision he ever made. He said he just followed procedures. When Klein wanted to see the procedure manuals, the firefighter said, "It is not written down."

What Klein found was that the firefighter was not taking decisions in the classical sense. Before taking the decision, the firefighter did not generate a set of options, and then compared their pros and cons. Klein asked him a rephrased question. "How have you handled cases where you had struggled, cases where you might have made mistakes earlier in your career?"

The firefighter thus described one of his firefighting experiences. Since the smoke was coming from the back, the firefighter presumed it was probably a kitchen fire. He sent one of his crews inside the house to knock the fire out.

Klein asked the fireman, why he sent a man inside the house when it is customary to go out of the house when a house is on fire? Why did he not break a window and use hoses to tame the fire?

The fireman told him that he did not do it because if he did that, he would have pushed the fire back into the house. This might have allowed it to spread wider into the house. Obviously, one wouldn't want to do that.

The fireman also told him that an interior attack is not always possible because if there is another house right next to it, it could catch fire also. In such cases, the firefighting starts externally.

Klein concludes, "That's what 20 years of experience buys you. You build up all these patterns, you quickly size up situations, and you know what to do. Experts know what to ignore, and what they have to watch carefully. Experts know what to expect next, so they get ready for that." These are intuitive decisions. By intuition Klein means the way we are able to use our experience.

Intuition is not magic. It is based on experience. It allows us to "build a repertoire of patterns" that allows us to quickly frame situations, size situations up, and know what to do. It is not mere intuition, but intuition laced with mental simulation. Our mental simulation does the analysis. Klein calls such decision-making "recognition-primed decisions." The decisions are primed by their ability to recognise situations balanced by the monitoring of mental simulation.

Intuition is about expertise and tacit knowledge. It prepares us to see things that we couldn't see before. It gives us the ability to make fine discriminations. It helps us to better our pattern-recognition capabilities, and alerts us to possible dangers. Intuition is a consequence of the experience we have built up.

"The intuitive mind is a sacred gift, and the rational mind is a faithful servant. We have created a society that honours the servant, and has forgotten the gift", Albert Einstein wrote years ago.

-16-

HUNGRY MIND

Our brains are hungry organs. Brain constitutes 2% of our body mass, but consumes 25% of the energy used by the body. Anthropologists say that our body's biological apparatus for getting energy became smaller over the last few million years and during this period, our brains enlarged.

Scientists say that the brain of Homo erectus was 50% larger than that of its predecessor, Homo habilis, and during this time, there was a big drop in the tooth size of Homo erectus. As more energy was routed to the brain, our biological apparatus (teeth, jaw muscles, stomach, guts) got diminished in effectiveness. They became less and less capable of processing food of all sorts. In spite of the decreased efficiency of jaw and gut, our ancestors managed calorie drought. The choice for them was between 'better food' and 'better food processor'. They chose better food. They preferred to use better techniques to extract more energy with less effort. They invented fire and cooking. Changing the diet decreased the energy requirement of the bigger brain. Anthropologist Richard Wrangham (39) writes, "The steady, accelerating pattern of brain growth was likely supported by shifts in diet as new food-procuring and preparation techniques steadily lifted the energy constraint on the brain's development."

Every animal in the animal kingdom would have liked to have bigger brains. But most animals don't have brains like humans have. It is because most animals don't know how to manage big brains. They don't know how to meet the energy demands of the big brains. As our brain uses energy, it generates heat, and in the process it gets overheated. Fortunately, our ancestors resolved the problem of overheat by developing a system of sweating that is managed by the brain.

The secret of our big brain is cooking. Cooking is one of the most important innovations for softening food. This is perhaps the reason why we are called coctivores (those who love to eat cooked food). Food scientist Heribert Watzke says, "Our dental anatomy is actually made, not for tearing down raw meat from bones or chewing fibrous leaves for hours. It is made for a diet which is soft, mushy, which is reduced in fibres, which is very easily chewable and digestible." If there was no cooking, our ancestors would literally be chewing the gathered food for the rest of the day to get enough calories to survive.

Life is easier if we understand the biological rules. Wrangham says that great apes have helped us a great deal to understand our own behaviour. It is estimated that sometime around 250,000 or 300,000 years ago cooking really got going. There is archeological evidence that shows the presence of earth ovens during that time. Wrangham, however, thinks we have learned to cook long before earth ovens came along.

Once cooking happened, it showed us completely new ways of utilising our resources. We began to look at the environment with new eyes. We began to see male-female relationship from a new perspective. Wrangham's idea is that once females were ready to make a meal by collecting food and cooking it, they became vulnerable to big males (he calls them "scroungers") who took away their food. Rather than collecting and cooking the food, the easier option for the males was to take it when it is ready. This necessitated the need of females protecting themselves from 'thieving males'. Perhaps, as Wrangham suggests, this is the origin of human male-female relationship.

-17-

OBESE MIND

Obesity is not good as it threatens our life span. We know that we should eat less and exercise more. Then why we don't follow what we know. The fault lies in our heads. The urge to eat too much is wired into our head.

Neurobiologists say that a multitude of systems in the brain encourages eating. Targeting one neuronal system is therefore, not enough, and as Dan Hurley writes (40), "No single silver bullet will ever work." The brains of overweight people are wired to feel more pleasure in response to food. Our brains seem hungrier than our stomach. We simply enjoy eating more.

This habit of overeating evolved in us because we were not sure of the next meal. Our brain's prime directive thus has been to equip the body to meet this challenge. A consequence of this is that we developed obese prone 'default eat' system. We now need remedial measures to counter the effects of the system.

The sensory experience of eating food can be seen in the gustatotry and the somatosensory regions of the brain. The fMRI brain scans of these regions showed greater activation in the obese. Striatum, a region near the centre of the brain that is known to respond to stimuli associated with rewards, showed decreased activation. The researchers observed that those who experienced less pleasure were at greater risk for weight gain. To clarify the matter, researchers say that reduced pleasure among the obese is a result of years of overeating. They compared it with a phenomenon seen in drug addicts who require ever-greater amounts of their drug to feel the same reward. Chronic dieters are more susceptible than average to overeating, say the researchers.

Eating behaviours are also linked to areas of the brain associated with self-control (such as the left superior frontal region) and visual attention (such as the right middle temporal region). Researchers showed that successful weight losers had greater activation in those regions, compared with normal-weight and obese people, when viewing images of food. When under stress, people like to eat high-calorie food. Researchers say that this is due to the association of stress pathways in the limbic system to the areas of the brain associated with seeking rewards. Eating high-calorie food is reward-seeking behaviour.

Taming obesity probably lies in taming a hungry brain. Resetting the brain temporarily seems possible, but the problem is that the reset brain wants to come back to the original setting. Another issue is the development of effective obesity therapy. This may require a combination of drugs that work simultaneously on multiple triggers of eating and metabolism. The therapy may also include, besides drugs, psychological or psychiatric approaches as well as exercises.

-18-

MORAL AND VULNERABLE MIND

Who or what decides our moral decisions? Some think that our unconscious biases decide our moral decisions. There are others who think that social environment is the dominant factor. "The largely unquestioned modern scientific view is that the brain gives rise to the mental mechanisms governing our cognitive existence," writes Michael Gazzaniga (41).

Studies indicate that morality is highly influenced by local culture and learning, and that all decision-making processes resulting in outward behaviour are carried out before one becomes consciously aware of them. Moral action is rational action. It is governed by a conception of the way that you ought to act. "To be a moral being is to be capable of being motivated to do what you ought to do because you believe you ought to do it".

Marc Hauser (42) says that morality is grounded in our biology. He thinks, "Inquiry into our moral nature will no longer be the proprietary province of the humanities and social sciences, but a shared journey with the natural sciences." He holds the view that we are born with abstract rules or principles that guide us toward the acquisition of particular moral systems. He believes that in us exists a "moral organ".

Does a moral organ really exist? Some analysts are not so sure. They say thus far we have reprogrammed ourselves reading histories, novels, philosophical treatises and ethnographies. These have helped us to update our moral software. Maybe someday in the far future biological hardware will be used for updating our moral software.

It is said that an intelligent and unethical mind is the most disastrous combination. It is also good to know that an intelligent and ethical mind is the most desirable combination, and we should strive for that, biologically or otherwise.

There are plenty of honest minds among us. We are generally honest in spite of the fact that we have resorted to some sort of dishonesty some time or the other. Often we behave dishonestly even when our intentions were not so. Honest minds don't intentionally misrepresent facts, intentions, or opinions. Honest people don't get tempted to behave dishonestly.

The 'grace hypothesis of honesty' says that the decisions of honest people don't get affected when they get an opportunity to increase their reward by being dishonest. The 'will hypothesis', on the other hand, says that honest behaviour can also result from the intentional resistance of perceived temptation to behave dishonestly.

Honesty and intelligence don't necessarily go hand-in-hand. Often brilliance and talent are the most dishonest combination. We often become so convinced about the rightness of our own theories that we start believing that we only have the right to be right. We tend to push threatening information away from us, and pull friendly information close to us.

We don't like to change our mind. We love to protect our sense of the self. We dislike arguments that try to change our mind and opinion. We like arguments that help us to hold our views (even though wrong). In a strongly competitive environment ambition and vanity sometimes completely outweigh our ethics and sense of fairness.

Honesty often is not the best policy as truth hurts. Honesty is shifty. We can be truthful even if what we say is not actually true. We can deceive and mislead others without telling a lie. Keeping quiet when one supposedly should speak is a form of dishonesty. An act of silence that is intended to cause another person to believe something that isn't true is deception.

Our rationality often is the causes of our dishonesty. We want to maximize our own payoffs. The higher the reward from being dishonest, the higher is the extent to which we engage ourselves to dishonest means, says Dan Ariely (31).

One way to limit dishonest ways is to restrict benefits of dishonest ways. Ariely, however, notes that people tend to be dishonest enough to give themselves an advantage. We try to balance our desire for personal gain with our willingness to be a good person.

We are vulnerable. We are vulnerable to attack, criticism, even temptation. We get easily wounded or hurt. Our vulnerability and susceptibility are subjective and depends upon our cognitive abilities, personality, and our social background.

Scientists say that certain variants of behavioural genes make people more vulnerable to certain moods and behaviours. "Your genes don't doom you to these disorders. But if you have bad versions of certain genes and life treats you ill, you're more prone to them", writes David Dobbs (43). The "upside" to vulnerability could be an asset, say some scientists. An alternate vulnerability hypothesis says that bad genes can create dysfunction in unfavourable contexts, but can enhance function in favourable contexts.

Scientists speak about "dandelion" and "orchid" children. Dandelion children are normal, healthy, and "do pretty well almost anywhere, whether raised in the equivalent of a sidewalk crack or a well-tended garden." Orchid children, on the other hand, "wilt if ignored or ill-treated, but bloom spectacularly with greenhouse care."

The "orchid hypothesis" shows us a new way to think about human behaviour. It says that, if care is given, an orchid child can become a dandelion child. The orchid hypothesis accepts the proposition that certain gene variants underlie some of the human kind's most grievous problems, but it also suggests that these troublemakers can play a critical role in our success.

A sizable population among us is known to carry gene variants for depression, anti-social and violent behaviour as well as anxiety. If these gene variants had created mainly dysfunction, they would not have survived natural selection, and thus would not have remained with us. Since gene variants exist, they must have done something good to ensure their survival and succession. So vulnerability has inherent goodness embedded in it.

The wise advise us not to take advantage of someone's vulnerability. This is because, once the situation changes, the vulnerable prey is no longer the defenseless prey. The vulnerable prey doesn't forget what his predator did to him. He waits for his sunny days to return, and when that happens, he doesn't lose the opportunity to pounce on the predator. And also don't ever forget that when a vulnerable acquires power, he is no less ruthless than a monster.

Corruption is one of our major problems. We can no longer afford to be indifferent towards the issue of corruption. To fight corruption, more than structural and legal reforms, moral renovation of the self is necessary. We need to reinvent our moral codes. We need to develop innate values so as to keep us moral even in the most amoral situations. We need to elevate consciousness and to revive spiritual awareness in us. We need to refurbish ourselves with the lessons of trustworthiness, compassion, forbearance, generosity, humility, and courage.

Corruption is generally associated with our moral decadence. Its modus operandi is infinite. It can take the form of misplaced justice, misuse of authority, manipulation of public money, use of unfair means, fabrication of evidence, plagiarism and manipulation of data, use of or provision of banned substances to enhance performance, among others. Motivations for corruption may include economic gain, status, power, sexual gratification.

A measure of corruption is highly subjective, and depends on a person's ethical, moral, cultural and religious beliefs. Depending on the observer's ethical and moral background, an action is labelled as corrupt. In spite of the fact that people's perception and the extent of corruption vary greatly across the world, but the general agreement is that corruption damages society, democracy, and economic progress.

It is said that we are not born corrupt, but we become corrupt. A corrupt person wants to win at any cost, and is willing to make any compromise. His overconfidence in his abilities leads him to take unjust, immoral and faulty steps. He becomes impulsive, and his thinking is prejudiced by greed. Francis Bacon said, people have a natural inclination to accept, believe and even prove what they would prefer to be true. Our prejudices and beliefs are dependent on our family background, childhood experiences, education, social class, and the market place.

A corrupt mind misuses the fertility of the mind. And as they say, a fertile and a vulnerable mind with no values is the most disastrous combination. The cortical region in the frontal lobe in our brain is involved to plan, control and coordinate our behaviour. The cortical region of the corrupt mind does the same, but in its own crooked way.

Ivan Petrovich Pavlov (44) in his studies on dogs observed that they start salivating when they see food, and salivation happen even in the absence of food, when there was some stimulant. The stimulant for the dogs was the lab coat of a person who served the food. Seeing the lab coat the dogs thought that food was on its way. Pavlov received similar response with ringing bells; the dogs learnt to associate the sound of the bell with food.

Pavlov's concept of 'conditioned learning' says that events that previously had no relation to a given reflex (such as a bell sound) could, through experience, trigger a reflex (salivation). Pavlov's work suggests that positive reinforcement cause repetition of the behaviour pattern, and also repetition causes the reactions to become more developed over time.

Another important offshoot of 'conditioned learning', called 'extinction', is that an established conditioned response (salivating in the case of the dogs) decreases in intensity if the conditioned stimulus (bell) is repeatedly presented without the unconditioned stimulus (food). Something similar must be happening in the minds of the corrupt, suggests Gary Novak.

The corrupt becomes bolder with repeated stimulus. After tasting and liking the 'blood', and if he is not caught, a corrupt becomes doubly aggressive the next time. He can do anything (like lying, bribing, killing) to fulfil his desire. If not stopped, he becomes a bloodsucker.

The problem is that the stimulus-response behaviour is so spontaneous and subconscious that it escapes the thought process of the corrupt. Pavlov's dogs tell us that if positive reinforcement works, so do the negative enforcements.

One of the positive reinforcements for the corrupt is power to prevail over others. To offset the positive reinforcement one would need negative reinforcement. Disqualification from holding a public office is one of the desirable negative reinforcements.

In the 'corrupt space', there is a need and still a hope for fairness. People will abuse power if we let them do so. We need to remind ourselves of our social responsibility. The least we can do is to identify, isolate, and avoid the corrupt.

-19-

MIND OF LOYALIST AND WHISTLE BLOWER

The loyalty landscape is enigmatic. Families expect it. Organisations demand it. Friends respect it, and countries foster it. Loyalty needs faithfulness and willingness to make sacrifices. It needs steadfast dedication in the face of temptation. If one is loyal to oneself, he or she is loyal to others too. Loyalty is often blind. Loyalty has dual nature. It is essential as well as fallible, argues Simon Keller (45). It requires complaisance as well as servility. It is virtuous, vice as well. In sum, not all loyalties merit our allegiance.

As the saying goes, "When an organisation wants you to do right, it asks for your integrity; when it wants you to do wrong, it demands your loyalty."

One can't be good to all. Similarly one can't be loyal to all. There is a size limit to loyalty. Sociologist Robin Dunbar says that our brains only allow us to get to know about 150 people, particularly well (a requisite for loyalty).

There is a thin line between loyalty and disloyalty, and this line is broken at the slightest temptation. We hardly remember who has been good to us, but it is hard to forget who has been bad to us. Evolutionarily speaking loyalty, compared to disloyalty, seems more profitable.

Whistle blowers are generally seen as disloyal. Whistle blowers are generally construed as if they are against the system they are serving. But that is not always the case. Whistle blowers can also be loyal. They also care for the organization they serve. It is true that whistle blowers are not afraid to raise the alarm once they see things like corruption, fraud, waste but they do this for the good of the organization. The sad thing is that whistle blowing loyalists are fast becoming an endangered species. This species needs to be preserved for the good of the system.

We come across many rule breakers in our day-to-day existence. There are people who don't break the rules, because they think breaking the rules is not the right thing to do. There are also people who don't break the rules, because of the fear of being caught and punished. There are also many among us for whom breaking the rules is not a big deal.

Among the following who is better on the integrity scale – the one who has the opportunity to break the rule but doesn't, or the one who possesses no such opportunity and therefore, doesn't? Obviously, the first one. If I don't steal because I think it is wrong to do, so I am morally more right than the one who doesn't steal because he is afraid of being caught.

It is not so difficult to get away with rule bending, but if you know you won't get caught, and even then, you don't bend the rules or lie or cheat, you are a master achiever in the integrity scale.

Let us say, you are appearing for a competitive exam. After entering the hall, the first thing you are told is that the room is fitted with cameras to keep a check on your dishonesty. Let us consider another situation. After entering the hall, you are asked to sign an integrity pledge that you will not use any unfair means during the exam. I suppose you will prefer the system that has no surveillance system.

The basic premise of conducting exam at the above two systems is different. There is less probability of cheating in the first system compared to the second. Is it the only reason for you to prefer the second option? Perhaps you chose the second option because this option assumes that the students can be trusted. The first option doesn't believe in such a supposition. This brings to our mind another question - Is surveillance a good idea?

Our attitude to surveillance is different in different settings, and thus the surveillance levels are set according to the goals of the system. In the competitive exam setting, perhaps, signing an integrity pledge is not enough. In a school setting, an integrity pledge (not only for examination but also for general conduct) is perhaps more relevant, because schools have a broader mission. Surveillance signifies a lack of trust, and therefore its effect on any relation is corrosive; closer the relationship, more corrosive is the effect.

The relation between surveillance and morality is a complex issue. It is said that if one regards the development of moral character completely irrelevant then one would be less troubled by the practice of surveillance. In some contexts, surveillance helps to keep us on track, and thereby reinforces good habits that become our second nature, says Emrys Westacott (46). "In other contexts, it can hinder moral development by steering us away from or obscuring the saintly ideal of genuinely disinterested action. And that ideal is worth keeping alive."

We should do what is right, because that is the right way to do things, and the notion that someone, somewhere may be watching strengthens this belief.

-20-

GOSSIPER'S MIND

Gossip - we may not like it; we may denounce it, but we can't avoid it. Gossip provides relief from monotony. Gossip keeps us aware of the world we are surrounded with. We can't be present everywhere, but we want to know what is happening everywhere. We thus depend upon intermediaries. We often forget to check how dependable these intermediaries are. Moreover, who has time to check the veracity of the information thus collected? We accept what pleases the 'soul'.

A gossiper doesn't mind to trespasses into other's private territories. Gossiper's reputation in the group is essentially determined by the potential and factual access he has to information about others' private lives.

Gossip is not 'background noise'. We invest time and effort on it. On an average, we spend 6 to 12 hours a day in conversation; gossip time varies between a fifth and two-thirds of the daily conversation time.

It is a myth that women gossip more. "The only time when men spend less time gossiping than women do is when women are present" seems to me a very sensible general observation. The 'perception' of gossip among women and men, however, are different. What is known among women as 'kitty party chit-chat', men call it 'networking' or 'exchange of ideas'.

Gossip can be used for gathering or disseminating information. Entertainment or recreational value is another function of gossip; "nothing is enjoyed so thoroughly or treasured so preciously" as gossip is. Gossip is less likely to take place between casual acquaintances or strangers. This is because shared social meanings and history are essential to understanding the subtleties of gossip. Only an 'insider' gets the privilege of becoming a member of the gossip club.

Gossip is necessary for survival. It allows us to integrate a large number of social relationships, says anthropologist Robin Dunbar. By talking, we can find out a great deal about how other individuals are likely to behave and how we should react to them. "Gossip is a policeman and a teacher. Without it, there would be chaos and ignorance" thus summarises Jonathan Haidt.

-21-

LIAR'S MIND

We are quite good at playing lying games. We play these games as per our own convenience, and as per the requirements of our emotions. Some of us are habitual liars. We lie even when there is no apparent gain. Lying often is very stressful and defending a lie is not easy.

We often lie out of respect for others. Some of us lie to reinvent ourselves. Some of us feel elated by fooling others. It seems all fantasists find the experience of lying very rewarding. They find it very exciting that they can impress people. Perhaps their 'chronic feeling of emptiness' drives them to lying. Lying gives them an opportunity to become what they are not. Liars often find it very difficult to stop.

Yudhisthir was an expert liar. In Mahabharata, an elephant named Ashwatthama was killed. The rumour was spread that Drona's son (also named Ashwatthama) was dead. Drona wanted to check the veracity of the rumour from Yudhisthir. Yudhisthir said Ashwatthma (he said 'elephant' under his breath) was indeed dead. After hearing this Drona laid down his arms. Draupadi's brother, who was waiting for an opportunity to kill Drona, cut off his head. Yudhisthir lied, and also did not.

Lying can be as complex as truth is. Not everyone can become a good liar. Professional liar masters the art of 'telling lies, the whole lies, and nothing but lies' in a manner as if it is 'the truth, the whole truth, and nothing but the truth'. Lying often becomes inevitable as telling the truth is not always desirable.

We are born liars argues Ian Leslie (47). In many situations, we take the umbrage of untruth. There is always more than one way to give a truthful description of an event. One can describe a situation highlighting a particular aspect that suits one's own perspective. Without lying, one can send across a wrong picture. If the intention is to deceive, in spite of no-false statement, a statement can be made with 'plenty of economy with the truth'.

Accuracy and sincerity are two positive virtues of truth, writes Julian Baggini (48). "People who claim we should never lie, not only neglect the second (sincerity), they also have an impoverished understanding of the first (accuracy)", says Baggini. It is true that truth requires accuracy, but it does not mean that everything one says is 100 per cent accurate. Truth must include all the relevant truths for truth to become 100 per cent correct. In other words, 'whole truth' is the sum of all 'part truths'. Unless all part of the truths are available, 'truth' can't be 'whole'. More often than not, it is difficult to know the complete truth. And as someone said there are only two ways of telling the complete truth — anonymously and posthumously.

We like to withhold some 'naked truths'. "Truthfulness is largely a matter of deciding what it is reasonable to withhold," Baggini says. The idea that one should always say what one truly believes is narcissistic nonsense, argues sociologist Steve Fuller. His advice: one should say what needs to be said in a given situation.

We value truth. The ability to sort truth from a lie can be our most valuable asset. Truth should be the default. Lying should be an exception and that should require a special justification. Like all other valuable things, truth has a shelf life, and the half-life of truth is very short.

Most of us lie, but we are poor lie detectors. Research suggests that supposedly stereotypical behavior of liars, such as "averted eyes or fidgeting", may not be all that indicative of an untrustworthy person. Research also suggests that conscious awareness may hinder our ability to detect whether someone is lying. Researchers say that "the unconscious mind could catch a liar — even when the conscious mind failed."

-22-

BELIEVER'S MIND

We see patterns not only in ourselves, but also in what others see in us. We like to believe that we can correctly read the intentions of others. Our 'believing brain' finds meaning and pattern even when there is none. Our brain tends to ignore information that contradicts our beliefs. Belief looks for patterns and these patterns shape our understanding, writes Michael Shermer (49). Even our beliefs dictate our seeing. If it is true that belief dictates our seeing, it is also true that seeing dictates our belief system.

Simple logic says that something has a better chance of survival if it is advantageous to us. One of its corollaries is that belief in something can sustain only if that thing proves its worth. The belief system will fizzle out if it is not worth believing. God, for example, would not have survived had he not proven his worth. What could be the evolutionary advantages of believing in God?

Psychologist Jesse Bering (50) says that we all experience the illusion of God. The illusion is that someone up there is constantly watching us, and is also concerned about our moral lives. When we know someone is watching us, we tend to behave differently. The feeling of 'being observed', both in adults and kids, makes one stop cheating.

'Someone is watching you' is our basic nature. Bering says that even committed atheists possess this nature; even their mind turns in a supernatural direction. Studies indicate that supernatural beliefs promote altruistic behaviour and adherence to social norms, at least among the adults.

Researchers say that "belief networks" operate across the brain and invoke spirituality. Some even say that atheism is probably the unnatural way to be.

We evolved to believe in God, writes Richard Alleyne. It is also said that religion is our survival instinct because religion brings us closer to each other, and that results in better chances of our survival.

It is quite possible that God is an evolved projection of our understanding of what God should be. But it is also true that our belief in the supernatural is natural. Our belief in the supernatural shall continue to remain so as long as the supernatural is useful to us. Even the bread-giver has to earn his bread.

-23-

'I' AND 'ME' MIND

Individualism prompts us to take necessary initiatives and actions to propagate the self and service the ego. An individualist often overvalues his own qualities and overestimates his importance in the group effort. A strong individualist doesn't feel embarrassed to attain his goals and pursue his happiness. He doesn't mind even being branded selfish and self-centred.

'I' and 'Me' are two different forms of individualism. Philosopher George Herbert Mead (51), the well-known contributor to the understanding of distinction between 'I' and 'me', says that 'me' can't be conceived without an 'I' because 'I' projects 'me'.

The self is a complex mix of 'I' and 'me'. As 'I', at the interface of 'me' and 'you', it responds to the attitude of others. 'Me' provides the self the perception of others. As 'me', a person receives, reacts and responds to himself in terms of the projection of the perception of people, events and society. His self-appraisal is based on his appraisal by others.

'I' is created by the ego or vice-versa. Reactions or actions of an individual, whether in response to others or self-initiated, are the artifacts of 'I'. Every response that 'I' makes is somewhat novel, not necessarily desirable. Mead said, "The 'I' gives the sense of freedom, of initiative. The situation is there for us to act in a self-conscious fashion. We are aware of ourselves, and of what the situation is, but exactly how we will act never gets into experience until after the action takes place. The true nature of reaction and response of 'I' becomes understandable when the situation slips into past and becomes an attribute of 'me'."

The summation of many 'I's is 'We'. 'We' works like a 'super organism', where the claims of individualists are minimal. It means, 'I' must surrender to the wishes of 'We'. In order that 'We' survives, 'I's must melt, and 'Me's must fuse with 'Us'. It is important to say, "It's me."

The issue is, as Amartya Sen said, whether one could claim to be a friend of the self. An individual can't remain an island, and also doesn't want to remain in an island. Can anything really be understood in isolation?

A part tries to remain a part of the whole to increase its value. A whole wants to keep a part of the whole only if that part is useful to the whole. There are certain things whose real value can only be known if they are part of something bigger. Their value exists only in relationships.

One of the ways to better understand a whole is to dissect it and see how the isolated parts perform on their own. We may use different methods of dissection and isolation, but the conclusion will be that the whole can't exist without the parts, and vice-versa. A nut is useless without a bolt, and vice-versa.

A whole can be less than the sum of the parts. One bad violinist is enough to spoil an orchestra. What we want is a whole that is more than the sum of its parts. That is possible if the level of the whole is higher than the cumulative level of its parts. One likes to be an integral part of the whole, but doesn't like to get lost in the whole.

How parts become whole?

Take building. We need bricks, cement, steel, etcetera to build it. These diverse components are put in a fixed pattern to build a building. There is fixity.

Think of a river. It moves from one place to the other. It doesn't have any fixed shape. It takes the shape of the place where it is flowing. Streams of diverse shape join the river, which itself is changing its shape as per the local conditions. There is no fixity.

Now think of a complex living system. A living system can be viewed from various perspectives. The perspective will depend upon who is viewing it. The perspective could be microscopic or macroscopic depending upon, for example, if the viewer is a molecular biologist, or a system biologist, or an ecologist. One could view a living system as a continuation of microscopic to macroscopic world, a world having multiplier effect and vulnerability. In this world order emerges out of the chaos.

Fritjof Capra (52) says that the key to a comprehensive living system lies in the synthesis of pattern (form, order, quality) and structure (substance, matter, quantity). The world is systemic. It is interconnected and interdependent. The problems of this world can't be resolved by remaining isolated. In this thinking emphasis is on the whole. Emphasis is on system thinking, which says that the properties of the parts are not intrinsic, but can be understood only within the context of the larger whole.

Take our society. It values relationship among its constituents. The structure of society so often changes. There is disorder, but it works. Network specialist Albert-Laszlo Barabasi (53) asks an important question — how some networks continue to function even after the vast majority of their nodes have failed? Networks are 'scale-free', says Barabasi, and these networks have shown remarkable resistance to accidental failures. But the networks have also shown extreme vulnerability to coordinated attacks. Our society functions somewhat in the same manner. Society can withstand accidental onslaughts. It takes time to overcome coordinated attacks. It comes back, nevertheless.

-24-

CONFABULATED MIND

There was a man. He was a stroke victim. He could describe a conference that he never attended. He constructed false answers and thought he was not lying. William Hirstein (54) talks about another patient who is paralytic, but she won't admit it. She would say she has arthritis. She too was not lying or pretending. There are some neurological patients who construct false answers while genuinely believing that they are telling the truth.

Confabulation is genuine lying. It is genuine because it "lacks the intent to deceive". It is an attempt to fill in memory gaps by fabricating information or details. In confabulation first a false response is created. Then the patient fails to recognise its falsity. A normal person, on the other hand, has the capacity to correct the falsity if he has created it. Confabulation appears in a wide variety of other syndromes, such as Anton's syndrome (denial of blindness), Capgras' syndrome (the illusion that an impostor has replaced a person close to the patient), and schizophrenia.

Our memory is reconstructive. During the reconstruction process, the memory is pieced together from fragments. While doing so errors creep in. The errors could be due to our own biases and expectations. The error can also be due to the damage in frontal lobe (due to tumours, head injuries or ruptured arteries). Our memories are usually reliable as the errors that creep in are small. In extreme cases, memories can be completely false.

Confabulation is unintentional false memory. It occurs due to the confusion of imagination with memory, or the confused application of true memories. It involves the absence of doubt about something one should doubt.

Provoked confabulation (milder form of confabulation produced in response to a question) can be healthy. People with provoked confabulation are fully in possession of most of their cognitive faculties and, thus are able to respond correctly to all sorts of situations. The provoked confabulation suggests that caution is good, but excessive caution can be counterproductive. Excessive caution is especially counterproductive when it occurs in someone in a position of power or responsibility. Imagine your over-cautious boss doing nothing, as he is always doubtful of doing things the right way.

We love to tell stories to others. More so if the story is about ourselves. If we get an opportunity to tell others how honest, ethical, successful and interesting, we are, we try to seize it. "Perhaps confabulation arises in part from this natural inclination toward telling stories about ourselves," writes Hirstein.

-25-

FICTIONAL MIND

We love to be in the fictional world. We love to have a fictional mind. Fiction involves visualisation. We like to roam freely in the visual world, but we don't want to go far away from our comfort zone. A thought is always accompanied by an image. The moment we hear or read a story our mind visualises the scene and the characters. The process continues even after the story has ended.

Yann Martel (55) says that fiction is selective transformation of reality. Our reaction to fiction is almost the same as in real life. The writer creates a world consisting of fiction and reality. Fiction follows its own form of reality. The credible fictional world must be logical, must have some amount of emotional complexity and elements of surprise. It is said that the story must be sufficiently complex to engage attention, achieve suspense and surprise and excite emotion, but not so complex that the unity, clarity, and coherence of its parts are lost. "The story must be probable, but it also must be a story. In other words, fiction is like history, but it is not history," writes Mortimer Adler.

David Novitz (56) says that imagination plays a crucial role in the acquisition and growth of empirical knowledge. Tilottama Rajan (57) thinks it is the reader who, in fact, creates the "meaning". It is the reader who bridges the gap between "conception" and "execution" by engaging the reader's memories and experiences.

Studies reveal that reading fiction develops the brain. The studies also reveal that fiction makes one more socially perceptive. At least, that is what researchers proved after reading a Franz Kafka story (The Country Doctor). The difficulties encountered while trying to find meaning in the Kafka text made the brain smarter. I don't know how long the effect lasted. Even if it lasted for few brief moments, it was worth taking the trouble of reading Kafka.

Fictional experiences enhance our mental fitness. Our brains, unlike computers, work more efficiently when more software are loaded into it. More the software one loads into the brain, more internal connections are forged. Spending time in the fictional world is thus an investment. The evolutionary psychologists J Tooby and L Cosmides say that the pay-off in such investments is greater earlier in the life cycle, when competing opportunities are lower, and adaptations less well developed.

Fictional experiences provide opportunities in which adaptation-organising experiences can occur. The more fictional stories we hear, the more circumstances we become familiar with, without having to actually experience them. The best thing is that our brain can separate pretence from reality. It can store not just absolute facts but information that may be true only temporarily or locally or to a specific individual. This is one of the reasons for our flexibility and adaptability.

-26-

DECISIVE, TRUSTWORTHY AND BIASED MIND

Though we take a number of decisions every day, we are not as rational decision makers as we wish to be. Our decisions are coloured. What goes on in our minds when we take decisions? What specific neuronal circuits in our brains are responsible for our thoughts and actions? Decision neuroscience tries to answer these questions. It investigates the neural basis of human decision-making.

The part of the brain that is linked to emotion is nucleus accumbens (nacc), the peanut-sized area that becomes active when we expect a reward of a primary nature, such as water when we are thirsty. The part of the brain that is linked to anxiety, anterior insula, lights up when a person sees disgusting, repulsive stimuli or when someone anticipates physical pain. According to the researchers, if the emotional states of individuals are included in rational decision-making models, people will make better financial choices.

Pure rational decision-making is difficult, if not impossible, as decisions are always coloured with emotions of the person who is taking the decision. Neuroscientists say that people with damaged part of the brain responsible for emotional reactions are unable to decide; the rational mind vacillates endlessly over the possible rational reasons. Extremely emotional decisions, on the other hand, also lead us to wrong decisions. Both 'cold reasons' and 'hot emotions' are needed to take a 'right decision'.

The essence of thinking during decision-making is mental simulation. Mental simulation means, says Daeyeol Lee (58), "you are trying to predict the outcome before you take an action by using analogies of your previous experiences, or by observing and remembering the outcomes of other people's behaviours". We do mental simulations for many different actions before we actually make a choice.

Some parts in our brain, being 'perceptual system specialists', place a value on what we see. Daniel Salzman (58) says that we tend to assign a value to different options we observe. Rewards are often the major parameter that affects our decisions. We thus develop a tendency to manipulate our decisions in the hope of better rewards. Reward could be immediate or delayed. Neuroscientists want to know how uncertainty about the reward or risk is represented in the brain and influences decision-making. They also want to find out how the brain handles the trade-off between the overall magnitudes of the reward and how immediately one receives the reward. Neuroscientists want to understand how neurons represent rewards, and how information on rewards is integrated over time in order to reach a decision.

How do we value our choices? Behaviour is very adaptive when we make choices, says Xiao-Jing Wang (58). "You can really watch how your choice behaviour adapts and changes from trial to trial, according to environment and task design, and such changes are reflected in the recorded activity of single neurons." Wang also talks about reinforcement learning. It occurs when you are not explicitly taught what you are supposed to learn, but rather learn it by trial-and-error.

Researchers working in the area of decision neuroscience want to understand the computations performed in different brain areas, how they are similar or different, how different areas communicate with each other, how the information is transformed as it moves around in the brain, how different variables come together and form a decision. Wang says, a decision involves many processes. One needs to accumulate evidence for or against different choice options, evaluate their possible outcomes and risks and suppress certain learned responses and biases. Thus, it is important to understand how different parts of the brain do different computations in a coordinated way.

There can't be a set of universal laws of decision-making. Brain is like a toolbox with random tools, says Lee. You take out one particular tool to solve a specific problem. The problem is, how so many tools interact to solve an interrelated problem. Another challenge for neuroscientists is to understand how the brain represents new situations in order to find out how the brain makes decisions about such new situations. Salzman says our brains are not big enough, and we don't have requisite neurons to represent every situation that we might possibly encounter.

Among the many practical applications of decision neuroscience research, one is to understand the biological basis of mental disorders. It is hoped that it will tell us more about the mental disorders resulting from dysfunction of neural circuits, like how these dysfunctions produce different cognitive and emotional symptoms, and thereby affect decision-making. It will tell us about the implications of treatment on neural network. Salzman says we need to understand how cognition and emotion work in the brain to produce a decision, and how they become dysfunctional. We need to understand why different individuals make different decisions, and why they make different choices when they face the same situation. Are the differences due to genetic differences, or due to the differences in experiences and learning environments, or both?

It gives a good feeling that decisions in a happy state of mind are happy decisions.

Trustworthy decisions emanate from a trustworthy mind. Trust begets trust. Trusting the self is the first requirement of trusting others. You can't trust others unless you trust yourself. Matters related to trust occupy a huge amount of our mental energies, writes David DeSteno (59). DeSteno makes a very important observation: "Although it's true that cooperation and vulnerability require two parties, no one ever said that the two parties had to be different people. To the contrary, the parties can be the same person at different times." DeSteno says being realistic, honest, and forgiving with yourself and others are helpful to deal with challenges of tough times.

Trust influences practically every aspect of our life. One of them is togetherness. Out of togetherness grows trust. One of the big challenges our ancestors faced was the need to solve the dilemmas of trust, writes Maria Popova. Because of the dilemmas of trust, the mind constantly tries to ascertain the trustworthiness of others. Trust has inherent risks. But we also believe that trust is kind of a risk that is worth taking.

In the matters of trust illusions are as good as hard facts. There are trusts that are 'calculation-based'. These trusts calculate the value of creating and sustaining trust in a relationship relative to the costs of sustaining or severing the relationship. The 'identification-based trust', on the other hand, values another person's identity as an individual. More trustworthy and sustainable relationships grow out of identification-based trust. Then there is 'benevolence-based trust'. In this, an individual does not intentionally harm another when given an opportunity to do so. The other kind of trust is 'competence-based'. In this, an individual believes that another person is knowledgeable about a given subject area and therefore, can be trusted.

Under vulnerable circumstances, we tend to depend more on trust. We shift from one mode of trust to the other, depending upon our life circumstances. Competence and reliability are the two traits that determine and establish trustworthiness. Both competence and trust are important for managing a system. One of the most essential ingredients of a knowledge-based system is knowledge sharing. Knowledge sharing is not possible unless trust is embedded in the system.

Trust evokes a feeling of confidence. A trusted person enjoys many advantages; even his vulnerability is accepted. A person can be trusted in some contexts, but not necessarily in all the contexts. Distrust, on the other hand, evokes a feeling of doubt and fear. The reasons of distrust could be purely imaginary, resulting out of misplaced feelings. Such feelings unnecessarily create vulnerability. Putting all the eggs in one basket is excessive trust.

A little distrust is often helpful. It can avert herd mentality. Relationship experts say that trust is valuable so far as it is appropriate to the context, and that a healthy amount of distrust can protect against the risk of exploitation. Does trust need periodic validity checks? Yes, it does if the trust is event-based, as the continuance of event-based trusts generally depend on future events. If the trust is process-based, it is more likely to become permanent.

We often go wrong even when we weigh all the facts and consider all evidence. Bias is one of the main reasons of our taking wrong decisions. Our biases and prejudices are subjective. We rely more on a certain piece of information as we think other alternatives might not work that effectively. Because of distorted perceptions and wishful thinking, we see things more positively than they really are. We even distort our memory to suit our perception. Then there is a problem of conformity to peer pressure. We accept the arguments of those whom we like and reject the arguments of those whom we dislike. We attribute our success to our abilities and talents, and our failures to bad luck, external factors and destiny. We use one yardstick to judge success/ failures of the self and another yardstick for others. We underestimate the influence of self-interest on our own judgments and decisions, but overestimate its influence on others. We underestimate future uncertainties. We cross-check the bad news, but readily accept the good news.

We all have 'bias blind spots'. We take biased decisions based upon the irrational decisions we have taken in the past. We accept things, not necessarily based on merit, but merely because of our familiarity with the thing. We take hasty decisions to escape the feeling of doubt and uncertainty. We overestimate the degree to which others should agree with us. We underestimate others' ability to understand us. We overestimate our own ability to know others. What was said matters less than who said it.

Our brains are highly attuned to negative biases. Almost all our decision-making biases favour conflict rather than concession. Hawks see only hostility in their adversaries. Doves often point to subtle openings for dialogue. In fact, a bias in favour of hawkish beliefs and preferences is built into the fabric of the human mind, says Daniel Kahneman. Since decision making is subjective, bias is inevitable in the decision-making process.

Biases don't die. They take new forms. Bias of some kind is always present in our decisions. We find it almost impossible to ignore the "subjective first person view of things." It, however, doesn't mean that all biased decisions are unfair and bad. In other words, it must be recognized that biased decisions can be fair. A fair decision ensures impartiality, consistency and transparency.

It is a subjective perception and experience. Some of us like familiarity and certainty. Some of us like uncertainty and novelty. People in the first group are less receptive to new ideas and are biased towards predictability and clarity. People belonging to the second group love to face new situations and are biased towards such people/issues.

-27-

LONELY MIND

Loneliness is a strange phenomenon. Some people are socially isolated, but they are not lonely. Some people are lonely, even if they have a lot of social contacts. In the absence of social connection, many things can happen. Loneliness undermines one's ability to self-regulate. Lonely people, not only drink more, they also eat more. Food presumably tries to fill the space created by loneliness. Lonely people tend to find greater fault with themselves and also those around them. Lonely people report more daytime fatigue. The quality of relationship matters in loneliness.

John Cacioppo (60), leading researcher on loneliness, has created a new way of thinking about the biology of interpersonal relationships. He thinks we are hardwired to find life unpleasant outside the safety of trusted friends and family. Cacioppo, however, thinks: "Given their feelings of social isolation, lonely individuals may be left to find relative comfort in nonsocial rewards." The anxiety that accompanies loneliness is a warning that an individual's social ties have gotten too weak. This signal tells us to get ready to change our behaviour in a way that's good for our survival.

Loneliness not only increases wear and tear by keeping the body in alert mode, but also prevents people from recharging their batteries with rest and relaxation. Loneliness is good if it is short-term. Loneliness is bad if it is too prolonged. Cacioppo says that loneliness is a survival impulse like hunger or thirst. We need food when we are hungry. Similarly, lonely people need the nourishment of human companionship.

How loneliness survived all these years in spite of the fact that persistently lonely people are unhealthy, depressed, withdrawn and hostile? Cacioppo says loneliness at the individual scale is hostile, but at the species scale, it is beneficial. In loneliness, there is interdependence of social and biological processes. In the presence of others, possibility of survival seems better. Cacioppo believes loneliness is moderately heritable, and the symptoms of loneliness outlast loneliness. It is also true that the benefits of feeling connected to persist even after the connections wither. Cacioppo and his colleagues devised a loneliness scale, based on a questionnaire that tries to size up how people perceive their social situation. They found that people scoring high on the loneliness scale tend to exhibit several physiological changes that effectively put the body in a state of alert.

Loneliness undermines health in many ways. Apart from conditions such as depression or stress, health risks include the rise in blood pressure, deterioration in immune system, and acceleration in aging. Social disconnection may impair the ability to control thoughts, emotions, and impulses, and also may contribute to Alzheimer's disease. Loneliness makes sleep less restful. Brain still hears that ancient warning that people are most vulnerable when they are asleep.

Prolonged loneliness transforms the brain. According to the studies, social isolation affects the behaviour of the people by changing the operation of the brain. Researchers found that ventral striatum, a region of the brain which is critical to learning and associated with rewards, is much more activated in non-lonely people than in the lonely when they view pictures of people in pleasant settings. On the other hand, the temporoparietal junction, a region associated with taking the perspective of another person, is much less activated among lonely than in the non-lonely when viewing pictures of people in unpleasant settings. Researchers also found that lonely people exhibit higher vascular resistance, resulting in tightening of the arteries that raises blood pressure. Why lonely people feel stressed even under moderately stressful situations? Cacioppo's thinks it is due to the rise in the cortisol and epinephrine levels in saliva and urine.

The studies have also shown that prolonged loneliness makes one feel less related to peers even after the period of loneliness. The studies conducted on adult mice have shown that long isolation (eight weeks to induce a depressive-like state) produce less myelin in parts of the brain. Myelin, made up of protein and fatty substances, is an insulating layer that forms around nerves, including those in the brain and spinal cord. Myelin sheath allows impulses to transmit quickly and efficiently along the nerve cells. If myelin is damaged, the impulses slow down. Myelins are responsible for complex emotional behaviour. These studies, says Karen Dietz the lead researcher, reveal the role of myelin in adult psychiatric disorders (61).

The socially isolated mice were found to imbibe the spirit of social avoidance and withdrawal. The good thing the researchers observed was that once the social integration was re-established, myelin production went back to normal. This indicated the possibility of reversal of negative consequences of adult social isolation by environmental intervention. These neurosocial studies, researchers believe, will give new insights on mental activities when one is experiencing loneliness.

-28-

SENSIBLE MIND

Senses have their own novelty. No particular sense is more important than the other. Senses don't lie, but our sense perceptions often lie. "The senses do not deceive us, but the judgment does". Our senses help us to observe things around us. But mere observation is not enough; it only tells part of the story.

We like to see, hear, taste, smell, and touch the world. Through these five basic senses, we read the story that goes around us. If we want to understand the story more comprehensively, we need to soak our observations with emotional sensibilities. A sense without this understanding is like a machine that collects information but doesn't know how to use it.

We are often blind about many things around us. We look at things for the sake of 'looking', not for the joy of 'seeing'. Senses give us sense data. When memory joins sensation, it becomes experience. When the mind acts on experience, it becomes knowledge. When the mind acts on knowledge, it becomes thought.

C S Lewis made a very interesting observation: "Five senses; an incurably abstract intellect; a haphazardly selective memory; a set of preconceptions and assumptions so numerous that I can never examine more than minority of them - never become conscious of them all. How much of total reality can such an apparatus let through?"

Thus to make sense of the senses, we "require abilities of a different order, without them, we should be unable to recognise form, pattern, regularity, harmony, rhythm, and meaning, not to mention life, consciousness, and self-awareness". This ability of a different order is our sixth sense, the conscience.

It is the sense of 'mind-in action'. It is the sense of right and wrong. It is the policeman of the community of senses. Its voice is the 'voice within', which can lead different people in quite different directions.

Unless we have the common sense, the seventh sense, the other six senses are of no use. This sense, though called common, it is not always common. What is obvious to one person may not be so obvious to the other person. Since our perceptions differ, our sense of perceptions is also different.

Albert Einstein included a time factor in his definition of common sense: "Common sense is the collection of prejudices acquired by age 18."

'Uncommon Sense' and 'Common Nonsense' are the two outcomes of common sense. Uncommon Sense is 'out of the box' type. Someone has rightly observed - such people are so deeply in the box that they can never get out of it. Common nonsense types are abundantly available. Such varieties are a "reflection of a flawed brain with a capacity for being interested in more things than it can comprehend."

Let me conclude with what William Makepeace Thackeray had to say on this subject: "I never know whether to pity or congratulate a man on coming to his senses."

-29-

MIND'S EYE

Eyes have a rich and varied vocabulary. Eyes are a great social navigator. Eyes can read others' minds as well as allow others to read their mind. Eyes appraise us the emotional and mental states of others. Eye-gaze perception is our guide to social interaction.

Eye contact signals attraction between people. Looking straight into the eyes indicates that you are a straight person. Prolonged eye contact, on the other hand, is perceived aggressive and can be threatening. Disengaged eye contact is a sign of distraction. It happens when we try to conceal our true feelings. We can notice that we are being noticed. We prefer to look at objects rather than empty space. Researchers have shown that when a person is seen to move their eyes to engage in eye contact, they are perceived as more likable and attractive than if they are seen to disengage eye contact.

Eye contact influences perception of another's attractiveness. This effect is modulated by the perceived relationship between the observer and the observed party, says Alexandra Frischen. The capacity to use another person's eye gaze, as a cue to attention, develops early in life. Children can detect deception. They know from eyes what people want to hide from them.

We possess a great sense of gaze direction. This is due to the small dark region (pupil and iris) and large regions of the white sclera to either side of iris. Our visual system is sensitive to gaze direction of other people. It is also known that other person's gaze shift produces a shift of an observer's usual attention in gaze direction.

Gaze cueing is a phenomenon whereby we pay attention to our peers by following their gaze and looking in the same direction as them. The work of scientists of the University of Padova (62) reveals that we pay more attention to people who have a higher status in life. The studies suggest that students pay more attention to faces when they are told that they are looking at high achievers. The researchers say, "We rapidly encode the relative social status of the individuals populating our environment, and we shape our social attention processes accordingly."

The meeting of eyes tells many tales. It tells different things to different people. One can see in it curiosity, while the other may see in it challenge. Trust can be developed almost immediately through eye contact. To look into someone's eye non-verbally is generally viewed impolite. But if you look too long, particularly if the other person is of the opposite sex, this might also land you into trouble. If you hold eye contact too long (usually more than five to seven seconds) it may be interpreted as a stare and can become a source of discomfort to the person being eyed. Often, a shy person or a person who lacks confidence is afraid to make eye contact. Liars and people who have social anxiety problems experience trouble maintaining eye contact.

In a group meeting or in a lecture or in a one-on-one conversation, eyes give feedback on how others are receiving the speaker. In a classroom, one can tell from the student's eyes if the teacher has talked enough. Then, there is eye contact favouritism; looking at certain people more than others. Research indicates that we tend to look more at those people who give us the most positive feedback, and also at people who matter the most. On the other hand, if you ignore some people (as demonstrated by the lack of eye contact) they too close the eyes on you. 'Eye contact equality' is a sure way to demonstrate fairness and respect to the listeners.

At some places, eye contact with strangers in an enclosed space (such as lift) is considered impolite behaviour. At these spaces "it is appropriate to gaze at the door or the floor indicators", advises a sociology professor. But such "appropriate" behaviour can be quite stressful, particularly if the lifts are of co-ed colleges.

At many places (for example, many of our villages) gazing into the eyes of others (elders and persons of the opposite sex) is not the norm. At these places, eye contact has different implication; it can even be taken as a sign of disrespect. People at these places should know that eye contact builds better rapport, and looking into the eye does not convey any form of disrespect. In the staring contest blinking is taken as a sign of submission.

Eyes, being the best communicators, can see the soul. Not only do eyes convey, they can also tell what is going on inside other's mind. We should all remember the wise saying of Benjamin Franklin: "Keep your eyes wide open before marriage, and half shut afterwards."

Seeing is realising the highest truth. It is a gradual and an elaborate process. Seeing requires more than just eyesight. According to a Buddhist text, before a man finally sees he goes through several intermediate steps. A man comes, having come he listens, by listening he remembers, he examines the sense of things, he ponders, he mentally realises the highest truth and penetrating it by means of wisdom, he finally sees. The relation between seeing and knowing is more complex than we commonly assume. For instance, people with normal sight have a blind spot, although we are not usually aware of this handicap in our sight.

There are people who can 'see' in spite of their visual disability. Their navigational feat is due to blindsight - "a weird ability to respond to visual information despite having no conscious knowledge of seeing anything". Cognitive neuroscientist Beatrice de Gelder (63), in a carefully conducted experiment, found that a visually impaired man could walk unaided through obstacles lying on the way. She says that the brain has a number of alternate routes that can be mobilised when the main avenues to vision are blocked. It is because the projection of images is not only restricted to the visual cortex, but also to other parts of the brain related to vision and emotion. She says that the mind could subconsciously process some visual information. She says, though we tend to concentrate on major visual systems in the brain, we have hidden resources.

Our conscious vision depends on a region of the brain, called the primary visual cortex. If this region is damaged how can one see? How could people see without knowing that they can see? This feat is possible due to the auditory assistance, say some experts. Some blind people have the ability to sense the reflection of sound waves, and that assists them to locate obstacles. Experiments have also revealed that people can unconsciously detect a wide range of visual attributes, including colour, simple shapes, simple motion, and the orientation of lines or gratings. Large shapes, as well as very fine details, seem hard to detect.

There are people who can't see, but don't want to believe that they can't see. They bump into objects while walking, but deny the visual impairment. The visual disturbance is a result of brain abnormality or damage rather than eye abnormalities. They have a rare symptom of brain damage, called Anton's syndrome, named after Austrian neuropsychiatrist Gabriel Anton. Anton was later joined by the brain pathologist Francois Babinski to understand this uncommon visual loss.

Anton's syndrome (AS) is caused by damage to the occipital lobe, which extends from the primary visual cortex into the visual association cortex. It is mostly seen following a stroke, but may also be seen after head injury. AS patients not only are unable to volunteer the information that they can't see, they also mislead others by behaving and talking as though they are not blind. They not only experience difficulty in finding their way around, says neurologist Macdonald Critchley, they begin to describe people and objects around them, which as a matter of fact, are not there at all. AS patients lack self-perception of their deficits.

George Riddoch, a temporary officer in the Royal Army Medical Corps in the late twenties, while studying soldiers blinded by enemy's gunfire observed that they were able to detect the presence of motion. One of his patients observed the moving thing having no distinct shape, and it looked like shadowy grey. For another patient, moving something was like a shadow. It neither had form nor colour. Yet another patient said he knew that something moved through his blind field, but would not know what that object was. They are

Riddoch Syndrome patients. They have the ability to perceive motion in the blind field crudely but consciously. Another manifestation of impaired visual perception is Charles Bonnet Syndrome (CBS). CBS patients experience visual loss with complex hallucinations like images of unfamiliar people or buildings, "Lilliputian hallucinations" in which the characters or objects are smaller than normal.

"Not the eye, only the mind, can determine the grade of significance." There are people who can see with a special eye; the mind's eye. These people are an inspiration even for people with eyesight.

The French author Jacques Lusseyran (64) became blind when he was only seven. He could feel light "rising, spreading, resting on objects, giving them form, and then leaving them". He saw light only when he was happy and thought well of people. But the light faded when he was afraid, angry, and impatient. When he was jealous or unfriendly, it was as if "a bandage came down" over his eyes.

Lusseyran lost his sight, but in exchange got many other extraordinary abilities. He seemed to hear well. "My ears were hearing no better, but I was making better use of them". He believes that the blind suffer greatly "from the inexperience of those who still have their eyes." Lusseyran's important message to parents of the blind is noteworthy: Parents should never say, "You can't know that because you can't see" and "Don't do that, it is dangerous." Lusseyran says, "For a blind child, there is a threat greater than all the wounds and bumps, the scratches and most of the blows and that is the danger of isolation."

Zoltan Torey (65) became blind when he was 21 years. He met with an accident in a factory. Naturally, he was depressed. One day he thought, "It was not quite fair for me to turn to God for assistance now that I was in a pretty deep mess, when, in fact, I had had no need for the relationship before." He asked himself, "instead of asking what God and the Universe can do for me, why don't I ask what I can do for God and the Universe?"

Torey's doctors advised him to leave all visual imagery behind and rebuild his mental representation of reality using hearing and touch. The doctors' instructions did not appeal to Torey. He did just the opposite; he simply pictured the world around him through his now hyperactive visual imagination. Torey discovered his world by continuously visualising the surroundings, "a world which became increasingly intense, accurate, and sharp." He took time to master this art. After some months, he was living in a visual reality. "Often, people forget that I can't see. I wear sunglasses all the time, and once somebody even said to me - it was very funny - she said, "Don't 'look' at me that way."

Torey believes that vision gets in the way of people with eyesight; "without being troubled by the continuous bombardment of actual sight, enables you to have a kind of mental freedom that can be very creative. Often, in fact, people close their eyes when they think. So in that respect, I was able to utilise my abnormal situation as a real advantage." Torey's most useful message for all of us is that "fate is one thing", but "what we make of it is another."

-30-

INVISIBLE MIND

Just ignore him. This statement is the most humiliating advices one can give to someone. It is said that anger is a nobler emotion than indifference. You say something, and you are not heard. You ask something and there is no response. This is a form of invisibility. Ralph Ellison (66) says, "I am a man of substance, of flesh and bone, fibre and liquid - and I might even be said to possess a mind. I am invisible; understand, because people refuse to see me."

Nobel Laureate José Saramago (67) gives a fictional account of a contemporary city where all the people suddenly go blind. No one knows the reason for collective blindness. The first victim is a man who loses his vision while in his car waiting for a traffic light to change. Blindness then spreads very quickly as an infectious disease.

All the blind people are put in a former mental hospital, in an effort to isolate them. The mental hospital becomes over-populated very quickly. There is a revolt. There is collective despair. The only person, who apparently is not affected by the blindness, is the ophthalmologist's wife. She makes the blindness 'visible'. Suddenly, when all hope seems to have vanished, everybody is able to see again. "I can see, I can see," the people in the street shout and sing. The lack of vision ends as abruptly as it had begun. But why did they become blind in the first place? Did they really go blind?

At the end of the novel Saramago writes, "Do you want me to tell you what I think, Yes, do, I don't think we go blind, I think we are blind, blind, but seeing, blind people who can see, but do not see." Saramago points to the vulnerability of our society. The main threat our society face is collective blindness - when we lose the ability to see, when the visible disappears in front of our eyes, when the society itself, becomes blind. How can we communicate our thoughts and emotions when we are blind to each other is the question Saramago asks.

Fritjof Capra (68) writes about a session conducted by a therapist. A man tells the therapist about problems related to his job and his family situation. The therapist asks him a few questions. At the end, the man bursts into tears and says: "For the first time, I have felt like a human being."

The meeting between the man and the therapist established the necessary resonance that was required between them. Capra described it as "an authentic meeting between human beings." The patient placed before the therapist all his inner feelings, and the therapist simply gave the patient an honest hearing. The therapist helped him to remove his cloak of invisibility.

Blindness, perhaps, is one way to remove the cloak of invisibility. As Jaques Lusseran, the blind French author (64) writes: "I stopped caring whether people were dark or fair, with blue eyes or green. I felt that sighted people spent too much time observing these empty things...."

Why we constantly fail to notice few things that are right in front of us? According to the studies (69) we are constantly overlooking much of the world around us because our attention is selective. We don't like to get distracted. We love prioritizing one thing and neglecting everything else. Research also suggests that our brain is 'selectively selective'.

-31-

SYNESTHETE'S MIND

Some people see numbers in objects, hear colours and taste sounds. They have muddled senses, called synesthesia. Synesthetes are otherwise normal, except that every time they see a number, the number would evoke a specific colour. Synesthesia literally means 'joined perception'. Just about any combination of the senses is possible. There are some synesthetes who hear sounds in response to smell. There are some who smell in response to touch, and so on. Synesthetic perceptions are specific to each person. Different people with synesthesia almost always disagree on their perceptions.

Synesthesia is a sensory experience, and not a pathological problem. It is not hallucination, nor a metaphor. It runs in family and so it may have a genetic basis. Synesthetes are not crazy people, says Vilanayur Ramachandran (70). There may be unconscious synesthetic propensities in all of us, says Ramachandran. "People often don't come out and say that they do because they're worried you might think they're crazy."

What causes synesthesia? There is a structure called the fusiform gyrus in the brain where the colour area of the brain is. Right next to this structure is the number area of the brain. The two areas are almost touching each other, and there may be an accidental cross-wiring between these two regions of the brain, says Ramachandran. The functional magnetic resonance imaging studies have shown the evidence of the occurrence of cross-activation in synesthetes. Because of the cross- wiring, the colour neurons get activated. Due to cross wiring every time synesthetes sees a number they see a colour.

Neuroscientists have proposed that synesthesia results from a genetically driven overabundance of neural connections in the brain. These over connections, they believe, cause a breakdown of usual modularity of the brain resulting in synesthesia. Researchers also say that these cross connections are present in everyone at birth, and the connections are simply refined later. They say adult synesthetes may have simply retained these crossed connections.

Synesthesia is more common among creative people. Observers claim that synesthesia is seven or eight times more common among artists, poets, and novelists. These are the people who can see "hidden links that most of us lesser mortals have difficulty in seeing."

Imagine if the synesthesia gene, instead of being expressed selectively in the fusiform gyrus, is expressed throughout the brain. In that case, says Ramachandran, "If you have these long-range connections, then it permits greater opportunity for linking seemingly unrelated concepts." For many researchers, this aspect of synesthesia is of utmost importance.

Researchers are interested in the study of synesthesia because they believe someday it may reveal something about human consciousness. No one knows how we bind all of our perceptions together into one complete whole. Studying synesthetes we may probably understand how we perceive our world.

Synesthesia genes are not really useless. If they were, they would have been eliminated from the gene pool years ago. If these genes are good, if the genes can make one artistic, then why doesn't everyone have it? Ramachandran says we must wait; evolution takes time. Maybe in another hundred thousand years everybody will have this gene, and we will all be creative people. Perhaps, this situation is also not desirable, because besides creative people, we also need people who can give shape to and benefit from creativity.

-32-

PATIENT'S MIND

Our two-year-old son had dysentery, which was becoming quite worrisome for us. A colleague suggested a doctor and said, "If you believe that those doctors who don't charge a big fee can still be good doctors, you may take your son to him."

This doctor was the most unassuming person I had ever met. We talked for almost an hour about us, our family, and many things totally unrelated to the problem our son was facing. In this one hour, he created enough confidence in us about his abilities. He understood our feelings as young and inexperienced parents. He told us that our feelings were absolutely normal. He said he felt the same when he was our age under similar circumstances. Before the treatment had even begun we felt that the doctor was caring and compassionate. We became, not merely his patients, but also his friends.

The Doctor let us talk. He listened quietly, generating a feeling that we knew more about our son's illness, and he respected that. He prescribed some medicine, but before doing that he gave the first dose after saying some prayers. Before the healing process started, he was able to create a bond between us. When we came out of his room we knew we met not only a good doctor, but also a good man. This man became our family doctor.

Obviously, both 'technology' and 'human touch' is important for curing an illness. They have a symbiotic relationship. The purpose of technology and human touch is healing and comforting; healing comes from medicine and comforting is done by the doctor. A doctor's job, I believe, is half finished if the patient thinks that the doctor has heard and understood him. A patient is not merely a machine. A patient has emotions, and that's why "find it and fix it" mode of treatment doesn't work. The feelings and emotions of a patient need to be understood, though it may seem unreasonable at times. Impatience could be the trait of a patient, but not of a doctor.

Our doctor, before coming to his chamber, always visited a nearby temple. One day, the doctor told me that he prayed for the well-being of his patients who came to him with a lot of anxiety and also had a lot of faith in him. For them, he was a great healer. The doctor prayed so that he could do justice to this faith. He believed that prayers help in the healing process.

The story in the adjoining chamber, which his son occupied, was different. Most of us preferred to consult the father. It was embarrassing not only for the son, but also for his father. Though the junior doctor respected his father, he was unhappy about our 'neglecting' him. He was well equipped on the 'technical' part, but bereft of the 'human' part. He did not blame his father, but also did not realise his own shortcomings. For a patient, a doctor's technical qualifications are important, but also important is the doctor's other side. It is true that for a doctor, an illness is a faulty process in the body. He tries to identify it through laboratory tests and clinical observations. But a doctor can't afford to be uncaring and hurried. He also can't afford to be disrespectful to the patient, whatever 'technology' or 'status' he might have acquired.

A patient's dependence, optimism and faith in the doctor make him a better doctor. One day, my doctor friend told me, "I wish my son understand, sooner the better, that the soul of a doctor lies in the heart and mind of the patient."

-33-

TRAPPED MIND

Some people have the habit of jumping into a ditch knowingly. They jump into the ditch because they think the risk is worth taking. They expect good returns from "the risk". It is also our greed that pushes us into a ditch. Sometimes we jump into a ditch without understanding its implications. Sometimes we jump into a ditch even after understanding the implications.

We jump into the ditch hoping there would be a saviour. Jared Diamond (71) writes that such people "feel safe because the perpetrators are typically concentrated (few in number) and highly motivated by the prospect of reaping big, certain, and immediate profits, while the losses are spread over large numbers of individuals." According to Diamond, the inclination of the elite to ruin a society grows in proportion to their ability to insulate themselves economically from the society as a whole.

Competition often is the reason for our jumping into a ditch. No one likes to lose. We all want to win even if it comes by adopting dubious means. We the human beings, it is generally believed, can be made to behave in any imaginable way. But this is not always true. We all have our threshold. We know that we will break if we allow ourselves to stretch beyond our threshold.

Some of us have 'dysrationalia disorder'. This disorder is "the inability to think and behave rationally despite adequate intelligence." This disorder makes the brain to believe that something is real, when in reality, it is not. It afflicts some of the smartest people. In the ditch, these afflicted people see lots of opportunities, which, in fact, are not there.

-34-

PAINFUL MIND

Pain is an unpleasant sensory and emotional experience. It could be in the mind due to, for example, rejection by someone you love. It could be in the body resulting from, for example, shoulder dislocation. It is said that the pain of the mind is worse than that of the body, and emotional distress lasts longer in the pain of the mind than when caused by physical injuries. Those who are in pain don't adapt with the situation as others do. But then one gradually adjusts to the pain and learns to live with it.

There are many factors that cause pain of the mind. The prominent ones are emotions, social context and background, beliefs, attitudes and expectations. The meaning of pain to a person also matters. It can be less painful if one knows how to deal with it. Fear and anxiety associated with pain is more disabling than the pain itself. In fact, both pain and depression share a common pathway to the emotional region of the brain. That's why depression aggravates pain. Researchers indicate that emotional arousal may influence how much pain a person perceives because of how well other physiological systems are working.

Pain basically is one's private affair. It is a subjective experience. It varies with one's family background and cultural attitudes, childhood experiences and so on. No one can understand someone else's pain. Emotional fractures are more difficult to heal. When we share our joys, our joy increases. When we share our pain, our pain lessens. At times, tolerance can also aggravate pain.

A non-emotional response to an injury may be a sign of bravery in certain cultural or social groups, but this behaviour can also mask the severity of an injury to an examining physician. Depression and anxiety can lower pain thresholds. Anger or excitement can obscure or lessen pain temporarily. Feelings of emotional relief can also lessen a painful sensation.

The intensity of the pain depends upon how an individual perceives it. If one believes that she is in pain, then she will be in pain. For, pain is like sleeplessness; the more one wants to sleep, more one gets incapacitated to fall asleep. If you want to sleep, do the opposite; try to stay awake. The lesson: confront pain head on to let it off.

In spite of the unpleasantness that is causes, it is essential to have pain perception. In fact, it is a curse if one does not feel physical and emotional pain. In some senses, it is like sickness. It is dangerous not to have symptoms of sickness when one is actually sick.

The spiritual teacher Ram Dass said, "Resistance to an unpleasant situation is the root cause of suffering." And so don't try to resist pain. The only way out is to face it and learn to deal with it.

-35-

WISE MIND

The great challenge for us is to be knowledgeable as well as wise. Knowledge is evolving at a fast pace, and as Bertrand Russell said, "If knowledge continues to increase, the world will need wisdom in the future even more than it does now." Wisdom is an evolving concept. Like truth, the concept of wisdom changes with time. Knowledge can be easily shared and needs regular updating. The goal of wisdom is to comprehend the deeper meaning of known facts, and for that a combination of cognition, self-reflection and openness are necessary.

Wise look at phenomena and events from different perspectives. Wise can accept the realities of the present moment. Wise can filter out noise from the pattern. Psychologist William James rightly said that wisdom is about knowing what to overlook. A truly wise mind can comprehend the inherent limits of knowledge as well as of wisdom.

Knowledge comes from information and facts. Wisdom comes from experience and living. A knowledgeable has the ability to compare options and solve problems. A wise has the ability to intuit the options before they become problems. Knowledge makes a person wise only if he experiences it. As one wisdom researcher says, "One can have theoretical knowledge without any corresponding transformation of one's personal being. But one cannot have wisdom without being wise." The difference between a wise and a clever person, according to a Jewish saying, is that a clever can extricate himself from a situation into which the wise would never have gotten himself.

Wisdom is understood at the experiential level; it cannot necessarily be found in what a person says but is expressed through an individual's personality and conduct in life. Wisdom is not necessarily conveyed through the content of a statement but through the way the statement is delivered.

Monika Ardelt (72) says that wisdom does not automatically grow with age, but the association between wisdom and age is potentially positive. The functions of biological "hardware" of the mind deteriorates with age, whereas the capability of "software" of the mind has the potential to increase with age.

Conventional wisdom is situational. Wisdom can be taught. It is possible to acquire wisdom by interacting with the wise. Though wisdom is learned more easily than it is taught, but unless taught, it is learned the hard way.

We supposedly 'know' much more than our ancestors knew. But have not we forgotten many things that our ancestors knew and remembered. We can cure dreaded cancer, but we are forgetting the ways to lead a simple, content and happy life.

-36-

ROBIN HOOD MIND

Robin Hoods rob the rich to feed the poor. They root for the poor, the weak, and the needy. Why do Robin Hoods have such powerful hold on the public imagination? Why do some people have Robin Hood mentality? We all have some amount of 'fairness instinct'. We get angry when we experience disparity, when we see injustice being meted to the deserving. It is fair to express anger if the reasons for anger are justified. Often people are angrier than the situation demands. That is not fair. It is said that the differences in merit are indeed often exaggerated by those seeking to justify departures from fairness. Like everything else, reciprocity requires fair play. A fair Robin Hood is respected, and his generosity becomes his asset.

We have 'inequity aversion'. We are generally not happy with what we have. We are more concerned about what others have. We turn down a good offer if others are getting a better offer. It is not simply a matter of how successful one is, but the question we ask is how successful others are. In the Darwinian language, it is not 'fitness', but 'relative fitness' that really matters.

Maximisation of one's fitness is not enough to optimise relative fitness. Monitoring others' fitness and success is equally important. Relative fitness is related to 'relative deprivation'. Relative fitness doesn't get imbalanced if relative deprivation is under control.

Robin Hoods aim to reduce imbalance. The Robin Hood mentality is a kind of altruism: You scratch my back, I scratch yours. Robin Hoods expect reciprocation from the beneficiaries. They prefer generous reciprocators. They try to avoid cheaters as cheaters unhesitatingly accept favours, but do not return the favours. The Robin Hoods don't like those favour-seekers who fail to reciprocate their favours in some form. Their conviction prompts them to choose favour-seekers. Sympathy and gratitude (to those who helped the favour-giver in the past) play a big role in deciding the beneficiary. Robin Hood can get cheated if he can't see the difference between a genuine and a fake favour-seeker.

It is generally moral rationalisation, rather than moral reasoning, which is the basis of taking a decision, says Jonathan Haidt. People "begin with the conclusion, coughed up by an unconscious emotion, and then work backward to a plausible justification." Steven Pinker says, "We are born with a universal moral grammar that forces us to analyse human action in terms of its moral structure, with just as little awareness." We generally like to reciprocate favours, reward benefactors, and punish cheaters as these behaviours are considered "fair" in all societies.

Since "natural selection" generally prefers the strategy of "keeping everything to yourself", can one have the evolution of fairness in the Darwinian world? Evolution of fairness is possible. In the Darwinian world, there is space for other norms. We do many things that benefit others more than it does to us. Robin Hood mentality is a kind of moralisation, and as Pinker says, "Moralisation is a psychological state that can be turned on and off like a switch, and when it is on, a distinctive mindset commandeers our thinking."

-37-

VIOLENT MIND

Aggression is natural part of our psyche. We love watching violent films, but we generally are not really violent. We may fantasize killing but we generally are not killers. Steven Pinker (73) says we are becoming nobler as we are living in the least violent phase of human history. According to Pinker, we are more peace-loving than our ancestors were. It is absolutely fine if you don't agree with what Pinker says.

Some scientists postulate that prefrontal cortex of the brain functions to suppress impulsive behaviour, including violence. It means that this part of the brain has the ability to restrain negative behaviour. Damage to this area may cause an intelligent and respectful person to become fitful, impulsive, and rude. Studies also indicate that some individuals come into the world predisposed to developing a violent or aggressive behaviour pattern. Violence has been linked with high amounts of testosterone and low levels of serotonin.

Stressful environment leads to aggression and vice versa. Debra Niehoff (74) says that brain is an organic historian. It keeps track of our experiences through the language of chemistry. Any change in our response to stress also gets recorded. When we confront an unknown person, we try to judge him/ her through our previous experiences stored as recorded messages. Based on the 'chemistry of those feelings' we respond. Based on this response, the unknown person reacts.

Is there a possibility of pre-empting violent tendencies in us? Marc Hauser's hypothesis suggests that it is possible to pre-empt violent tendencies in us if we have an 'intention detector' that can read people's intentions before they act. Though a great idea it doesn't seem a feasible solution to pre-empt violent tendencies. The total elimination of murderous impulses can be another way to end violent tendencies. Perhaps, that is possible in the future by biologically manipulating the quantities of testosterone and serotonin.

Another interesting observation has been made about the mode of violence. It says that modus operandi of the crime may change; "robberies would be achieved with trickery rather than at the point of a pistol; gang members might attack each other with insults and taunts rather than razors; governments might play chess to decide on tricky border issues." Such 'elimination' is possible in remote-controlled robots, but not in human beings. Unhealthy amount of violent tendencies is certainly not desirable; perhaps, a streak of it is welcome. It is boring to live in a totally peaceful world.

-38-

FOOL'S MIND

The Latin word 'follis' means "a large inflated ball". Fool, a 'windbag', is generally considered ignorant. We generally think fools can't judge or understand properly. But all fools are not necessarily ignorant or stupid. Michael Dirda (75) has put fools in three categories: real fools, professional fools, and unsuspecting fools.

The innocents and simpletons are real fools. They can't act because they are so real. They speak their mind without restraint. But they often unknowingly utter words of wisdom. In fairy tales, real fools ultimately find the treasure and also win the princess. Though they are often unsure of themselves, these fools are saintly and humble.

The mind of a professional fool is pretentious. The professional fool deliberately makes others feel important. He is good actor. Yes-men, con artists and clowns fall in this category.

An unsuspecting fool considers himself to be wise. He thinks he is wise but he gets fooled so easily. His vanity is like a windbag that deflates mid-air. You must have seen the ad on TV that showed the deflation of a ballooned man after getting his annual increment, which was much lower than his expectations.

Literature in every language is full of interesting and sympathetic 'foolish minds'. Rabindranath Tagore's 'Taraprasanna's Fame' is the story of a writer who writes all the time. He has no time for anything else and thus knows very little about the world around him. But the stuff he wrote had never been published. Naturally, others did not think very highly of him. Finally,

Taraprasanna's work not only gets published, it is even praised by reviewers. The reviewers become highly impressed by the complexity of the book. They couldn't understand a word in the book. Who is the bigger fool, Taraprasanna or the reviewers, is for you to decide.

The mind of Sir John Falstaff, a Shakespearean character, is essentially like a professional fool. Fallstaff, a fat ("lying tub of lard"), vain glorious and cowardly knight is a party man. Wherever he goes it is party time. What makes Fallstaff so entertaining? "Possibly his openness in his crimes, his lack of loyalty being so apparent — essentially his frankness (not so much honesty) in life and his grinning self-determination, self-observance," writes Kenneth MacLeish (76).

The historic Akbar-Birbal king-fool pair of the 16th century is so well known. Birbal (1528-1586) was indeed witty and entertaining, but he was also powerful, being one of the 'nau rattans' (nine jewels) of the most powerful emperor. He was well versed in Hindi, Sanskrit, and Persian. The wit and poet was also a gifted singer. Should we really call him a fool?

Tagore's poem 'Old Servant' is about Keshto. No one likes this witty and faithful, but good for nothing family retainer. Being the old servant, he manages to remain in the house. Once on a pilgrimage, the master of the house gets sick. It is time for Keshto to come to the fore. His dedication and service rescues the master from the fatal illness. In the process, he becomes ill. His illness proves fatal. The master had to return home, but without his beloved old servant. Keshto was not a wastrel after all.

The so-called fools can't be overlooked as they play a significant role in society and as Alexander Pope said, "Fools rush in where angels fear to tread."

-39-

FRIENDLY MIND

Friendship is a special relationship between two individuals. This relationship is voluntary, informal and personal. It is essentially a relationship among equals. A child can be a friend of his parents only when both are 'equal'. Until then, it is parental love. Among friends suppression and inhibition are unnecessary. A friend feels happy at his friend's success. A friend feels sad at his friend's failure.

Friendship is not used for achieving status. Our experience of friendship alters with age. "Our earliest friendships are coed, then imprecisely homoerotic, as we reach the age at which tribal people form cadres of hunter-warriors to protect and feed the clan, then homophobic for the sake of family life, and at last relaxed and coed again", writes Edward Hoagland (77).

Friends know one another's soft spots. Often, we take friends for granted. Often, we don't mind hurting their feelings. Often, we go out of bounds. Often, the pain caused by a friend is beyond repair. To lose a good friend is a real tragedy.

Aristotle defines friendship under three categories: friendships of utility, friendships of pleasure, and friendships of the good. In the friendship of utility, 'friends' are friends because they benefit each other. In the friendship of pleasure individuals seek out each other's company because of the joy it brings. Most pristine is the friendship of the good. This friendship is based upon mutual respect, admiration for each other's virtues, and a strong desire to aid and assist the other because one recognises the essential goodness of the other. The friendship of virtue remains as long as friends remain virtuous in each other's eyes. Only a few fortunate have such good friends. Friendships of utility and pleasure are much less intense and less permanent.

Adam Smith explored the effect of commercialisation on friendship. He said that when a man performs a generous action, not out of fancy but with proper motives, he feels himself to be the natural object of their love and gratitude. And when he looks back, he applauds himself for the sympathy and approbation he got for the offered generosity. His mind is filled with cheerfulness, serenity, and composure. "He is in friendship and harmony with all mankind, and looks upon his fellow-creatures with confidence and benevolent satisfaction, secure that he has rendered himself worthy of their most favourable regards."

Friendship, as understood by C S Lewis, arises out of mere companionship. Some common insights or interests lead to companionship. We find it quite gratifying when we find that someone also thinks like we think. Often, similar thinking people become a 'burden'. We feel what we thought our own 'unique treasure' is in fact, not so. It is in fact, being shared.

Friendship is an important part of everybody's life. Those of us who don't have enough friends (for some reason) would like to imagine that we have friends, even when we know that these so-called friends don't acknowledge our friendship in any manner. We look upon friends for support and a sense of personal identity, and at the same time, we like to have our own space. Friendship is a matter of choice, and so it operates within the constraints of class, gender, age, ethnicity and geography.

Can a man and a woman be just friends? The answer is both 'yes' and 'no'. Those who say 'no' say that 'the sex part always gets in the way'. They say we seem to understand only romantic relationships. Some say 'just friends' type of relationships between the opposite sexes is definitely possible.

We have seen several patterns of relationships between man and woman. One can have friendship and then get married. One can have marriage and then develop friendship. One can have friendship and remain only friends; marriage is unimportant. Many people think it is not necessary to 'sexualise' every relationship. People are open to a wider range of emotional possibilities. Many people believe in platonic friendships, but they say that once physical attraction comes into the picture or when people are in a committed relationship with someone else, the relationship gets complicated.

One of the aspects of friendship is sharing emotions, and sharing emotions doesn't come naturally. It requires an enormous amount of energy. "Women often mistake this emotional exchange as an act of friendship, because that is what comes naturally for them", writes Brian Lee. One view is that when a woman sees someone as a friend, she finds it difficult to accept him in any other role. Friendship is informal, but love is not. Once friendship transforms into love, it loses informality. Love comes with strings attached. We have trouble accepting asymmetric relationships. For example, an intense relationship between a student and a teacher is not liked. But things are changing fast.

Man and woman can't be "just friends", is another view. Adrian Ward says that "platonic coexistence is merely a façade, an elaborate dance covering up countless sexual impulses bubbling just beneath the surface." We may think we're capable of being "just friends" with members of the opposite sex, but the opportunity (or perceived opportunity) for "romance" often complicates the relationship.

Many observers believe that the perception of friendship between the opposite sexes is a matter of gender differences. It simply means that the meaning of friendship is different for a man and a woman. Men are much more attracted to their female friends than the other way. Men suffer more from the "misguided belief" that their female friends were attracted to them. "As a result, men consistently overestimate the level of attraction felt by their female friends and women consistently underestimate the level of attraction felt by their male friends."

Generally, women are not good at reading the minds of their male friends. In platonic relationships, men look for opportunities of romance. Women, on the other hand, see platonic relationships purely from that perspective. Platonic relationship for a woman means that she can talk and share her feelings with someone close. Men, on the other hand, typically define their best friend as someone with whom they can do something worthwhile.

John Mac-Murray (78) says that greater the fundamental difference between two persons is, more difficult it is to establish a fully personal relation between them, but also the more worthwhile the relation will be, if it can be established and maintained. If one draws an analogy from this observation of Mac-Murray, it would seem that the nature of man-woman relationship depends upon how one establishes and maintains a relationship with the opposite sex, in spite of the fundamental differences between them.

-40-

MIND THAT TOUCHES HEART

Touch is one of the nicest human expressions. A supportive touch makes a big difference. A sympathetic touch soothes depression and strengthens a relationship. Touch lessens pain. Touch is a medium of social exchange. It helps to form strong attachments and alliances. A touch can be worth a thousand words.

Our emotions have various forms, and they cause variety of responses. The response can be physiological (for example, increase in heart rate), behavioural (for example, to run away or come closer), or subjective (for example, feeing happy, or sad). Certain kind of touch conveys specific emotion, researchers say. Fear, for example, can be expressed by holding and squeezing with no movement. Sympathy requires holding, patting and rubbing. Says a touch researcher, "Most touches were only about five seconds, but in these fleeting moments, we're capable of communicating distinct emotions, just as we are with the face. This is a sophisticated differential signalling system that we haven't previously known about."

When someone touches us, we first perceive the physical properties of the touch, such as its speed, its gentleness, and the roughness of the skin. "Only thereafter, in a separable second step based on who touched us, do we believe we value this touch more or less." Neuroscientists have reported a relationship between touch and emotion via the brain's primary somatosensory cortex, the brain regions that encodes basic touch properties, such as how rough or smooth an object is.

The researchers at Caltech say that emotion is involved even at the primary stages of social touch. The researchers at the University of Chicago say that the timing and frequency of vibrations produced in the skin when you run your hands along a surface play an important role in how we use our sense of touch to gather information about the objects and surfaces around us. As the frequency of vibrations on the eardrum conveys information about sound, the researchers say, the precise timing and frequency of these neural responses convey specific messages about texture to the brain.

Our perception is shaped by how we feel about the things we perceive. The researchers hope that their work can help reconfigure social responses to touch for people diagnosed with autism. One of their findings (that gentle touch leads to more positive reception) can be used to develop methods to assist victims of physical and sexual abuse or torture. "Now that we have clear evidence that primary somatosensory cortex encodes emotional significance of touch, it may be possible to work with early sensory pathways to help children with autism respond more positively to the gentle touch of their parents and siblings," believe the Caltech researchers.

Too often, we underestimate the power of a touch. We must remember that we are not machines. We can't afford to lose faith in human touch. Touch a lonely heart with a tender hand and you will know what a wonderful feeling touch conveys.

-41-

MIND AND WILLPOWER

The habits of highly effective people, as outlined by Stephen Covey (79) are: be proactive, begin with the end in mind, put first things first, think "win-win", seek first to understand, then to be understood, synergise and undergo frequent self-renewal. Knowledge, skill and desire are required to form these habits. In order to form a habit, we should know what to do, how to do, and most importantly, we must have the desire to do. We often lack the desire to do.

Roy Baumeister (80) says, virtue is hard work. We often don't give enough efforts to do something worthy of efforts. For example, eating right kind of food can't be so difficult, but we eat junk food knowingly and unhesitatingly. We know smoking cigarette is not good, and we also know that getting rid of these habits is not such a big deal, but we continue doing them. Our willpower often becomes so weak that we can't resist the alluring temptations of vice or bad habit.

One assumes that people with high self-control can resist temptations more effectively than people with low self-control. But the researchers tell us a different story. They say that people with strong self-control are less likely than others to resist desires they come across in their daily lives. Baumeister says that people with good self-control avoid temptations and problem situations, rather than battling with them. There are other researchers who say that self-control works most effectively by means of controlling habits, rather than by using willpower, for direct control of one's actions in the heat of the moment.

Self-control is desirable for forming good habits, and following virtues are indicators of good self-control. Self-control, or lack of it, can make or break good habits. Researchers tell us that self-control is most effective when it operates through habits. Some even say that habits are more reliable than willpower. Willpower is limited, and it fluctuates. When willpower is used to resist impulses and desires, one encounters natural reluctance. A consequence of this is depleted action or no action.

We are made to acquire habits. Habits are formed with repeated practice. Habits can be helpful in conserving willpower. So the advice is — Don't waste your self-control over mundane matters; preserve them for the time when you encounter more serious situations.

Virtuous habits are extremely helpful in conserving willpower, as these habits prepare us to deal with strong temptations. The sources of temptations are both inside and outside. It could be due to external objects. It could arise entirely from inside the mind. "It takes both, a suitably inclined person and the compromising situation, to create the maximum temptation", writes Baumeister. In the situations of maximum temptations, one will almost certainly require willpower. In these situations, habits may not be of much help. Virtuous habits may be more effective at avoiding temptation than at resisting it. It is not easy to eliminate desires, particularly sinful desires. It is thus, good to be virtuous as "virtue is not the absence of desire for sin — it is the absence of sin despite the desire to sin".

In the moment of weakness, our willpower could be low. We may like to smoke a cigarette, but if it is not available, virtue remains intact despite the fact that the person is briefly willing to give in. Many good goalkeepers know that preventing the shot is easier than blocking all the shots. As Baumeister tells us, every day virtue is best achieved, not by such heroic feats of willpower, but rather by avoiding such situations in the first place.

-42-

SHY MIND

Shyness is one of our common traits of character. Even though shyness makes us uncomfortable, it is essential part of our psyche. It becomes evident on our faces and in our deeds that we don't want to talk about this 'odd state of mind'. One can observe it in our heartbeats or upset stomachs. Shyness must have benefited us; otherwise it would not have existed, evolutionarily speaking.

From a survival standpoint, perhaps, shyness has evolutionary advantage. There was time when shyness was not that evident. One lived far more in public; whole families would eat, sleep and socialise together in the same room. "As greater physical and psychological boundaries grew up around individuals, particularly among relative strangers in public, there were more opportunities for awkwardness and embarrassment about when these boundaries should be crossed", writes Joe Moran (81). Shyness increases as the possibilities of human contact and interaction decreases.

We are not shy in all situations, but in certain situations. We feel shy when we are talking to a stranger. In the presence of some strangers, we feel threatened and try to protect ourselves from the perceived threat. Because of the perceived threat, we feel inferior to that person, and if the person is 'attractive', we feel even more threatened. We become more concerned about this person's thinking and how to deal with it. As a result, we struggle to communicate. We feel shy and try to avoid eye contact.

Are introverts shy people? Introverts tend to make frequent strategic withdrawals from social life. Introverts prefer solitude to social activities. Shy people long for contacts with other people, but generally feel awkward and fearful to make such contacts. Shyness is generally associated with gentleness, but there is nothing in shyness that makes one, more likely, a nice person. Shy people often find social life painful and burdensome. Little shyness is understandable, but too much of shyness is a kind of social anxiety disorder.

Shyness has no logic. It is situational. We may feel shy in the presence of an authoritative figure. We may feel shy when we are in unstructured and unfamiliar settings. Shy people look for closer bonds with people who are close to them. One may feel shy in intimate encounters. Shyness can impact our self-esteem and control our ways of living in society. Shyness is subjective. In some of us, it is mild social awkwardness. In some of us, it is a social phobia. Shy people try to avoid situations that involve contact with others. Social phobia may lead to loneliness. Excessive self-focus and our preoccupation with our own thoughts can lead to shyness.

I don't know if we came to this world with a certain 'shyness default setting'. But I know that shyness is culture dependent and can have interactive effect on our emotional problems. Shyness is a habit that can be moulded. Confident people are, perhaps, less shy. One way to overcome shyness is to overcome fear and develop confidence. There are behavioural and cognitive interventions to overcome shyness. Shyness interventions, perhaps, work better in group settings when they are with other people experiencing similar problems.

If one is comfortable with what one is, there is less possibility of self-doubt, there is less fear from failure, and there is less possibility of shyness. Here, one also needs to be careful. Too much 'comfortable' with oneself makes one a narcissist. And as Andre Dubus said, "Shyness has a strange element of narcissism, a belief that how we look, how we perform, is truly important to other people."

-43-

TEARFUL MIND

Tear is one of the expressions of emotions. Tears can mean many things. It can also mean nothing. Not only do tears relieve emotions, they also reduce stress. We cry when we are sad. We also cry when we are happy. The secretion of tears can also be due to any irritation caused by foreign irritants in the eye. Public weeping to draw attention is nowadays a common phenomenon. Then there is 'shower weeping' and there is 'stream weeping'. During shower weeping, one weeps inordinately, shedding floods of tears. During stream weeping, quiet streams trickle down the cheek.

Intense situations, happy or sad, can provoke overwhelming mental reactions, and that may take the form of tears. Emotional isolation can also produce tears. Crying often signals vulnerability and it can lessen a person's aggressive behaviour. Crying signals submission, and promotes a feeling of trust. It promotes a feeling of sympathy or unity in associates. Besides helplessness and loss, the factors that promote weeping, according to psychologist Ad Vingerhoets (82) includes personal conflict, anger, rejection, feeling of inadequacy, self-pity, joy and the emotions produced by music and films.

Tears lubricate the eye. Crying is a process like exhaling, urinating, defecating and sweating. Tears release potentially toxic substances from the body. They act as a safety valve by releasing excess stress hormones such as cortisol. As stress often precedes a good cry, the sense of calm often felt afterward is, at least in part, due to hormonal release. Our traumatic memories need to be flushed out of the psyche. Crying is one way of getting rid of such memories.

Tears can be "a kind of overflow or discharge of previously repressed emotion." It can also be "some sort of return to infantile, even prenatal, experiences and emotions," writes Thomas Dixon (83). Tears have healthy as well as pathological implications. The healthy implication of tears is to function as a channel for the discharge of a strong feeling. "Affect is conceived as a psychic fluid that needs to be drained out of the system; weeping is one way to achieve that," writes Dixon. Tears also have hysterical symptoms. Confusion and sleeplessness may result in bouts of tears that may last for hours. There is a view that says weeping serves no purpose other than to get rid of 'increased cerebral excitation,' and to allow the excitation to 'flow away.'

Sandor Feldman (84) believes that there is no such thing as weeping for joy. Feldman argues that weeping for joy (for example, after seeing the happy ending of a film, or experiencing a moment of pride or joy such as the birth of a child) in fact, are "merely cases of a delayed or displaced discharge of negative affect." For Feldman the moments of pride or joy are awareness of the transitory nature of life and happiness. Feldman says, there are no tears of joy, only tears of sadness.

Emotional tears differ from onion tears. Emotional tears contain higher levels of stress hormones such as adrenocorticotropic hormone, prolactin and the painkiller leucine enkephalin. The levels of hormones and prolactin levels rise with stress, researchers observe. Emotional tears contain more manganese than onion tears. Chronically depressed people often have high levels of manganese in their systems. Researchers say manganese helps regulate mood.

'Crocodile tears' don't have the biochemical or psychic weight of the deep emotional ones. Psychologists Jonathan Rottenberg, Lauren Bylsma and Ad Vingerhoets (85) analysed 300 crying experiences. They say the benefits of crying depend on what, where and when particular crying episode took place. They found that in the majority of cases, improvements in the mood followed a bout of crying. According to their study, one-third of the survey participants reported no improvement in mood and one-tenth felt worse after crying.

Without a context, tears mean nothing, believed Charles Darwin. For him, weeping was an incidental result, and its sole effect was to give relief to individuals who were experiencing the agony of pain. Tears assume meaning only when they have a particular mental, social and narrative context.

Darwin (86) listed three reasons for the secretion of tears: "The primary function of the secretion of tears, with some mucus, is to lubricate the surface of the eye, and a secondary one, as some believe, is to keep the nostrils damp, so that the inhaled air may be moist, and likewise to favour the power of smelling. But another, and at least equally important function of tears is to wash out particles of dust or other minute objects which may get into the eyes."

Tears have a history that is as old as the human history. "We came out of the ocean more than 400 million years ago, but we never completely left the sea water behind. We still find it in our blood, sweat and tears," is how Fritzoff Capra sums up million years of human history.

-44-

MIND THAT DRIVES

Our most basic purposes, survival and reproduction, are met through family, extended family and community. Next in the hierarchy of purposes are our psycho-social needs; security, bonding, acceptance and affection evolve to meet our needs of cooperation and altruism. Among the higher purposes come love, family commitment, meaningful work and career, social and political involvement, transcendence and spirituality.

The fundamental motives that drive us, according to Paul Lawrence and Nitin Nohria (87), are the drives to acquire, to bond, to learn and to defend. These drives have both bright and dark sides. Those lacking the drive to acquire are more likely to lack self-esteem. On the other hand, the drive to acquire makes one insatiable. Addicts are driven to seek more. Both ambition and envy stem from our drive to acquire. The drive to acquire can lead to competition and restlessness. It is desirable to align our competitive energies for a larger, rather than an individual goal. The drive to bond with others reduces discontentment, and makes life more fulfilling. But the drive to bond is based on distinction between 'us' and 'them'. The drive to bond brings us closer to each other. When the bonds are severed, we feel a deep sense of betrayal. In the bonding mode, one likes to enter into a caring commitment with others, be it with an individual or a group. The balancing between acquisitive and bonding drives at all levels — between individuals, between groups, and between individuals and the larger goal — is thus desirable, but is not easy to achieve. An uneven balance can lead to cutthroat competition or totally collusive bonding; harmful either way.

The drive to defend prepares one to protect oneself from unjust attacks. It helps one to defend his identity and reputation. The dark sides of defending and learning drives are that these also leads one to dysfunctional extremes; obsessed learners are good for nothing, and becoming too defensive can lead one to paranoia. Excelling in one or two drives is not enough. To really excel, one needs to balance all the four drives. When any one drive gains dominance, for whatever reason in a given social setting, it soon becomes self-reinforcing.

It is our brain that helps us to prioritise and set our goals. Our brain receives signals in various forms. Our emotions influence these signals. Due to the clashes in emotions, the likelihood of clashes in our drives always exists. Our brain sorts out the priority, based on our past experiences, skill sets, and cultural leanings. Our brain sees what matters to us the most, and then it takes us there. It also takes us away from irrelevant goals. Arjuna saw only the bird, others the tree.

-45-

EXPERT'S MIND

An expert is a person who is capable of making mistake even in his narrow field of expertise. An expert knows more about the future of others than their past or their present. As one expert said, "An expert knows all the answers - if you ask the right questions." We all are experts.

A committee consisting of deserving experts is an expert committee. Although the members of the expert committee possess different expertise, they think alike in one sense. They are not keen listeners. They don't care to listen when the presenter is presenting, but their amazing enthusiasm can be noticed at the question hour. The expert committee always keeps some decoration pieces. These decoration pieces look good in the vases. Obviously, they are expensive to maintain.

The mutation rates of experts are quite high. That is the reason committee members are taken for a specified period. Fortunately, getting freshly-minted experts is not a problem. They are available in plenty. Those who constitute an expert committee believe wisdom comes only with age. Thus, 50+ is an ideal age to become an expert committee member. Retirees are preferred as they create less fuss regarding fixing of the date for the meeting. Moreover, having them as member is a way to resolve another problem, the problem of a quorum. They are the best 'fillers'. More flexible an expert is more sought after he is for the committees.

Experts are 'experts' in concluding that "this can't be done", and also in explaining why this can't be done. At the smallest pretext, they reject proposals. They love using riders while accepting a proposal. One good thing about experts is that they don't think too much. They know that they are advisors, not implementers. They also know that their report will not be read, so why bother.

No one should deny the need of a committee, particularly when some want (for various reasons) to kill someone's initiatives or push it to the future. As Fred Allen remarked, "A committee is a group of people who individually can do nothing, but who, as a group, can meet and decide that nothing can be done." C Northcote Parkison likened a committee to a plant. Perhaps that's why experts are sometimes planted in the committee as watchdogs. Their only work is helping the committees to achieve their mandated objectives.

I am a member of several expert committees. I have acquired the above qualifications the hard way. My experience has taught me a few important lessons. I wish to share a few of them here: (i) An expert is a person who avoids the small errors while sweeping on to the grand fallacy, (ii) "If Columbus had an advisory committee he would probably still be at the dock", (iii) If you see a snake, just kill it, rather than appointing a committee on snakes, (iv) "Some experts have no differential abilities from the rest of the population, but for some reasons, and their empirical records, are believed to be experts. They dress up their expertise in beautiful language, jargon, mathematics and often wear expensive suits", and (v) Remember there is no better expert than the one who uses all his six senses; the sixth being common sense.

-46-

MEANINGFUL MIND

We all seem to possess a meaningful mind. We all want to lead a meaningful life. We all try to understand the meaning of life in our own way. Meaningful life may mean different things to different people. The definition of 'meaning' depends on our requirement and interest. It is understood in relation to an individual's basic needs, experiences and emotions.

Meaning is interactive, selective and value-driven. Our intentions often differ from our actions. We are more committed towards our intentions than our actions. Due to the intention-action gap, what we say is sometimes not what we mean. We perhaps somewhat know our mind, but we are not so sure of the others' minds. But knowing others' mind is equally important to understand meaning. Rabindranath Tagore said, "I miss the meaning of my own part in the play of life because I know not the part that others play." A really meaningful mind understands others' mind as much as one's own mind.

Social connection is important for meaningfulness. One generally learns meaning from the group. "Meaning is like a large map or web, gradually filled in by the cooperative work of countless generations." Meaning is thus, more linked to one's cultural identity.

Neuroscience says that the construction of meaning is a biological property. Neurobiology proposes that "meanings arise as a brain creates intentional behaviours and then changes itself in accordance with the sensory consequences of those behaviours". Arnold Modell (88) says that events within

143

the body, mind and brain are the original sources through which the meaning of experience is constructed.

A meaningful life makes one feel worthwhile and happy. Meaningful, however, does not ensure happiness. Unhappy life could still be meaningful. Moreover, meaningfulness does not always have to bank on morality or goodness. A good athlete need not necessarily be good to his competitors. It doesn't, however, mean evil life is acceptable if it is meaningful. Meaningfulness, howsoever meaningful it is, must not cross certain moral limits. The goals of happiness and meaningfulness are not necessarily the same. But the problem is that people seek not just happiness, but also meaning of life.

Is there a need for 'meaning' in a world that has truth, beauty and love, asks Arthur C Clarke. "If we waste time looking for life's meaning, we may have no time to live — or to play", felt Clarke. It must also be acknowledged that purposeless life is not worth living. It is true that life online is not easy. But it is also a fact that life offline also doesn't have much worth. It is said that evolution has 'no purpose'. But can we ignore the fact that it happens. And when it happens, it must have a purpose. Perhaps evolution had no purpose to begin with, but slowly it emerged as we progressed. Unless purpose is backed by the driving force of possibilities, how can it emerge?

Why are we here for? "We are here because one odd group of fishes had a peculiar fin anatomy that could transform into legs for terrestrial creatures; because the earth never froze entirely during an ice age; because a small and tenuous species, arising in Africa a quarter of a million years ago, has managed, so far, to survive by hook and by crook", said Stephen J Gould.

What are we here for? One might simply say we are here to witness our generation and our times. Some might say we are here to make new structures that are needed to make an even universe. One might like to say that universe has a purpose, and we are here to serve the purpose of the universe.

What is the purpose of the universe? One of the purposes of the universe is to provide and prepare ground for the emergence of intelligent life. The purpose of the intelligent life is to ask profound questions, and probe the nature of the universe itself. We are a miniscule part of a multiverse. No species is guaranteed its tenure on this planet. Ours is the only universe that supports biological life. Our universe did exactly what it was supposed to do. We are thankful to our universe that we are not sterile and lifeless. We are unique because we can 'think'.

-47-

TALKATIVE MIND

One often wonders what is more difficult, talking or listening. Those people who are eager to tell too much about themselves, may not have similar eagerness to know about others. Lonely people look for an opportunity to meet and talk to people. They even invite themselves to gatherings where they expect to get an outlet for their outpouring. It becomes a means to them to pass on the pain of loneliness.

All professors seem to believe in the logic of Oscar Wilde, who said: "I like to do all the talking myself. It saves time, and prevents arguments."

One likes to talk to beautiful minds. The beholder sees the beauty of the mind through two drives: 'sense' and 'form'. The sense drive seeks for immediate gratification. The form drive, on the other hand, looks for abstract understanding and rational order. These drives, however, are in conflict with each other, says Friedrich Schiller (89). "Comfort and ease struggle against a sense of duty and responsibility. The allure of freedom clashes with the longing to be steadfast and rooted in existing commitments." Though in conflict, we need both the drives to see the true beauty. The logic of seeing beauty perhaps applies to the art of conversation.

Politeness is one of the main ingredients of the art of conversation. It is said that good nature is 'natural politeness'. It has also been said that politeness is 'artificial good nature'. Exuberant politeness perhaps, is not the desirable attribute one needs to possess. Sycophancy is as despicable as rudeness is. "Politeness is a sort of social benevolence, which avoids wounding the pride, or shocking the prejudices of those around you", writes Maria Popova.

Arthur Martine (90) has given us some guidelines on the art of conversation. It includes: know when not to speak (silences are often more flattering than compliments), mind the rudeness of laconic response (avoid giving sharp answers that look uncivil). Martine's list of ill-manners includes: the loud talkers don't allow anyone to utter a word; the excessive life-sharers are the biggest bores, they think what interests them interests others too; the clever bores don't like simple conversations to go on, they try to intercept it with 'idle speech' to show their wisdom; the apathetic bore yawns on your face deliberately, bad taste is the falling of these bores; the lingering bores overstay; the eternal bores talk about the same subject all the time; some people possess special gift for choosing the least appropriate topics of conversation, like to the blind they will speak of fine pictures and scenery; the egotistical bore is most revolting as they are "ready to slime over every subject of discourse with the vile saliva of selfish vanity."

What about the conversations in the techno-bulged age? Sherry Turkle (91) thinks that the world has become more talkative, but feels that we are talking at each other rather than with each other. In other words, technology-based conversations are becoming less interesting. It seems everyone is talking but in fact no one is talking. "You can't always tell, in a conversation, when the interesting bit is going to come," Turkle says.

-48-

STRESS, FAITH AND MIND

Ayurveda has been saying for centuries that mood causes or influences the course of various disorders. It is no longer merely a Ayurvedic belief. Researchers have established a definite link between stress caused by behavioural and psychological events and the immune system. The immune system alters neural activity and thereby behaviour, thoughts and moods.

Stress could cause fever, can change liver metabolism, reduced food and water intake, reduce sexual activity, and increase anxiety. The study of how the immune system responds to stress, has given newer insights about how our bodies process stress, how neurological and hormonal activities are connected with stresses, and how stress interferes with the body's immune system.

Another pillar of stress-human health structure is the faith factor. Biologists, social scientists, and religionists are working on the role of faith vis-à-vis stress and well-being. Their aim is to explore ties between spirituality and enhanced action of human immune system. Scientific evidence suggests that religious belief and spiritual practices are associated with health. Some believe that our biological immune system has a higher, more profound spiritual counterpart, and spiritual and psychic immune systems are deeply related. And as our subconscious minds are the first to react, it is from here our spiritual immune systems emanate. Function of religious and spiritual coping in adjustment to serious illness, including cancer, is getting due attention and recognition. US National Cancer Institute supports the possibility that spiritual coping is one of the most powerful means by which patients draw on their own resources to deal with a serious illness such as cancer.

-49-

BLIND MIND

The blind age ('Andha Yug'), Dharamvir Bharati's landmark book, set in the last days of the Mahabharata war, was written in the years following the partition of India. It speaks about destruction, not only of human lives, but also of ethical values. In Mahabharata, both the victor and the vanquished loose eventually.

HG Wells tells the story of stagnation in The Country of the Blind. The story is about a mountaineer, who by accident finds himself in a valley cut off from the rest of the world. All the inhabitants of the valley are blind. These people are self-sufficient but are insular and close-minded. The villagers of the valley have no concept of sight, nor do they want to understand it. Even the woman the mountaineer loved dismisses the concept as his imagination. The mountaineer's 'unstable obsession with sight' becomes the symbol of his defective thought process. These sightless people of the valley wish to deprive the mountaineer of his own eyes. The mountaineer tries to flee from the valley.

Sight can be confusing. This is the theme of a story by Brian Friel, based on Oliver Sacks' case history of a patient. In this story, a born blind gets sight in midlife, but finds it profoundly confusing. The patient can't make sense of anything she sees and thus wants to return to her original state of blindness.

Various metaphors have been used to symbolise blindness. Dharamvir Bharati has used blindness to represent dehumanisation of individual and society. HG Wells's blindness represents a restricting society, and the struggle of the individual against social conformity. Sight can lead to confusion, says

Friel. Saramago uses blindness as a metaphor for both personal misfortune and social catastrophe.

In 'blind' times, we need icons and role models to take us away from the blindness. We look forward to some torch bearers to take us out of the dark tunnel.

-50-

QUESTIONING MIND

'What's the time' is a simple question. 'What is time' is a complex question. 'How are you?' is not a question.

Take this simple question that was circulated on the internet: Would you give your honest opinion about solutions to the food shortage in the rest of the world? It is a simple question but from the responses received from various continents, it seems it was not a simple question. In some parts of the world, people did not know what 'food' meant. In some other parts, people didn't know what 'shortage' meant. Some people didn't know what 'honest' meant. And, in some parts, people did not know what 'opinion' meant. In some parts of the world, people didn't know what 'rest of the world' meant. It also means that simplicity or complexity of a question doesn't lie only in the question but also in the responses.

We all have a questioning mind. The nature of our questioning mind varies. Some questions reflect our ability of reasoning, understanding and learning. Some questions reflect our hollowness. A convergent question has specific answer and is close-ended. Divergent questions are open-ended and have many answers. Close-ended questions are 'saturated'. Open-ended questions are 'unsaturated'. Some questions have both 'yes' and 'no' answer. Some questions have no answer. As Milan Kundera says, "it is questions with no answers that set the limit of human possibilities, describe the boundaries of human existence." Questions can be 'deeply satisfying' as well as 'deeply troubling'.

One of the ways of growing up and moving forward is to step outside our comfort zone. Questions take us away from our comfort zone and help us to move forward. A questioning mind stops working when true happiness dawns, says Sri Sri Ravishankar. It is good that we never achieve true happiness.

Voltaire said that a man can be judged by his questions. Right kind of questions, to oneself as well as others, can be very helpful. Some people have the innate ability to frame good questions. A good question is the one that causes people to really think before they answer it, and one that reveals answers that had previously eluded them, writes Phil McKinney (92). It is thus important to effectively phrase, and ask questions. By asking the right questions, one can proactively make their own discoveries. One, therefore, shouldn't be ashamed of or afraid to ask questions to themselves as well as others. The ability to form a question might be the key cognitive ability that separates us from all other beings. "The desire to ask a question shows a higher level of thought, one that accepts that your own knowledge of a situation isn't complete or perfect", writes McKinney.

The ability to think inquisitively is one of our critical survival skills. Researchers say that the true genius has high levels of cognitive disinhibition. These are the people who have the mental agility to process and use all the absorbed information in an organised way. McKinney believes that anyone can develop and harness this power through the use of provocative questioning and the discovery that follows.

We face as well as ask all kinds of questions; good, bad and indifferent. There are questions where the questioner doesn't expect any answer; the answer is implicit in the question. The questioner expects only agreement. Such questions are asked by the people who want to appear to care about another person's opinion, but really want their instructions carried out without discussion. Such a questioner is, writes McKinney, either overly confident of his beliefs, or so insecure that he has to bully others into agreeing with him. Such questioners don't believe in considering an alternative point of view. Such questioners want to take away your power of answering the question, but it may so happen that you are unwilling to surrender this power of yours. You want to present your viewpoint that is different from that of the questioner. You don't want to ignore his question, nor do you want him to ignore your answer.

If you have to say something contrary to the expectations of the questioner, you try to say it with conviction, and you make sure that it gets heard at the appropriate level.

Socrates liked to ask questions, and that was his way of teaching. Socratic questions have been divided into various types: questions for clarification, questions that probe assumptions, questions that probe reasons and evidence, questions about viewpoints and perspectives, questions that probe implications and consequences, and questioning the question. McKinney says that the Socratic Method is a good way to generate good investigative questions. Socratic questions challenge you to justify your beliefs about a subject, often over a series of questions, rather than responding with an answer that you have been taught is 'correct'. Socratic set of questions don't assume you are right or wrong. Socrates's goal was to help his students unveil their own thoughts and their own beliefs. Socrates believed that the first step toward knowledge was recognition of one's ignorance. Questions help us recognize this and drive us forward. Tony Wagner (93) says, "don't take things at face value; don't go in with preconceived ideas that you're trying to prove." To ask questions one needs to apply reasoning and logic to unfamiliar ideas and situations. A questioning mind needs to have 'critical-thinking skills'. Daniel Gilbert says questions are not the problems. He was particularly talking about questions in his area - psychology. Gilbert thinks the problem is "we have a tendency toward irrational exuberance." He thinks we have not yet asked the questions that are going to be the 'most delicious' in the coming years.

A questioning mind asks both small and big questions.

The John Templeton Foundation (www.templeton.org) has been asking big questions from time to time; questions like, Does the Universe have a purpose? Does evolution explain human nature? Does moral action depend upon reasoning? Does science make belief in God obsolete? Does contemporary neuroscience support or challenge the reality of free will? Can you learn to control your mind? Does quantum physics make it easier to believe in God? Do we have souls?

Every year Edge (www.edge.org) asks the most interesting question. Some of the questions are: What scientific idea is ready for retirement? What should we be worried about? What is your favourite deep, elegant, or beautiful explanation? How is internet changing the way you think? What will change everything? What are you optimistic about? What do you believe is true even though you cannot prove it? The best thing about these questions is the quality of answers given by the stalwarts in their own respective areas. They reflect diversity. One question can have many answers.

Gemma Elwin Harris' compilation (94) of Big Questions is interesting because the simple answers are given by Great Minds. It has questions like (the great minds who have given the answers are in the bracket): Why is blood red, not blue? (Christian Jessen), How are dreams made? (Alain de Botton), Where does mind come from? (Antony Woodward & Rob Penn), Why do monkeys like bananas? (Daniel Simmonds), Why can't animals talk like us? (Noam Chomsky), Can a bee sting a bee? (George McGavin), If the universe started from nothing, how did it become something? (Simon Singh), Where does 'good' come from? (A.C. Grayling), Are we all related? (Richard Dawkins), Why does time go slowly when you want it go fast? (Clandia Hammond).

Then there are small questions that are asked by ordinary people, such as, Can one ask an unbiased question? Should one always accept what one is told? Should one ask questions to only those who presumably know the answer? If there is a difficulty in understanding a point of view, where is the difficulty, in explaining or in understanding? What gives us more stress – when we know too much or when we know too little? Why can't we walk straight, even when we know that the shortest distance between two points is a straight line? Should we encourage or discourage the appearance of more evolved species for our own survival? Will we ever be able to cure cancer? Can we live forever? Can we ever know what does a woman want?

-51-

SHOULD WE DESIGN A PERFECT MIND

A perfect man is not confined to his time. He understands nature. He has wisdom and knowledge. He is creative and visionary. He has conscience, determination, reforming capabilities, leadership abilities, insight, and tolerance. He has weaknesses and shortcomings as well.

If I were to design a perfect man, I would like my man to have the above qualities. Taking the clues from genetic behaviourism, I would identify the genes responsible for these traits. Obviously, my search for the desired genes will begin with those men who have proved their worth in their chosen fields.

After an elaborate search I would pick specific genes of the following individuals for my "Designed Genome" project.

I would pick creativity genes of Rabindranath Tagore.

I would choose determination genes of Mahatma Gandhi.

I would pick visionary genes of Jawaharlal Nehru.

For leadership genes, I would go for Jamshedji Tata's genes.

I would make real efforts to get the reforming capability genes of Raja Rammohan Roy.

For conscience genes I would not find a better donor than Vivekanand.

I would have to work hard work to pick the scientific insight genes of Jagdish Chandra Bose.

The most difficult search for me would be to identify the donor of tolerance genes. After a long search perhaps I would get it from my next door neighbour, a common man.

While I was thinking about reassembling the genes into the genome of designed man, it occurred to me that genes of so many strong persons can't reside in one body. It also occurred to me that when systems are not engineered, instead they are allowed to build themselves, the resultant whole is greater than the sum of its parts. I was also cautioned that evolutionary approach is much better than strict engineering approach, if one is thinking about designing something as complex as human being. My colleagues told me that "humans were produced by a process that was not engineering".

My learned colleagues also told me that liberating human race from its biological constraints is a dangerous idea. Since genetic code is four billion years old, some of my colleagues believe that it is time to rewrite it. They say, "If we don't play God, who will". There are some other colleagues of mine who think that "to take God's place is insane arrogance, a risky and a dangerous venture." I saw merit in the arguments of my both sets of colleagues. But I felt that the futuristic concept that "humans must wrest their biological destiny from evolution's blind process", though quite tempting, is not really a workable idea. I felt no need to become stronger and smarter biologically. I did not want to become God. I decided to abandon the idea of designing a complete man. I decided to wait for the proper man to evolve naturally.

-52-

WHY ARE WE AFRAID TO TAKE A LOOK AT OURSELVES

We are afraid to take a closer look at ourselves because we think Pandora's Box might open. We are afraid that the box might contain some unpalatable truths. When we look closely to the self, we find many abnormalities, many imperfections, and many unpalatable truths. We also see ourselves as perceived by others and we respond accordingly. We try to fit ourselves into their thinking. The expectation of others gets reflected in our actions.

Ernst Schumacher (95) writes about a man who after his death meets many people in the other world. Among them, he dislikes one the most. He wants to know who that person is. Someone up there tells him, "Up here, we have special mirrors that are quite different from those in your world." He then says, "The man you hated the most is you."

When we look in the mirror, we see good as well as bad images. Distorted images disturb us. We try to remove the distortions. Often we are successful. But some distortions are not easy to remove. Should we try to remove all distortions? Can't one be beautiful with natural imperfections? Should we not be content with natural imperfections?

Cicero said, all mistakes are not foolish. Mistakes are helpful, particularly if others are making them. "Never interrupt your enemy when he is making a mistake" is the wise counsel of Napoleon Bonaparte.

Some idealists try to create the perfect, even at the cost of disastrous consequences these might lead to. One of Nathaniel Hawthorne's short stories (96) is about an otherwise perfectly beautiful woman with a birthmark on her left cheek. Hawthorne writes, "The fatal flaw of humanity, which nature, in one shape or another, stamps ineffaceably on all her productions." This 'marked' woman is married to a scientist. This scientist thinks that science can remove all kinds of blemishes, including the birthmark of his wife. In his scientific quest, this frustrated idealist discovers that it is her 'birthmark of mortality', and that removing it removes her from life itself. In Pied Beauty, on the other hand, poet Gerard Manley Hopkins thanks god for making 'freckled' things. The poem has only good things to say about "pied" (spotted).

It is said that "Beauty leads to a closer look". We judge good-looking people, not only more favourably, but also more accurately, say the researchers. A beautiful book cover prompts a closer reading. Another research conducted by psychologists suggests that people enjoy gazing in the mirror. They like to see what they see in the mirror. Narcissists go out of their way "to modify personal appearance in an effort to garner praise that bolsters self-views". This makes them successful short-term self-lovers.

-53-

WHAT KIND OF MIND IS NEEDED TO DEAL WITH INCOMPATIBILITIES

Fritjof Capra (68) writes about two great friends but with differing viewpoints: "(Heisenberg) gave me a vivid description of discussions between Erwin Schroedinger and Neils Bohr. Schroedinger's wave mechanics was a continuous formalism involving familiar mathematical techniques, while Bohr's interpretation of quantum theory was based on Heisenberg's discontinuous and highly unorthodox matrix mechanics, which involved so-called quantum jumps." Bohr tried to convince Schroedinger who exclaimed in great frustration. Heisenberg continued with a smile, "How poor Schroedinger was lying in bed at Bohr's home and Mrs Bohr was serving him a bowl of soup, while Neils Bohr was sitting on his bed insisting: 'But Schroedinger, you must admit...'"

It seems conflicting ideas do not necessarily lead to animosity. There are people who get along so beautifully in spite of differences. Take for example, Rabindranath Tagore and Mahatma Gandhi. Both had tremendous respect for each other's intellectual and moral capabilities, but their paths diverged on many occasions. Gandhi saw in Bihar earthquake "a vital connection between the calamity and the untouchability campaign." He believed "not a leaf moves but by His will". The calamity also disturbed Tagore, but he could not support Gandhi's argument equating it with ethical failure.

In some debates, there is never an eventual winner. Michael Madhusudan Dutt and Ishwar Chandra Vidyasagar were two very different persons. Vidyasagar was not a modern man in the conventional sense, but he was the propagator of the most modern concept of the period — widow remarriage. Dutt was a confused person; he changed religion and led a reckless life. Vidyasagar helped him to resolve his confusion. The convergence of contradictory thoughts and compatibility between two temperamentally different personalities is possible, if both are well meaning individuals. Such minds are becoming a rarity in the present century.

What kind of minds do we need for the present century? Howard Gardner (97) says that the most sought after minds for this century are the disciplined mind, the synthesising mind, the creative mind, the respectful mind and the ethical mind. For a disciplined mind, it is not enough to accumulate factual knowledge. A disciplined mind recognises the difference between subject matter and discipline. Discipline equips one in specific ways of thinking. This specific way of disciplined thinking sets one apart from others.

A synthesising mind can bind part information into a coherent whole. The creative mind goes beyond normal knowledge, poses new questions and offers new solutions. Too disciplined minds are often in conflict with synthesising and creative minds. The synthesising mind's approach is to seek order, equilibrium and closure. The creative mind is motivated by uncertainty, surprise, and continual challenge. The respectful mind respects, acknowledges, and views sympathetically and constructively the differences between people.

We need all five kinds of minds to succeed in a fast changing world. Overall, we need a balanced mind that values both empathy and system in equal measure. Balanced minds get along despite differences.

-54-

WHY TIME HAS NO MIND OF ITS OWN

Mind can choose its speed. Mind can move through time in any direction. Mind visits the future or revisits the past whenever it wishes to. Time can be compressed or stretched. Time seems to slow down when there is not much work. Time races when there is enough challenging work. An emotional event becomes more recent than it actually is. Time flies when one is having fun. The perception of time can heighten enjoyment and ease annoyance.

Physiologist Hudson Hoagland conducted time-perception experiment on his wife. She had flu. She made a usual complain that her husband is away from her bedside for too long, even if he had gone away only for a short while. A common complaint gave birth to such an important experiment.

Hoagland proposed to his wife quite an annoying experiment: Count off 60 seconds while he timed her with his watch. The result of the experiment: When her minute was up, his clock showed 37 seconds. In subsequent experiments he showed that his wife's mental clock ran faster, higher her temperature became.

Our illusions and distortions of time are consequences of the way our brain builds a representation of time, says David Eagleman (98). He says that time "slows down" during brief, dangerous events such as car accidents and robberies. Our brain processes different types of sensory information at different speeds by different neural architectures. The difficulty our brain faces is that it receives signals from different modalities at different speeds in different neural regions, but to be useful, these signals must become aligned in time and correctly tagged to outside events.

Daniel Gilbert says that we are a race of time travelers unfettered by chronology and capable of visiting the future or revisiting the past whenever we wish. We may get trapped in the present when our neural time machines are damaged.

Aristotle argued that time neither has beginning nor end. The end of one moment is the beginning of another moment. One doesn't want to retain all the past memories. One also doesn't want to completely wash off his past. One can't stop future vistas from taking shape. It is impossible not to remember the past or not to envision the future.

Past and present events can shape the future, but not always. It is like the 'seed and tree' situation. All seeds have potential to become trees, but not all seeds become trees. If the soil is not right, the seeds rot. For a seed to become a tree proper soil and sunlight are needed.

Janus is the god of the beginnings and the end. Janus (the month of January is named after him) is usually depicted as having two faces or heads, facing in opposite directions. It was the gift of god Saturn that Janus could see both the future and the past. Janus symbolises change and transition, such as progression of the past to the present into the future. Janus can see various facets of time in the same frame and at the same time.

We experience time as we create it in our mind. Claudia Hammond (99) considers time to be a friend as well as an enemy. The trick is to harness it and to work in line with our conception of time. Time slows down when we are gripped with fear. As one gets older, time seems to speed up. Hammond says often things seem closer than they really are. She calls this 'forward telescoping'. The reverse of it is 'backward telescoping' "when you guess that events happened longer ago than they really did." Some do not agree with these suppositions. They say it is the tempo of life that makes time faster or slower.

We can't, and possibly shouldn't, try to live long in the past or in the future. The past and the present are known and thus limited. The future is unknown and thus unlimited. It is hard to fathom the 'unlimited' on the basis of the 'limited'. Let us pray that we do not become the victim of 'endless now's'. Pray we can re-visit past, not to live there permanently, however, rosy it may appear to be. Pray we can create our future.

-55-

IS THERE A NEED TO KNOW THE FUTURE

Astronomers and astrologers are star-gazers. They study heavenly phenomena. Astronomer probes the cosmos. Astrologer interprets the impact of celestial objects on materials in the earth. There was a time when one could hardly differentiate between these two streams. There was no problem as long as astrologers were using 'physics of the universe' to explain earthly events. The problem started when astrologers extended their role and used the positions of celestial objects to predict future events. The bone of contention was science versus non-science.

Astrologers believe that the "universe is deterministic and fully or mostly predictable". Astronomers believe that astrology, as is generally accepted, is not connected to any known real world phenomena. In astrology, 'divinity', 'supernatural', 'metaphysics' play a big role, whereas these words are not part of astronomy's vocabulary. In simple language, astronomy is science and astrology is non-science.

Astrophysicist Jayant Narlikar is against granting legitimacy to astrology, which according to him is pseudoscience. Science journalist Biman Basu (100) writes about the incompatibility of star positions and prediction and control of human fate. Astrologer Bejan Daruwala takes a practical path when he says, "I don't care if astrology is a science or not. The fact is that it works".

Coming to the question of predicting future by using scientific methods, let us take the case of genetic behaviourism and personal genomics. Genes can't tell if someone will get a lottery or get promotion, but can predict one's likely future health scenario. We have begun to believe gene-based health predictions. One might say such predictions are statistically biased. It is more of a conjecture as astrology is. This science is yet to establish its credibility. But one must recognize the fact that there are better chances of establishing the correlation between genes and diseases than between star position and future prediction. This is because scientific methods are available with genetic science, but no worthwhile efforts have been made to evolve scientific methods in predictive astrology.

Another aspect of future predictability is that the future has two faces, one positive and one negative. Taking the cue from positive psychology, let us say that we shall confine only to positive future predictions, such as promotion or some such thing. The moment one reads in 'What the stars foretell' column that he or she is likely to get a promotion, the positive psyche gets activated. The person makes real efforts to get promotion. He gets promotion. He gets the promotion, not because of his stars, but because of his efforts. If he wants to feel happy that his promotion happened due to his star position, let him be happy. What ultimately matters is the state of our mind. If something bad is happening now, there is no harm in hoping that something good is waiting for you in the future. By thinking so, we are not hurting ourselves or anyone else.

But is there a need to know the future? At this moment, perhaps, that is beside the point.

-56-

WHY IT IS HARD TO WALK STRAIGHT

The shortest distance between two points is a straight line but we often fail to follow this simple geometrical instruction. What are the possible temptations that direct us to take routes that are not straight?

Our desires are always greater than our necessities. We are so eager to fulfill our desires that we forget what line or curve for the route we are following to fulfill those desires. Niccolo Machiavelli said, "Men are so simple and so ready to obey present necessities that one who deceives will always find those who allow themselves to be deceived."

Economic compulsion is one of the major reasons that lead us to take wrong paths. We come across situations where there is possibility of making bad money. Some of us can't resist such temptations and take the wrong way knowingly. We all love to put in the least efforts to achieve the maximum. There is nothing wrong if one follows the law of least effort; in fact, it gels well with the concept of following a straight line.

In majority of cases we get cheated because we want to follow shortcuts. We get cheated because we want to get cheated. We become, knowingly or unknowingly, willing partners of the cheating process. The situational contingencies lead us to behave inconsistently. We all like to behave like an idealist. But when we come nearer the problem, we falter, especially when the problem affects us personally. John Galsworthy said, "Idealism increases in direct proportion to one's distance from the problem."

Robert Thouless (101) has given a few helpful guru mantras for walking on not-so-straight line. These include: use emotionally toned words and gestures to get undue attention, emphasise the trivial and ignore the important to let down an opponent, contradict and misrepresent an opponent's position by diverting his attention to irrelevant issues, point out the logical correctness of the form of an argument whose premises contain doubtful or untrue statements of fact, use of pseudo-technical jargon to confidently present false credentials, use questions to draw out damaging admissions, angering an opponent deliberately so that he argues badly, and so on.

Creating controversy is another kind of crooked thinking. Arthur Schopenhauer's strategies (102) of controversy includes: claim victory despite defeat; interrupt, break, divert the dispute; meet the opponent with a counter-argument as bad as his, make him exaggerate his statement, appeal to authority rather than reason; and so on.

Misconceptions about ourselves and about the world surrounding us also lead us to wrong paths. One should know the rules of the game. If you know the rules, it doesn't mean you should apply them on others. But if you know the rules, others will find it difficult to apply them on you.

It is also handy to remember that straight-line solutions are not possible if problems are bigger than logic. It is difficult to teach a crab to walk straight. So either beware of the crabs, or if that is not possible, learn the ways of the crabs.

-57-

IS SURVEILLANCE A GOOD IDEA

There are people who don't break the rules because they think breaking the rules is not the right thing to do. There are also people who don't break the rules because of the fear of being caught and punished. Who is better on the integrity scale, the one who has the opportunity to steal but doesn't, or the one who possesses no such opportunity and thus doesn't steal?

If I don't steal because I think it is wrong thing to do, then I am morally more right than the one who doesn't steal because he is afraid of being caught. The person who is afraid to steal and therefore does not steal may be applauded, but doesn't deserve the moral credit for not stealing. It is not so difficult to get away with rule bending, but if you know you won't get caught and even then you don't bend the rules or lie or cheat, you are a master achiever in the integrity scale.

Let us say, you are appearing for a competitive examination. After entering the hall the first thing you are told is that the room is fitted with several CCTV cameras to keep a check on your academic dishonesty. Let us consider another situation. After entering the hall you are asked to sign an integrity pledge that you will not use any unfair means during the exam. In the first surveillance system is in place and in the second no such system is in place. Which system you will prefer? I suppose you will prefer the second system. But is it the better system for conducting competitive exams?

The basic premise of conducting the exam at the above two systems is different. There is less probability of cheating in the first system compared to the second. Is it the only reason for students preferring the second option?

The second system assumes that the students can be trusted, whereas, in the first system, the organisers are not so sure of such trust in the students. Is surveillance a good idea?

Our attitude to surveillance is different in different settings, and thus the surveillance level should be set according to the goals of the system. In the examination hall, perhaps, signing an integrity pledge is not enough. In a school setting an integrity pledge for general conduct is perhaps more relevant because schools have a broader mission. It needs surveillance of a different kind. Schools and colleges not only give us degrees or diplomas, but also give us opportunities to become what we ultimately become. A good school is one in which students need neither extrinsic motivators to encourage study, nor surveillance to deter cheating. Surveillance signifies a lack of trust, and therefore its effect on any relation is corrosive; closer the relationship, more corrosive is the effect.

The relation between surveillance and morality is a complex issue. "In some contexts, surveillance helps keep us on track and thereby reinforces good habits that become second nature", says Emrys Westacott (103). "In other contexts, it can hinder moral development by steering us away from or obscuring the saintly ideal of genuinely disinterested action. And that ideal is worth keeping alive". Westacott says that if one regards the development of moral character completely irrelevant, then one would be less troubled by the practice of surveillance.

We should do what is right because it is the right way to do things, and the notion that someone, somewhere may be watching strengthens this belief.

-58-

WHY SRK IS SRK

Some people have privileged existence. Some inherit it and some create it. There are some people who are called lucky because they can create their own luck. They know the paths of success, and they consciously and methodically try to follow those paths. They are not necessarily more talented than others, but they know how to maximise their potential better than others. They know what is important for them. Generally, they have the ability to get along well with others. They are ambitious. They have the capability to accept their failures intelligently.

In spite of so many success stories, we are still not sure what kind of rules success follows. It is generally believed that only those who deserve success get success. This supposition, however, is not always true. It is also not true that only the hardworking gets success. Success doesn't necessarily always involve some form of sacrifice or compromise. There are some people who get more than they apparently deserve.

The X-factors of success, according to some psychologists, are charisma, chutzpah, joie de vivre, and grace. Some people have these X-factors in plenty. Shah Rukh Khan (SRK) is one of them.

SRK is sharp and witty. He likes to make fun of others, but does not like those who make fun of him. He knows how to be brash or gentle as the situation demands. SRK is an excellent communicator. He is endowed with all the overlapping components "such as expressivity, sensitivity, control, eloquence, vision and self-confidence". His verbal fluency has its own charm. He is a natural attractor. He knows what could be interesting to the other person (particularly his female admirers). He is successful because he can envision his success. His films are ordinary, but very successful. SRK is not worried because he has understood that 'success' and 'ordinary' can go hand-in-hand. SRK is a charismatic person. It doesn't matter if he is not a charismatic actor. I too am not sure if SRK has chutzpah. He hardly challenges conventions.

Neuroscientists believe that people who possess originality and simplicity still need chutzpah to deliver on their potential. SRK is neither original nor simple, nor does he have chutzpah, but he delivers, much better than those who possess these characteristics. He is popular, in spite of his audacious behaviour. He doesn't like criticism. He is naturally provocative, but with his natural boldness he can break the boundaries.

SRK's joyous spirit is well known. Passionate exuberance is SRK's forte. Psychologists say exuberance is a stable commodity; it doesn't wane as one grows older. But, there is a problem. "When you are exuberant, you have your emotions out there on the line." The good thing about exuberance is that it is contagious, spreads quickly, and expands people's sense of possibilities. SRK knows how to make others feel important. People envy him. They think he gets more than he deserves. Does he? You may not like SRK but it is difficult to ignore him, at least in Bollywood.

This is how the magician Steve Cohen unlocks the secrets of influence, charisma and showmanship: "The trick itself is never important; it's having a presentational hook." SRK has learnt the ways of showmanship the hard way. He has known that charisma has more to do with his image than with his innate abilities. Someone said that wisdom increases between the age of 27 and 52. SRK is in the time zone when wisdom peaks. Let his star power not overshadow the substance in him.

-59-

WHY WE MAKE DELIBERATE MISTAKES

There is a saying that once the thieves have gone away wiser we become. Why do we go the wrong way or let others go the wrong way? It is because we don't want to confront problems that are likely to create further problems for us. We have an unconscious tendency to simplify the world.

Our approach to solve our own problems is different from the approach we make to solve the problems of others. When we see things from a distance, they are different than when we see them from close quarters. We often can't see things when we look at them from within the system. Often, we have to go out of the system to see things in proper perspective. Often, we don't see things we should have seen. We often watch the world with closed eyes.

Why do we go against our beliefs and wishes? Why do we make deliberate mistakes? Why do we let things go the wrong way? It is because we are afraid of being misunderstood. We don't like to be scrutinised by others, nor do we like to scrutinise others, particularly if the people are powerful. We prefer keeping our eyes closed as per our convenience. We are good at transferring our responsibilities to others, by convincing ourselves that it was not our job. We easily convince ourselves that the problem would resolve by itself, and any kind of intervention is not needed to resolve the problem. Why put fingers in the fire, particularly if the problem is created by the boss. Why take the chance of becoming disloyal to the boss by pointing his fault? We understand that it is not easy to change the boss. It is rather easier to change the job.

This problem is more troublesome in small groups where one of our motives is to exchange niceties. In small groups, it is important to maintain cordial relations with colleagues. "The cosier and the more close-knit the group, the less incentive you have to stir the waters," points out a management expert. Our loyalty often tends to overprotect, and often that tempts us to go the wrong way.

When you don't want to discuss an issue, you simply try not to discuss it. The matter is as simple as plotting points on a graph paper. The points that are not as they should be, either you ignore them, or should be willing to explain the deviation. It is easier to ignore than to explain. Why bother to find out if it was due to experimental error, or due to some new phenomena that was responsible for the deviation from the expected norms. Either way, it is additional work, so why bother.

Says a management consultant, we make two kinds of mistakes when an undiscussable issue is raised: one, we fix blames in a way that escalates stress and conflict, and two, we use ambiguous language that enables people to avoid the problem. When companies have a culture in which managers are more interested in hiding things than solving problems, there is little one can do. We, the humans are designed to make blunders and are all pretty sure we are way above average, says Joseph Hallinan (104). It is the way we think, see and remember that are responsible for our mistakes. We are subconsciously biased. We are overconfident of our own abilities and that leads us to making mistakes.

-60-

WHY ARTISTS PREFER SELF EMPLOYMENT

Job satisfaction is an important part of our professional life. It improves our quality of life. One expects his job to be hassle-free. Whatever little hassle one faces, one wants to get rid of it. Though one expects fair play, one generally expects more than what one deserves. Greater the differences in expectation and reward, bigger are our dissatisfaction. We expect our achievements to get noticed and get their due. Overlooked, or taken-for-granted attitude bothers us the most. We love the complexity and the variety in jobs. Routine is boring for most of us, but most jobs are only that. How to make our work more interesting is thus important for job satisfaction. Too much control from the top leads to job dissatisfaction. Some amount of control is, perhaps useful. It is good for those who control also to remember that employees' care is important part of job satisfaction.

Artists prefer self-employment. According to a study made on a group of workers, performance or visual artists have higher job satisfaction, in spite of the fact, that they earn lesser. Why are the artists more satisfied from their work compared to non-artists? It is known that autonomy has positive influences on job satisfaction. Perhaps, that is the reason self-employed people have more job satisfaction.

Autonomy in the workplace is one of the key factors of job satisfaction. Autonomy provides better possibilities of achieving commitment, involvement, performance and motivation. These are the factors that affect job satisfaction. Autonomy provides the freedom of work. It gives us the opportunity of better time scheduling and its control. One has better control over his or her performance due to autonomy. It also helps to meet the deadlines. These factors obviously improve one's motivation for the work and commitment for the organisation. Motivation prepares us to set proactive goals, a part of job satisfaction. Autonomy gives self-identity and a feeling of self-worth.

Autonomy means self-governance. An autonomous system uses its own information to modify itself and its environment to enhance the chances of its survival and viability. Autonomous systems use their own governance to maintain themselves. When people experience a sense of autonomy they experience affective, cognitive and behavioural benefits.

Traditional organisations entrust autonomy only at the higher levels. There are also some organisations that support autonomy at all levels. These institutions encourage the concept of 'working without guidance'. They even allow independent work. Some organisations, for example, allow their employees to spend a sizeable part of their working time on whatever they want to do. "They pay off, as well", is the experience of these organisations.

Autonomy is believed to have minimised some of the relational barriers between superiors and subordinates. Too much autonomy can sometimes lead to dissatisfaction. We must recognise that each individual is different. Their need of autonomy is therefore also different. Some of us feel uncomfortable with autonomy. We feel intimidated by the responsibilities of autonomy. Some of us are not well-equipped to handle autonomy judiciously. Many of us are either not adequately trained, or don't have the temperament required for autonomy.

One of the flip sides of autonomy, for both high and low level employees, is the possibility of developing unethical behaviour. A certain amount of vigilance is thus, necessary to prevent us from following unethical practices, particularly when there is a high level of autonomy.

-61-

WHY BOREDOM IS NOT FOR EVERYONE

Boredom is of various kinds. Milan Kundera's boredom has three kinds: passive boredom (the girl dancing and yawning), active boredom (kite-lovers), and rebellious boredom (people burning buses and smashing shop windows). Peter Toohey's boredom (105) has two types: simple and existential. Simple boredom (the kind of boredom which a child experiences trapped in a classroom) is an emotion. This kind of boredom is produced by temporarily unavoidable and predictable circumstances. The people most susceptible to it are those who are trapped in a situation and can't get out, "such as young children at school". Simple boredom is not for the intellectuals. Existential boredom, on the other hand, is a state and not an emotion. It is cerebral and is a reflection of sense of emptiness and isolation. Existentially bored persons find it difficult to concentrate. People have experienced boredom from time immemorial. Toohey argues that boredom is an essential aspect of human experience.

There is also a luxurious and dreaming kind of boredom. This kind of boredom is, says Will Alsop, vital to create something fresh. "It's the irreplaceable pause where we have the space to reflect from inside the process." The problem is to find time for luxury and dreaming. When there is so much entertainment, where is the time for imagination? "Without the kind of boredom that gives space for creativity and reflection, we risk the dullness of an uncreative life. The paint never dries and we make a muddy mire of things", writes Alsop. The effect of boredom can be devastating. Teachers, preachers, and government officials can make us sit indefinitely, and also expect us to behave properly. We often do that but at the cost of getting bored. Boredom can be artificially induced; one can get bored with old products, with dangerous ideas. Aviad Kleinberg says that boredom's "deceivingly innocuous nature" may be its greatest strength. Kleinberg and many others think we are becoming increasingly impatient. Hooked on constant entertainment, we need frequent fixes to maintain our high.

It is said that situations of prolonged boredom are dangerous and harmful as this affects brain's plasticity. Boredom is a biological warning that the circumstance you are in is not good for your brain. The younger generation is more prone to boredom. It is believed that it is due to excessive TV and various other kinds of entertainment. In the midst of too much one suddenly gets bored.

Kundera thinks boredom is much greater today, than it once was. The passionate involvement with our occupations was much more in the good old days. The peasants loved their land. The shoemakers knew every customer's feet by heart. The meaning of life was available to them at their workplace, in their field. Each occupation had its own way of being. Today, we are all alike, says Kundera, all of us bound together by our shared apathy towards our work.

Boredom is not for everyone. As Nietzsche said, only the most active animals get bored.

-62-

WHAT IS THE RIGHT DOSE OF GRIEF

Grief is a normal human experience. Grief is a personal experience. One feels sad when one loses someone or something. During this period, one experiences difficult emotions. One likes to be alone. Solitude gives time to the bereaved to adjust and recover. One becomes more susceptible to conflict situations. Since each relationship is unique, grief impacts the aggrieved differently.

Grief in a right dose is good, as shortening or suppressing the natural grieving process can be counterproductive. Researchers found that validation, rather than downplaying of grief, helps the bereaved to cope with their loss in a healthy way. "Grief is our innate adjustment process to loss, which when ignored or downplayed, can result in complications such as depression and other co-morbidities," say the researchers. However, it is difficult to spell "how long one should grieve" as grief is an individual process.

Abnormal grief, however, is harmful. When grief is persistently intense, it could lead to complicated grief disorder. The likely causes of complicated grief disorder are traumatic experiences such as premature, sudden, violent, or unexpected death of someone very close. There is painful yearning for his or her presence. The images of the deceased persist for too long. It may lead to denial of the death. Other complications are desperate loneliness and helplessness. Too much loneliness may cause restlessness, confusion in thought and feeling. Too much sorrow could lead to clinical depression.

Complicated grief disorder affects general health in several ways: fatigue, loss of motivation, sleeping problems, loss of appetite, pain and anxiety symptoms. A person with a history of depression is more likely to suffer complicated grief after bereavement. Too much sorrow allows the brain to lose its adaptability. Researchers say that when sadness spirals into depression, the production of new neurons stop, and over repeated episodes of depression, some areas of the brain actually shrink.

One way to decrease depression resulting from grief is to improve the process of neurogenesis. Regular exercise promotes neurogenesis in the hippocampus region by young and old alike. It improves mood and vitality, reduces anxiety, relieves mild depression, and helps to cope with stress. Research shows that better-educated people tend to experience lower levels of unpleasant emotions because "the knowledge and problem-solving skills provided by education can liberate us from irrational worries that would otherwise leave us prey to anxiety".

Physical touch eases sadness. Supportive companionship is good to overcome grief. But wrong companionship can worsen grief. Re-engagement with the world helps the bereaved to overcome grief. According to a group of researchers, in the absence of social interaction, a normally beneficial experience can exert a potentially deleterious influence on the brain. The studies found that exercise does not encourage neurogenesis if the subject is living in isolation. A promising treatment called "traumatic grief therapy" uses cognitive behavioural methods for symptoms and stress relief, along with interpersonal techniques to encourage re-engagement with the world.

-63-

WHAT MASCULINISES
THE BRAIN

Male brain is different from the female brain. Female brains, in general, develop empathy at a faster rate. Male brains, in general, have a stronger drive to figure out how systems work. Developmental psychopathologist Simon Baron-Cohen (106) says that, "It's your prenatal testosterone that might be very important in understanding this variability in patterns of development."

Testosterone 'masculinises' the brain, say animal researchers. Experiments on rats have shown that testosterone has long term 'organisational' effect on brain development. Baron-Cohen wanted to study the influence of this male hormone (males produce more of it than females) in humans. He wanted to know if the differences in human beings are "purely the result of culture and purely the result of postnatal experience, or whether biology might also be contributing to those differences."

Testosterone is a significant hormone. For this hormone to work, it has to bind with androgen receptors. These receptors are present all over the body, including the brain. Once bound, this hormone does many things, for example modulation of neurotransmitters. Testosterone also seems to affect connections that neurons make with each other. During the process of apoptosis (selective cell death) nerve cells in the brain are pruned so that we lose certain connections. Testosterone seems to affect the rate at which we lose those connections. Genes are one of the sources that can influence the variation in this hormone. Researchers say that there are at least 25 different genes that can influence how much testosterone we produce.

In one of the studies conducted by Baron-Cohen, he showed babies (just after 24 hours they are born) two very different kinds of objects, one mechanical and one animate and human. He wanted to see whether babies looked longer at the human face, or looked longer at the mechanical object. What he found was that more boys seemed to look longer at the mechanical stimulus, and more girls seemed to look longer at the social stimulus, the face. What he observed was that girls on average are more oriented towards people, more inquisitive about people. Boys, on average, are slightly more oriented in their attention towards the physical environment, and patterns in the physical world.

In another study, in order to see if testosterone level results in individual differences, Baron-Cohen did amniocentesis (when the baby is 12 to 19 weeks of pregnancy, and this is the time when their brain develops very rapidly) and analysed the fluid for testosterone level. He wanted to know how testosterone level in the womb affects a child's development.

Some of his observations were: higher the baby's prenatal testosterone, the less eye contact they made at their first birthday; higher the child's prenatal testosterone, the smaller their vocabulary at two years old; higher the testosterone during the pregnancy, slower the child develops empathy as a four-year-old; higher the child's prenatal testosterone the more interested they were in systems of one kind or another.

Baron-Cohen thinks that his research is going to "teach us something about those neurodevelopmental conditions like autism, like delayed language development, and potentially have us understand the causes of those conditions".

This research, however, has large ethical implications. Manipulation of the child's hormone level prenatally, or at birth, is one of the ethically frightening ideas. Baron-Cohen also feels it would be unethical to ask women to have an amniocentesis purely for research, because amniocentesis carries a risk of inducing miscarriage.

-64-

WHY POISON IS NOT ALWAYS POISONOUS

Fever is a nuisance, but not always. Often, it can help our immune system function better. Likewise, poison, when used sparingly and directly to the target, can be beneficial. Ancient medical wisdom says that it is the dose that makes the poison poisonous. After 'plant poisons', it is now 'animal toxins' that are proving their worth in a good way. Venom is proving to be a novel source of useful molecules.

We have been using snake venom as antisera for snake bites for decades and now we are making drugs from venom. For instance, a person suffering from a chronic autoimmune disease of the skeleton got bitten accidentally by a bark scorpion. The fierce pain from the sting subsided in about 30 hours as the anti-venom was readily available. But a few days after the sting, to his utter surprise, the gentleman found that the pain he suffered due to spinal arthritis also subsided. He did not know what the venom did, but he says: "If my pain came back, I'd let that scorpion sting me again".

Venoms are known as the most efficient killers. They contain toxic proteins and peptides that affect targets differently. Some, for example, affect the nervous system, some destroy the cells resulting in the collapse of the tissues. Some cause blood clotting, while some prevent blood clotting. "Ironically, the properties that make venom deadly are also what make it so valuable for medicine," writes Jennifer Holland in the National Geographic. Many venom toxins target the same molecules that need to be controlled to treat diseases. Venom works fast and is highly specific.

Animals that have evolved to produce venom include snakes, scorpions, spiders, a few lizards, bees, sea creatures such as octopuses, numerous species of fish, and cone snails. The composition of the venom of a single snake species varies from place to place and between adults and their young. An individual snake's venom may even change with its diet.

The potential of venom as medicine is huge, say toxicologists. They say fewer than a thousand toxins have been scrutinised for medicinal value, and a dozen or so major drugs have made it to the market.

Researchers have been able to extract a protein from the venom of the Asian sand viper that is found to be helpful to fight malignant melanoma. This protein is known for stopping blood clotting. Other medicines derived from reptile toxins include a modified version of anticoagulant from the venom of the African saw-scaled viper, a protein from the South American rattlesnake to treat lung cancers, a pain relieving agent made from king-cobra venom. A synthetic form of hormone that occurs naturally in the saliva of the Gila monster, a venomous North American lizard, has been found to have blood-vessel-relaxing property. Endocrinologists found a component in Gila venom that controls blood sugar and even reduces appetite. This hormone from the venom has the ability to deal with sugar overload but remain inactive when sugar levels are normal.

Researchers are now talking about 'designer toxins' — toxins but with therapeutic values. The millions of years of evolutionary wisdom preserved in venoms will find its applications in designing such toxins. "We're mining the molecular biodiversity in nature," says Zoltan Takacs, the leading researcher in this area. Indeed, advances in molecular biology have accelerated the ways to find better methods to understand venoms and their targets. Designer toxins, say the drug companies, have a bright future. But there is also a need to be cautious, as playing with venoms is indeed a dangerous game.

-65-

WHY WE REJECT OUTSIDERS

Prejudice has always been a subject of great interest for sociologists, psychologists and historians. Biologists have also been trying to understand the causes of prejudice. They are trying to understand prejudice from evolutionary and cognitive perspective. They want to understand why we welcome insiders and reject outsiders. They feel biology may offer effective counter measures to deal with prejudices.

One of the earlier theories of prejudice put forward by Henri Tajfel and John Turner (107), known as the 'social identity theory', explored beliefs and prejudices of the people based on their membership and status within different social groups. Their research suggested that our preference towards those who we perceive to be similar to ourselves over those who are different is innate. This inbuilt prejudice, it is believed can be masked. The neuroscience research, however, suggests that prejudices may still exist despite the conscious effort to hide them.

Research by Elizabeth Phelps (108) provides some interesting insights into different racial groups. Based on functional magnetic resonance imaging, Phelps and her team suggest that a network of interconnected brain regions play an active role in racial matters. This network consists of the fusiform gyrus, amygdala, anterior cingulated cortex (ACC) and the dorsolateral prefrontal cortex (DLPFC). Fusiform gyrus is associated with the processing of colour information and facial recognition. Intuitively, this region should play a simple role in the initial recognition of a black face. Amygdala is known for regulating emotion. The ACC is known to be active in conflict situations. The DLPFC is responsible for social judgement and other such complex mental processes.

A recent theory put forward by Carlos Navarette, Melissa McDonald and Mark van Vugt (109) and known as 'male warrior hypothesis' suggests that prejudice is programmed into our genes. Their theory integrates psychology with ecology and evolutionary biology. We the humans lived in tribes to protect ourselves from hostility and fear. We have thus always viewed outsiders with suspicion.

It seems "the human mind is shaped in a way that tends to perpetuate conflict with 'outsiders'." The male warrior hypothesis works on the notion that men evolved to show aggression against other men whom they think belong to an outgroup. That gave rise to race, ethnicity, tribe, nationality, etc. Research suggests that all kinds of human activities that pit one person against another may arise out of the same genetic package. The researchers are not saying that prejudice is exclusively a male thing. Their research, however, suggests that men more or less started it. Male prejudice against other groups is often motivated by aggression, while women's biases come from fear, researchers say.

Researchers also found that men and women play vastly different roles in group conflicts. These differing positions are responsible for their distinctive psychologies. Studies have shown that men are generally more xenophobic than women, and they are more likely than women to dehumanise members of other groups. One of their observations is that men identify more strongly and cooperate better with men in their own group than do women.

Research also points that "men were more likely than women to put aside selfish motivations in a public goods game". The researchers suggest that women may instinctually avoid people who pose the greatest reproductive threat. The researchers believe that women getting political power and being decision-makers would be helpful. Researchers say their studies can be an important step into improving the problems caused by our darker predispositions.

-66-

WHY FACTS ARE LESS FIXED

What is the relationship of truth with time? Some say truth does not change with time and some say it does. With the passage of time words change their meanings. "The nature of time is that it is slippery avenue on which the truth manages to balance", writes Aneesha Dharwadekar (110).

We are constantly changing and so are the facts associated with us. If we know the pattern of the changes, we may, perhaps, better handle uncertainties. The facts are less fixed than we assume, argues Samuel Arbesman (111). Some facts have very short half-life. These are fast-changing facts, like the weather, the stock market and the principles of politicians. We also experience very slow-changing facts; the facts that have very large half-life, like the height and the location of Mount Everest that changes from year to year. Arbesman says that fact changes are predictable and quantifiable. "Far better than learning facts is learning how to adapt to changing facts," writes Arbesman. Embrace change rather than fight it. Changing facts are a fact of life.

-67-

WHY WE MAKE MISTAKES

We make mistakes because we are naturally stupid and timid. We make mistakes because of our prejudice, emotional imbalance, inattention, distraction and aggression. We feel ashamed when we are caught making mistakes. We forget that going wrong is vital for our learning process. We forget that we can't be permanently right. We make mistakes because we can't ignore the "subjective first person view of things".

Bias is our evolved cognitive tendency. "As something becomes more familiar, we tend to notice less, not more. We come to see things not as they are but as they ought to be." We suffer from "reference dependence" bias; we take decision not on the basis of our own payoff, but payoff of others. We suffer from "loss aversion" bias; we prefer to avoid a certain loss in favour of a potential loss. We work twice as hard to prevent being in the list of losers than in seeking opportunities to be in the list of gainers.

It is human to make mistakes, writes Joseph Hallinan (112). Not seeing what is right in front of us, is just one of a stunningly large array of shortcomings of the human brain that cause us to err. Hallinan calls it, "Looked but didn't see" mistake. We can't blame our brains for all our mistakes. Our surroundings are equally responsible for us to make mistakes.

Since we haven't understood the root causes of making mistakes, we often keep on repeating the mistakes. We often don't want to learn from our own mistakes. We are biased, but we often don't realize we are biased. Sometimes we make more mistakes when we try to understand why we made a mistake.

Our memories are often the big culprits. Some of our memory sins often drive us to make mistakes. As is said, memory is often more a reconstruction than a reproduction. One idea is "Stop memorising things; memories can be outsourced to the cloud".

-68-

SHOULD WE ALWAYS HATE OUR ENEMY

Hate is among the most powerful of human emotions. It may originate from the negation of intimacy, as a result of passion, or decision-commitment. The thermally sensitive seven forms of hate, according to Robert Sternberg, editor of The Psychology of Hate, are: Cool hate (disgust), hot hate (anger/fear), cold hate (devaluation), boiling hate (revulsion), simmering hate (loathing), seething hate (revilement), and burning hate (extreme hate, driving a need for annihilation).

Erich Fromm's description of hate comes in two forms: Rational and irrational. Rational hate is reactive; it arises when one is attacked, and ends with the end of the attack. The attack may be directed against one's own life or freedom. It could be against those whom one loves. The attack may be against one's moral and spiritual values. There is promise of love in rational hatred. No one loves to hate or hates to love, but love can turn into hate, and hate can turn into love.

Irrational hatred is character conditioned. It arises due to the experiences a person has encountered, especially those in early childhood. It then becomes part of one's personality. Such haters can't conceal their hostility, and wait for an occasion to express, rationalise and justify hate. Hateful situations give them pleasure and relief. Irrational hate blinds a person as it blocks spontaneity, emotional and physical expansiveness and the development of the self. The irrational hater resents happiness. Such hate mobilises the worst traits in the self. Hatred of this kind affects one's rational judgement; the pleasure in satisfying one's hatred becomes more important than the practical task of defeating the enemy.

The irrational hater's concern is destruction. Fromm illustrates Nazi genocide to establish the truth that destructiveness is the result of an unlived life. Due to socio-economic reasons, a certain class of people in the then Germany led a frustrated life. It gave rise in them destructiveness and sadism. Nazis utilised this lingering hatred for their political purposes. They rationalised hatred and, thus, justified outbreaks of hatred of one group for the other.

Fromm writes, "Hitler understood that people were desperate not only for economic reasons but for the reason that life had lost its meaning to them, that they did not know what to live for." Hitler used people's loss of ability to think and feel spontaneously. He promised them that their life should have a meaning. "To be sure, what he gave them was the very opposite of what is the real meaning of life, but even these faked and sordid ideals appealed to people who were hungry for a vision of the future," according to Fromm.

Should we hate our enemy, Fromm asked. Yes, by all means, he said, if the enemy is worth fighting with. Fromm was not advocating hatred, but wanted to remind the people that to fight some enemies with "emotional business-as-usual attitude" is not sufficient. Hatred for some enemies is legitimate. Martin Luther King, Jr said that we must love our enemies to break the chain reaction of "hate begetting hate". Love can drive out some kinds, but not all kinds of hates. Fromm said, "We must not teach hatred but we must teach love for those institutions and ideals which are attacked."

-69-

WHY SOME QUESTIONS SHALL REMAIN UNRESOLVED FOREVER

Francisco Redi proposed that viable organisms arise from dead matter. But Louis Pasteur put Redi's proposition to permanent rest. Swedish scientist Svante Arrhenius suggested that life always existed in the Universe, and migrated across space, continually colonising new planets. This theory of 'seeding' has also not found many takers.

It is believed that life emerged from a 'chemical soup', which favoured the formation of complex molecules. Gradually, structures evolved and from them the first cell emerged. In order to stay alive, these cells equipped themselves to trap energy, water and food.

Earth is believed to be more than four billion years old. Homo sapiens (wise human), individuals very much like us, emerged around 100,000 years ago. Some believe that the earth is relatively young; perhaps only 10,000 years old. There are some other creation science believers who accept that earth has existed for millions of years, but argue that the various types of organisms, especially humans, could only have come about with supernatural intervention. This is the starting point of the creation-evolution-design controversy.

Charles Darwin said, "If a solution, consistent with the ordinary course of nature can be found, we must not invoke an abnormal act of Creative Power." Darwin was of the view that all living things gradually change, and during the process of change, most do not survive if they do not evolve.

Then came the concept of design in nature. English theologian William Paley argued that anything as complex as life must have required a Creator. It was he who observed that if you found a watch, you would be forced to conclude that somewhere there was a watchmaker. The proponents of 'intelligent design' movement believe that creation of the magnitude of such 'irreducible complexity' as human being is possible only by invoking an intelligent designer. Some adherents of this movement do not outrightly reject the evolution theory. They say that the 'designer' might have assembled the first cell, essentially solving the problem of irreducible complexity, after which evolution might well have proceeded by more or less conventional means.

The creation-evolution-design debate is still going on.

One side argues that "what is, is what was created". The other side says that "what is, is what evolved". One side believes that "nothing in biology makes sense except in the light of Divine Creation". For the other side "nothing in biology makes sense except in the light of evolution".

The outcome of this debate will depend upon our perception about the real world. Does it consist of matter, energy, and obvious things or it resides beyond the obvious? Darwin wrote in his autobiography that, "The mystery of the beginning of all things is insoluble by us; and I for one must be content to remain an agnostic".

The Big Bang laid the foundations of the beginning of our universe. It attempted to explain the transition from 'nothing' to 'something'. Our universe is believed to be 13-15 billion years old. Big Bang has no answer to what happened before that. It seems in the beginning our universe was a hot entity of infinite density. This 'primeval fireball' then started to cool and expand by a process called 'Big Bang'. Our universe that started expanding billions of years ago is still expanding. "Galaxies are moving away from us at speeds proportional to their distance" is Edwin Hubble's way of explaining that the universe is indeed expanding. Some doubt the sanctity of science, "Solidification and cooling of our once molten planet defies explanation by conventional physical and chemical laws".

How can something come out of nothing? When science can't answer, non-science comes to the rescue. One such non-science explanation is that the universe is divinely caused, divinely designed, and divinely created. Nobel physicist Leon Lederman writes, "In the very beginning, there was a void, a nothingness containing no space, no time, no matter, no light, no sound. Yet the laws of nature were in place and this curious vacuum held potential. Only God knows what happened at the very beginning?"

"Why should God create our universe?" is another question. There are many who believe that God cares for us and that's why he created a universe for us. But there is another view. Stephen Hawking writes, "We are such insignificant creatures on a minor planet of a very average star in the outer suburb of one of a hundred billion galaxies. So it is difficult to believe in a God that would care about us or even notice our existence."

God has a big advantage. If you accept him you will have to accept him unconditionally. You can question science's limits but you can't question god's limits.

Who should be credited for creating a universe for us is a difficult question. To understand our universe, as Carl Sagan said, "We would need a brain as massive as the universe." The cumulative brain capacity of our universe will never attain that proportion. But in this expanding universe there will always be big questions. The search will go on to find answers to these questions. At the moment we should be happy that "The ideal universe for us is one very much like the universe we inhabit."

-70-

WHAT SILKWORMS CAN LEARN FROM BUTTERFLIES

There are some who come to this world to spread colour. Their presence keeps everyone in good humour and spirits. They bring sunshine into the lives of those who work with them. They are like a colourful butterfly.

Butterflies, metamorphosed from repulsive caterpillars, are beautiful and graceful. They are like flowers. They can't fly straight, but know how to live. Though they have few moments to live, they think that is enough. As Rabindranath said, "They flutter for a day and think it is forever."

We think something is 'useful' only if it is 'economical'. But the time 'wasted' on some 'uneconomical' pursuits is not always a waste of time. The time 'wasted' for not so-useful purposes can give us a different kind of sense of fulfillment. For a butterfly, 'useless' is not always useless. A butterfly has no weight, but it spreads happiness. It knows the value of leisure. It knows the real meaning of 'useful'.

There are some who are like silkworms. A silkworm works day and night. It spits silk. It has cash value. People of silkworm mentality understand only cash value. They have no time to enliven their softer side. They have no time to enjoy new colours of life.

The silkworm people must imbibe the spirit of the butterflies. They must learn from the butterflies that bringing sunshine in their own lives and into the lives of others is not a waste of time.

-71-

WHY MEMOIRS ARE FABRICATED

There are some memories we want to retain forever. There are some memories we want to forget. I could not recall the old building that stood on a plot of land near our house for so many years. When one of my friends asked me about it, I said philosophically, borrowing from Marcus Aurelius' Meditations, "How swiftly all things wash away, both the bodies themselves in the universe, and the remembrance of them in time". Our mental apparatus has unlimited receptive and retention capacity. I wonder how then our memories get washed away. Memory failure is somewhat like breathing failure; we don't notice them until they fail. I wonder what is harder – remembering or forgetting.

Memory is used for different purposes; 'episodic memory' refers to the recollection of specific past events; 'procedural memory' refers to the ability to remember specific motor skills; 'fear memory' refers to the immediate sense of distress that comes from recalling a physically or emotionally dangerous experience. Researchers say that the purpose decides which particular pathway the neural system uses. Whatever the memory, whenever one retrieves the memory by whatever means, one essentially fetches a timeless narrative of an earlier event, say the researchers. Humans are thus the sum total of their fixed memories, writes Stephen Hall (113).

Our memories range from the profound to the most trivial. We possess both short term and long-term memories. Our short term memory reflects our current thinking, and it provides us the details about few things. Our long-term memory is a culmination of thoughts and experiences gained over a long time. Our long-term memory, though can hold many things, the details are often fuzzy. What we remember is the gist of what happened, the details are often missing. There is another view. It says that our long-term memories are not as fuzzy as we think they are. The studies by neuroscientist Timothy Brady indicate massive storage ability of long-term memories. He observed that these memories could also hold detailed and precise form of information.

Why do we forget? We forget when we can't retrieve a memory. When we create new memory, old memory begins to fade and disappear. We forget because of the competition between stored memories; similar information causes greater competition. Often old memories become the roadblocks of new memories; as our previously learned experiences get hampered by our new experiences.

We forget because of 'encoding failure' which prevents the information from entering our memory space. We often find it difficult to recall the name of a familiar face. This is due to temporary blocking of stored information. We often work actively to erase some of our memories. Our efforts to forget often boomerang. The memory nullifying efforts often make them stick stronger. Conscious forgetting doesn't work. We become the tragic prisoners of memory. Often our forgetfulness is deliberate. Often memory's vices become its virtues. "These mindbugs are the occasional result of the normally efficient operation of the human memory system," says Daniel Schacter (114).

Memory sins are responsible for memory failure. The first of the seven memory sins, as told by Daniel Schacter, tells us that memory is time dependent. Our memories wash away as time passes. This tendency is not abrupt, but gradual. Moreover, with time, the quality of memory changes, from specific to reconstructed. Specific memories are more reliable than reconstructed ones. The reconstructed memories are a result of inference and guesswork.

Neuroscientists say that our memories are fragile. They tend to break the moment these are formed. Over time memories, however, get strengthened. Once consolidated, these memories remain essentially static, stored in the brain, and can be used when the need arises. Neuroscientists Daniela Schiller and others (115) have shown that memories are malleable constructs that may be rebuilt every time they are recalled. This knowledge can be useful, writes Stephens Hall (116), to help patients block the fearful emotions they experience when recalling a traumatic event, converting chronic sources of debilitating anxiety into benign trips down memory lane. This landmark research indicates that emotional impact of a memory can be altered by adding new information to it or recalling it in a different context. One of the interpretations of the research is "Every memoir is fabricated, and the past is nothing more than our last retelling of it." Schiller's conclusion: Your memory is who you are now. "The only way to freeze a memory is to put it in a story."

Absentmindedness is common human phenomenon. This happens when our mind wanders resulting in divided attention to things and events. Failure of prospective memory is a major source of absentmindedness. Another memory sin is blocking, that is failure to retrieve information that is available in the memory. Blocking is generally accompanied by the feeling that one is on the verge of remembering the information; inability to recall the names of the people and places is the common example.

Memory misattribution is another sin. This is believed to be the primary cause of eyewitness misidentification. Some of us also develop a tendency to incorporate misleading information into our memory. This is called suggestibility. Suggestibility can create serious problems by implanting misleading information into the memory system.

Unknowingly or unconsciously, we often 'edit' or 'rewrite' our past experiences. Such memory distortions are due to the influence of our current knowledge and beliefs. People displeased with romantic relationship, for example, tend to have a disproportionately negative take on past state of relationship.

The seventh memory sin is persistence. It is precisely the reason that those memories we want to get away with never leave us. These intrusive memories are more the consequence of emotional experiences than non-emotional ones. The so-called memory sins are an integral part of the mind's heritage, and are essential features of the memory to work well, says Daniel Schacter.

Neuroscientists (115) tells us about another fascinating feature of memory. He says, in order to persist, retrieved memories need to be reconsolidated. When reconsolidated, the brain incorporates new information into the memory. Research suggests that reconsolidation can overwrite previous memories. The new memory could involve a "collage of old and new information". The focal point of reconsolidation research is that each use of a memory changes the memory. Sometimes the change can be striking. The most striking observation neuroscientists make is that "the only way a memory remains 'pure' and resistant to change is by never being used." It means the most accurate memories are indeed the ones never remembered. So be careful about what you remember.

There are some memories we want to retain forever. There are also some memories we want to erase, but can't. Researchers say that our brains are like faulty tape recorders. Some say our brains are like a doctored tapes. It makes mistakes during memory retrieval as well as acquisition. It mutilates memories and as a result reproduces faulty memories.

Some memories are very special. We like to remember our first kiss. Scientists say that when one experiences something for the first time, our brains store the information much more carefully. Says neuroscientist David Eagleman, you aren't embroidering a bank of previous experiences, you are starting afresh. Something as special as the first kiss appears to have lasted for ever. Eagleman found that the brain uses more energy to represent a memory when the memory is novel, and one enjoys recalling such memories.

We are so fond of our childhood memories. Memory is the glue that holds together our identity and functioning. The memories of the yesteryears begin to appear more and more frequently as one approaches the end. When people reflect on old age, they think of the people they grew up with. The more one comes nearer the end, the more one thinks of his/her childhood years. That is why childhood memories are so special. We want to carry our childhood always with us. It is said that when you finally go back to your old home, you find it wasn't the old home you missed, but your childhood.

Older people too have novel experiences. Psychologist Warren Meck says that "when you hit your 60s and 70s, and time is beginning to run out, experiences get more precious and once again you remember all the details". It is true that the older people increasingly have the feeling that time is going faster than they are. But it is also true that older people acquire the ability to inhibit irrelevant memories, and the ability to ignore insults.

We applaud the spectacular memory feats of some individuals. We are curious about their extraordinary memory capacity. One 'memory champion' tells us about his prowess, "My philosophy of life is that a heroic person should be able to withstand about ten years in solitary confinement without getting terribly annoyed." My purpose is not to deny the virtues of memorisation, but 'solitary confinement' and that too 'without getting terribly annoyed' seems to me a difficult proposition. Perhaps that's one of the reasons I am not a 'heroic' person.

Some people have the unnecessary appetite for memory accumulation. Besides knowing about everything they want to keep everything in their memory space. Should we hold in our mind everything we come across?

It is a common experience that we can't often remember what we want to remember. This is our ancient problem, and our ancestors devised a solution for it — write down what you want to remember. But then Socrates said, "If men learn this, it will implant forgetfulness in their souls. They will cease to exercise their memory and become forgetful; they will rely on that which is written, calling things to remembrance no longer within themselves, but by means of external marks."

Where is the necessity of storing so much information when we can make use of the unlimited external memory space now available with us? There is unlimited external resource, but availability of resources is one thing and its use is another. We take that for granted what is already available. We read borrowed books, our own books remain unread. We are more worried about our fading memory space, but we are less worried about our existing memory space.

Isn't it a good idea that many things lapse into oblivion? One of my friends once told me that whenever he buys a new shirt he disposes an old one. Our memory is like that old shirt. We follow a 'curve of forgetting'. Whenever we store a new piece of information, our memory's hold on it begins to loosen. But we want to maintain that hold. Since that is not possible after a certain time, we use external resources like books, videos or photographs. But the catch is that the more we are dependent upon external memory technology, the more we tend to lose internal memory capacity.

We know that books can be used for two purposes: to read and to decorate the bookshelf. We also know that Tagore on the shelf means less than Tagore in the mind. When there were fewer books, reading was more intensive and less extensive. Now we have more books and fewer things to remember. Memory technology, some think, has made us extensive readers, but has reduced our intimacy with knowledge. We are becoming good collectors, but bad contemplators of resources. We need to maintain a better balance between collection and contemplation.

-72-

WHY WE ARE NOT
TOTALLY DISHONEST

We live in a rule bound world. We make rules so that these can be flouted. If your child wants attendance without attending classes, he will get it. Some schools are run only for this purpose. If you have killed a pedestrian while driving recklessly, don't worry. You will find a merciful someone to take care of your mistake. Pedestrians, after all, are not endangered species. If you don't want, you don't have to follow traffic rules. Traffic rule protectors will follow you. If you want to visit a busy temple, but don't have the patience to stand in a long queue, no worries; for a price a separate line can be created for you. If you want to sell your product, hire an endorser who is more saleable than the product. If you want to dispose your 'waste', find a 'wasted' neighbour. It could be a country. If you want home/hotel comforts in a prison cell, you can get it for a price. If you think you look good in a mahatma's robe, wear it. You will be amply rewarded. This notional list suggests that we live in 'price-tag society'. In this society everything can be bought at a price.

The problem is that we want to buy many things, but don't have the capacity to pay. We tend to spend more than what we earn. Michael Sandel (117) writes, "Today, the logic of buying and selling no longer applies to material goods alone. It increasingly governs the whole of life." We live amid a widening want-need gap. One of its consequences is greed. Greed gives rise to irresponsible deeds, and that in effect gives rise to inequality and corruption. To purchase our 'wants', we become purchasable. We forget that values (like human dignity) we exchange for goods are often more valuable. "Hiring foreign mercenaries to fight our wars might spare the lives of our citizens, but, might also corrupt the meaning of citizenship", writes Sandel.

We should know that everything is not on sale. Many things are available for free, but, that doesn't mean they should be misused. If someone pays your bill, that doesn't mean you should try to overspend. We should remember that things like civic duties, education and health, among others are not merely economic, and thus, should be valued differently. We often go the wrong way. The standard economic perspective tells us to maximise our own payoffs. This often leads us to the wrong way. Two things, the possibility of being caught and the magnitude of punishment, deter us from going the wrong way. There is another perspective. It says that our internal reward mechanisms help us to overcome dishonesty. Researchers say that internal reward mechanisms exert influence on our decisions. Nina Mazar and Dan Ariely's research (118) demonstrate that people act selfishly, insofar as they maximise their own payoffs, but, they are also sensitive to the costs that their dishonest ways impose on others. Their research shows that people behave dishonestly enough to profit, but, honestly enough to delude themselves of their own integrity. This effectively means we are a little bit dishonest because it gives us a taste of profit without spoiling a positive self-view.

-73-

WHY ALL WORRIES ARE NOT WORTH WORRYING

We are living in the age of anxieties. As we are growing, our list of fears is also growing. We are in the fast expanding phase of worries. Everything — food, water, energy and environment — has started bothering us. Are all our worries worth worrying?

We become worried when we face uncertainty about the present or anticipated problems. Our worries make us anxious. The problem is that our neural worry engine is always on. It is always in search of its next target. "When we worry, there is an impressively complex array of interacting neural and endocrine activities that engages the whole person, brain and body", writes Donald Hoffman (119).

Worry can be unproductive nervous activity. Worry can also be productive problem-solving activity. Our cause of worry need not always be external. The level of worry one experiences varies with the individual. In some of us, the worry engine starts at the smallest pretext while in some others, the worry engine needs a lot of warming to start. History says that those who worried too little died and those who worried too much also failed to live. It means that we require a certain amount of worry to function effectively. The point is what is that 'optimal level of worry' to live optimally.

We also have a 'worry gap' — the gap between imagined and actual threats. Our worry gap often misdirects us towards the wrong targets, says Hoffman. Our worry gaps are widening. We are becoming more worried about our imagined threats. "Since the brain has limited energy, we should probably view worry as a resource to be conserved and efficiently allocated", says Hoffman. We can only lessen our worry gaps. Stop worrying about all the worries is probably good for us.

Worry has served us well throughout our evolutionary history. Robert Provine (120) says that worry pays off in a long life. Another aspect of worry is that it protects us from danger. It gives us direction. Worry helps us to prepare our 'to do' list. It helps us to update the list. Too much worry diminishes the significance of this list. Too much worry strands us in an agitated state of despair, anxiety and paranoia; too little worry leaves us without motivation and direction. A modest level of worry is usually the best.

How should we package our worries? Mary Catherine Bateson (121) says, "People empathise more easily with polar bears and whales than with honey bees and bats. They care more about natural disasters in countries they have visited." She says the social psychology of fear and anxiety is different from the individual psychology of fear and anxiety and this distinction needs to be understood more clearly.

Is there a relationship between intelligence quotient (IQ) and worry? Earlier studies have indicated that excessive worry tends to exist both in people with higher intelligence and lower intelligence, and less so in people of moderate intelligence. Studies have also indicated that excessive worrying may have co-evolved with intelligence. In a recent study, patients with generalised anxiety disorder (GAD) were compared with healthy volunteers to assess the relationship between IQ and worry. The study found association of high IQ with a lower degree of worry in a control group of normal volunteers. In GAD, patient's high IQ was found to be associated with a greater degree of worry.

-74-

WHY WE MUST LIMIT OUR EXPECTATIONS

Both science and religion are in search of truth; one discovers it, while the other reveals it. Both try to understand and explain the deepest puzzles of life. Both have remained exciting for us. Both are full of unsolved mysteries. We are standing in-between the two unpredictable. God is not dead, nor is going to die soon. Isn't it better if we change our conception about God? Why can't we conceive God in a new format? Perhapd God's anthropomorphic representation is going out of fashion. More and more we are realizing that God does not entertain private petitions. Many eminent practitioners of science have also started to say that there is no logical contradiction between faith and belief if God is clothed appropriately. There is nothing wrong if a Marxist participates in Durga puja and offers 'pushpanjali' on the Mahashtami day, or goes for Haj pilgrimage. A scientist can be an ordinary person of faith.

There is no contradiction if a scientist believes in God. Nobel laureate physicist William Phillips says, "A majority of the people I know have no difficulty accepting scientific knowledge and holding to religious faith." It is as difficult to prove God's existence as his non-existence; "science's tools will never be enough to prove or disprove the existence of God". Belief in God is not a scientific matter. It must also be understood that a religious statement is not a scientific statement, and vice-versa.

Conflict between science and religion can be resolved amicably provided both sides understand the merits inherent in each side. The real culprits are impure expectations from both the sides. Both science and religion need to be presented in more straightforward and meaningful ways. It is not possible to prove everything. At the same time, it must be understood that God's intervention is not necessary in everything. Let science confine itself to the realm of facts. Let religion limit its reach to values.

It is we the people who decide the confinements and limitations. It is important to recognise that "there are no 10 commandments in thermodynamics or molecular biology, no path to righteousness and charity and love in Euclidean geometry". Impure expectations from both the sides clash because both seem threatened by diversity each side offers.

It is quite acceptable if a scientist doesn't accept faith straight away, and vice-versa. If someone says that "earthquake is a divine chastisement sent by Gods for our sins" one may not necessarily support the argument of equating calamity with ethical failure. One may like to put a counter argument and say that "our sins and errors, however enormous have not enough force to drag down the structure of creation to ruin". It is absolutely fine if one is filled with doubt before accepting the other. It is said that doubt is part of true faith.

We need to demarcate the expectations from science and religion. Religion risks turning into fundamentalism if it ignores scientific reasons. At the same time, science should also try to listen to religion. Mutual incomprehension is not good for both. We expect science not to knock down the castles of human relations built by religion. It is also good to remember what John Naisbitt said, "The most exciting breakthroughs of the 21st century will not occur because of technology but because of an expanding concept of what it means to be human."

-75-

CAN KNOWLEDGE EVER EXCEED MAN

Knowledge is evolving at a fast rate. Bertrand Russell said, "If knowledge continues to increase, the world will need wisdom in the future even more than it does now." One of the great challenges for us is to be knowledgeable as well as wise. The concept of wisdom changes with time. The goal of wisdom is to comprehend the deeper meaning of known facts, and for that a combination of cognition, self-reflection and openness are necessary.

Wisdom is filtering out noise from the pattern. Wisdom is subjective. Wise has the ability to overcome his subjectivity. He can look at phenomena and events from different perspectives. Wise people can accept the realities of the present time. It is possible to acquire wisdom by interacting with the wise. Though wisdom is learned more easily than it is taught, but unless taught, it is learned the hard way. William James rightly said that wisdom is about knowing what to overlook. A truly wise can comprehend the inherent limits of knowledge as well as wisdom.

Knowledge comes from books and facts. Wisdom comes from experience and living. A wise has the ability to intuit the options before they become problems. The difference between a wise and a clever person, according to a Jewish saying, is that the clever can extricate himself from a situation into which the wise would never have gotten himself. Monika Ardelt says that wisdom does not automatically grow with age. She, however, says that the association between wisdom and age is potentially positive. The biological hardware of the mind deteriorates with age. The software of the mind has the potential to increase with age.

Knowledge makes a person wise only if he experiences it. As one wisdom researcher says, "One can have theoretical knowledge without any corresponding transformation of one's personal being. But one cannot have wisdom without being wise". Wisdom is understood at the experiential level; it cannot necessarily be found in what a person says, but it can be expressed through an individual's personality and conduct in life. Wisdom is not necessarily conveyed through the content of a statement, but through the way the statement is delivered.

Are we wiser than our ancestors were? It is generally said that the present generation 'know' more and 'understand' better than the previous generation knew or understood. But one must not also overlook the fact that the present generation has forgotten many things that the previous generation has remembered. The present generation can cure dreaded cancer but are forgetting the ways to lead a simple, contented and a happy life. A truly wise understand the limits of wisdom.

Can knowledge ever exceed man? If you want to know, you need to have an organ. Good thing is that we all have this organ. The organ is our head, and the size of the world is the size of each man's head. It simply means that if I want to see you, I must have the capacity to see you. You can see the beauty in me only if you are beautiful. It also means that a thing inaccessible to me does not mean that it doesn't exist.

Imagine a X-Y plot between size of the head of the knower and knowledge of the world. The origin of the plot indicates that a person with zero head size will possess no knowledge of the world. With an increase in head size one's knowledge of the world should increase proportionately. In some cases, however, as the head size increases the knowledge of the world increases or decreases disproportionately.

There are some people among us who know what they know. These people are in the first quadrant of the graph. This quadrant is important in the sense that it represents how adequate or inadequate one is toward knowing himself as well as the world. This person is conscious about his competence. In this quadrant, a person may have well-developed self-awareness, but inadequate information about the world. This could be a deliberately created situation.

Is there a possibility of a person who has a head size enough to know what he wants to know? I believe such persons exist. They may not know the world as much as many others know, but may know much more about their specific world (say, music or painting) than many others. Perhaps the world that is beyond their world of interest doesn't matter to them.

There are some people who don't know what they know. These people belong to the second quadrant of the graph. These people are unconscious of their competence. The people in this quadrant are unaware of their hidden talents.

There are also people who don't know what they don't know. These people in the third quadrant of the graph are the most ignorant, because they are unconscious of their incompetence.

People in the fourth quadrant know what they really don't know. These people are conscious of their incompetence. These people are good learners.

Knowledge is expanding at a rapid rate. The size of man's head is also expanding. If both are proportionately increasing then no problem is visualized. If the increases in the size of knowledge is more than the size of the head, man would need 'external' head to keep track of the knowledge expansion. One possibility is that the size of the head expands but doesn't get utilized. We all know that an unutilised mind is devil's workshop. It is like engaging a person for head and then make his head inconsequential.

-76-

CAN MACHINES EVER SURPASS HUMAN INTELLIGENCE

Computers, like brain cells, are interconnected. It is thus logical to assume that one day computers would work the same way human brain works. But both neuroscientists and computer scientists know that human brain is different from a computer in many ways.

They know that synapses are far more complex than electrical logic gates. They know that the interneuronal connections in human brain are much more than in any computer. The brain is a massively parallel machine; computers are modular and serial. The brain uses content-addressable memory, computers byte-addressable.

The democratic nature of the brain prepares itself to deal with contradictions for better solutions. Brain uses evolution; adults have far fewer synapses than many random synapses the toddlers have. There is no central clock in the brain, and its processing speed is not fixed. The human brain constantly rewires and self-organises itself.

No hardware/software distinction can be made with respect to the brain; the mind emerges directly from the brain, and changes in the mind are always accompanied by changes in the brain. Brain has body at its disposal so that it can "offload" its memory requirements to the environment in which it exists. Though the human brain has the capacity of learning things faster than computers, it is slower than computer in many functions, like multitasking capability and mathematically involved processes are better with computers.

The brain is capable of imagination, and is far superior to computers in matters related to common sense.

In the changing software landscape, artificial intelligence is becoming the most powerful tool to build a human-like machine. These developments raise mind-blowing (as well as frightening) possibilities. Some of these possibilities are welcome, but not all. The question that is most bothersome is, "Should machines surpass human intelligence?" The related question is "Can machines ever surpass human intelligence?" David Gelertner asks a counter question: Since computers are creating so much mess in the information cyberspace, should we not divert our attention to clear the mess, rather than creating additional mess? Should we not control 'out of control' cyber pollution, in addition to installing better security guards?

Gelertner thinks that no computer will be able to think like man unless it can 'free-associate'. By 'free associate' he means, "When you stop work for a moment, look out the window and let your mind wander, you are still thinking. Your mind is still at work. This sort of free association is an important part of human thought". Gelertner also says that no computer will be able to think like we think unless it can 'hallucinate'. We hallucinate when we fall asleep and dream, and in the hallucinated state our mind redefines reality for us; outside reality disappears, inside thinking remains.

Gelertner contends that our level of 'alertness' is basic to human thought. In the low alertness state, our thoughts tend to move by themselves with no conscious direction from us. In this state of free association, each new thought resembles or overlaps or somehow connects to the previous thought. With fall in our alertness we lose contact with external reality. Eventually we sleep and dream. In the hallucinated state the thinker and his thought stream are not separate. The thinker inhabits his thoughts. No computer will be able to think like a man unless it, too, can inhabit its thoughts; can disappear into its own mind.

-77-

THE FUTURE OF
NEURAL SUITCASE

"Houdini believed that true telepathy was impossible. But science is proving Houdini wrong", writes Michio Kaku (122). Kaku says it is possible to read our brain by combining the latest scanning technology with pattern recognition software. Kaku envisages a mind that can videotape dreams. Our consciousness can be downloaded onto machines. There would be possibility of transporting thoughts and emotions through the "internet of the brain". Kaku is optimistic about the future of mind. He thinks that future is not beyond reach. "Perhaps one day the mind will not only be free of its material body, it will also be able to explore the universe as a being of pure energy. The idea that consciousness will one day be free to roam the stars is the ultimate dream. As incredible as it may sound, this is well within the laws of physics." He says mind is a hard engineering problem and since fundamental laws of engineering are already known, it will be easier to understand and manipulate the "computer of meat". By mapping the "connectome" Kaku imagines it should be possible to reverse-engineer each and every person's brain. Using the connectome one can download oneself into a machine. When that is possible your mind can live as long as that machine lives.

There is worldwide interest in reverse engineering the brain. The major groups involved in the work have varied aims. The Human Brain Project aims to simulate the brain electronically on computers. The Brain Research through Advancing Innovative Neurotechnologies initiative aims to map the neurons of the brain directly. Another project aims to decipher the genes that control brain development.

Reverse engineering the brain is bound to raise many questions, both technical and non-technical. Are we merely the sum of our brain's connections? In the absence of a good working model to understand consciousness, should we envisage the kind of future of mind that are being envisaged? As Adams Frankmarch writes, "There has always been the temptation to take the latest technology, like clockworks in the 17th century, and see it as a model for the mechanics of thought. But simulations are not a self, and information is not experience."

-78-

MIND OF A POLYMATH

Rabindranath Tagore was a multifaceted visionary. He was a novelist, poet, and dramatist. In a creative span of 60 years he wrote and gave music to 2,500 songs and drew over 2,000 paintings and drawings. Leonardo Da Vinci, the Mona Lisa man, apart from painting studied anatomy, biology, mathematics, and engineering. He was known for his intellectual, artistic and physical pursuits. If he was proud of his artistic creation, he was also proud of his ability to bend iron bars. Aristotle was known as a philosopher, politician, ethicist, logician, astronomer, biologist, and what not. These beautiful minds were polymaths. T H Huxley thus described a polymath – someone who knows something about everything and everything about something. "The only thing that I know is that I know nothing," said Socrates. This is typical humility of polymaths.

Often an odd thought strikes me - why do we have people who know so much and those who know so little? Why are my set points of assimilation and dissimilation so different from the ones who have more beautiful mind? Why the beautiful minds understand things so easily while they are so difficult for me? What is responsible for this difference - my sense organs or is it because I lack effort?

My simple mind says it can't only be the senses that are the differentiators. It is true that resolve and effort makes one different from the other. But there is something else besides resolve and effort. What is that? E F Schumacher writes, "Beethoven's musical abilities, even in deafness, were incomparably greater than mine, and the difference did not lie in the sense of hearing; it lay in mind."

Malcolm Gladwell thinks that anyone who works hard enough over a long period of time can end up at the top of her/his field. He claims that "greatness requires enormous time". By this he means that if you have time and you are willing to spend it on something special, there are good chances of achieving it.

Psychologist Howard Gardner, however, has other view. Gardner says that talent and expertise are necessary, but not sufficient to make someone original and creative; "achievement is not just hard work: the differences between performance at time 1 and successive performances at times 2, 3, and 4 are vast, not simply the result of additional sweat." Gardner believes that the answer to the question — why some minds are more beautiful — will come through a combination of findings. Genetics will give some insight on why highly talented individuals have a distinctive, recognisable genetic profile. Neuroscience will explain why there are differences in structural or functional neural signatures. Cognitive psychologists will tell us more about the psychology of motivation of talented individuals. They will tell us why the talented individuals develop passion to master their art.

We are now living in the age of specialists. We use many tools and data to arrive at a conclusion. We often don't give importance to the fact that we are best when we use our minds to do many things. "The real master has no tools at all, only a limitless capacity to improvise with what is at hand," writes British poet and explorer Robert Twigger. He says carrying too many tools is the sign of a weak man.

Over-specialisation often limits us to our own sphere. Experts develop a tendency to defend what they know. They are afraid to make new connections. A polymathic expert is perhaps a better expert; "the further afield your knowledge extends the greater potential you have for innovation." Can polymathic tendencies be created? Is age a bar to become a polymath?

There is no doubt that our learning capabilities are better when we are young. It is also known that early years of childhood can shape many adult outcomes. But we also know that our learning capabilities don't stop with age. Nutritious diet, physical fitness, social engagement, and mentally stimulating activities are potential factors that help our learning abilities. We need to make better connections with the outside world. We need to keep our learning abilities young, even when we are no longer young. The best time for making new connections in our neural suitcase is until the age of ten-eleven. As we grow old our brain becomes more selective.

-79-

MIND OF AN IDEALIST

One of the ideals of a teacher is to imbibe among students "an idealist's view of life". One may ask, does the idea of ideal make sense in the non-ideal world? A teacher would say it does make sense.

In the early 19th century, Sadi Carnot conceived an engine that was 100 per cent efficient. Man conceived an omnipotent and omnipresent superman. Mathematicians conceived infinity, an abstract concept that has no limit. Ideal is like Carnot's engine. Ideal is like god. Ideal is like infinity. Ideal is a goal post that can't be reached. Why then do we want to reach the ideal? If a concept can't be achieved, it doesn't mean we shouldn't try to achieve it. We need a goal post, even an imaginary one, to reach near that.

We are subjective idealists. We have our own idealism. It's just that our ideas about idealism are different. For example, some think paranoia leads one to death. Some think paranoia is helpful for survival. Some think independence abolishes slavery. Some think slavery continues in spite of independence. We also ask questions, such as, if there is possibility of slavery to continue, why should one aspire to be free?

It is not easy to hold on to one's idealism. When we face reality, we generally go away from our idealism. The problem is that our purposes and values are dynamic, and thus our idealism is provisional and tentative. It so happens that an idea that makes sense to one may not make any sense to the other. The idea changes according to the circumstances one is in. We expect others to like our ideas. We ask for advice, but we expect approbation. When one's idea is not accepted, one of the possibilities is that one accepts other's idea by ignoring one's own ideas. The other possibility is that one rejects other's idea and prepares oneself for confrontation. Philosopher Philip Kitcher suggested a way to deal with such tricky situations that takes care of the one as well as the other: "There are various ways to understand entropy... I shall follow the approach of classical thermodynamics, in which entropy is seen as a function of unusable energy. But the points I make will not be affected by this choice." Amartya Sen doesn't like the idea of an idealist. He says, "There are some words I try not to use, and idealist is one of them. That could mean someone who was hopelessly unrealistic or someone who was so enamoured of his ideas that he would not examine the opposite argument."

An ideal needs an ideal world, and that is missing in the real world. In order to survive in the non-ideal world, one has to dilute his idealism. In the process, he becomes somewhat non-ideal. How much is one willing to bend oneself is a personal choice. "Ideal" is unattainable, yet an useful concept. It teaches us to minimise 'losses'. The designer of Carnot's engine presumed no losses. If there wasn't the concept of an ideal engine, we wouldn't have been able to design almost perfect engines.

It is not easy to think of an ideal self. Only an ideal can think of an ideal. Even though it is 'hopelessly unrealistic' to think of an ideal self, how about sparing some time and thinking about such an odd thought? No doubt, the gap between real and ideal shall always remain. But this gap will be a constant reminder to us that we are not what we want to be.

Ideal is like a thought experiment that can be thought but can't actually be performed. Even then it is performed because a thought experiment has useful implications. "Contemporary philosophy, even more than the sciences, would be severely impoverished without them", writes Stanford Encyclopedia of Philosophy.

Sri Aurobindo was a difficult to understand idealist. "No one can write about my life because it has not been on the surface for man to see", he said. Aurobindo believed four layers of mind are the 'instruments' of education. The first layer is the reservoir of past mental impressions ('chitta') on which all other layers stand. "It is the active memory, a higher but less perfectly developed function, which is in need of improvement." The second layer is mind proper ('manas'). Its function is to receive the images of the five senses and translate them into thought. The third layer is the intellect ('buddhi'). It orders and disposes of the knowledge acquired by the other layers. The fourth layer, says Aurobindo, has not yet entirely developed in man, but is gradually developing. "The powers peculiar to this highest stratum of knowledge are chiefly known to us from the phenomena of genius." These powers are rare though many possess them imperfectly or by flashes. Aurobindo says, though largely distrusted, humanity could not have advanced to its present stage if it had not been for the help of these faculties. The most important point Aurobindo makes is that "The mere instructor does his best to discourage and stifle genius, the more liberal teacher welcomes it." (123).

-80-

MIND OF YUDHISTHIR

Yudhisthir in the epic Mahabharat is portrayed as weak, indecisive and less confident. He has least inclination towards wealth, and no regal aspiration touches him. He is portrayed as too dependent on the counsel of Krishna and on the prowess of his brothers. He is portrayed as poor gambler. Yudhisthir was not bestowed with the boons of God (as Arjun was), nor was he put under any curse (as Karna was). All his boons and curses were hidden within him. His major concern was the welfare of his subjects. He fails Drona's archery test. In the test, he notices tree, his teachers, and his brothers. He misses the target.

"His personality is so weakly attractive that no poet from Kalidas to Rabindranath has ever composed a 'kavya' or 'natak' with Yudhisthir as the central figure", writes Budhadev Bose (124). Budhadev adds, "It is our great good fortune he is just a man, a very ordinary man". Yudhisthir taught us that insignificance is the locus of true significance. Yudhisthir (meaning the "steady in war") is not the most worthless and the most insignificant warrior of the Kuru clan, as some have tried to portray him.

We find in Yudhisthir a great learner. During exile ('Vanparva') he did not waste time in perpetual discontent nor did he indulge in combat with others, but learned the attributes of humanity. He learned to deal with the angry laments of his wife. He patiently learned to tolerate the rebukes and rash exhortations of his violence-prone brother. He listened to 'puranic' tales from 'rishis' and 'munis'. These tales were not the 'conventional eulogy of ancestors', but the ageless and unfading tales of wisdom.

From the tales Yudhisthir understood inner life of the Universe. He listened, not alone, but along with his brothers and wife. He listened attentively, asked questions and sought clarifications. It was this school of learning that taught him to deal with the higher nuances of life and living. It was this school that prepared him to answer all the questions put forth by the mysterious crane ('Yaksha'), and as a reward brought back all his brothers to life.

Yudhisthir, in this school found the greatest of teachers. Their instructions were not only in the use of arms or in the acquisition of orthodox learning, but also in the ways of self-searching and self-discovery so essential to grasp the true meaning of the universe. In this school Yudhisthir learnt the art of detachment.

At the end Yudhisthir so calmly and graciously accepted the departure of his brothers and his wife. He did not look behind. He walked steadily carrying the "riches of his deprivation, relying on the conviction that has hardened in the heat of misery and the pressure of delusion." The terrible blow of war did not turn him into a stone. He walked by himself, but was not entirely alone. A dog followed him.

"If we pause here for a moment, at this peak of Yudhisthir's great departure, where he confronts Indra's divinity with his own humanity, where he refuses to be persuaded by Indra and is ready to forsake entry into heaven for the sake of a dog -- if we recall at this point many other past events, then we shall realise that this noble and human poem is but an account of Yudhisthir's life. It is he who holds together all the incongruities." Budhadev Bose writes, the central male character of Mahabharata is Yudhisthir.

-81-

MIND OF A TEACHER

Our teachers are our guides. They tell us the difference between drawing and tracing. When we draw, we encounter discontinuities. These discontinuities disappear when we trace. But, thanks to our teachers, we want to draw our own picture. Discontinuities form our driving force to move forward on our own terms.

Aristotle believed that "those who educate children well are more to be honoured than they who produce them; for these only gave them life, those the art of living well." Mark Twain called Anne Sullivan the "miracle worker". Anne Sullivan, teacher and companion of Helen Keller, herself was blind for much of the first part of her life. Undoubtedly, Sullivan's own partial blindness gave her insight into the closed-off world of Helen Keller. Maria Montessori, one of Italy's first female doctors, is a name we shall always very fondly remember in the field of education. She believed children essentially teach themselves; the teacher's primary responsibility is to create the appropriate environment for learning and provide the spark that allows children to develop naturally.

Teacher makes a difference to what a student becomes. It is great teachers who make a great school. A teacher who knows his subject very well, but doesn't know his students, can't be called a great teacher. Great teachers are not necessarily dynamic personalities or dramatic performers. They are compassionate and caring. They refuse to "surrender to the combined menaces of bureaucracy, and budgetary shortfalls."

Great teachers are aware of the potential of their students. They know the way to unlock that potential. They give the students as much as they are capable of receiving. Great teachers set big goals for their students. They are demanding. They don't feel inhibited to push the students if that is needed. Effective teachers try to ensure that students are really learning. Great teachers can hold the attention of the class. It is believed that students can't learn unless the teacher succeeds in capturing their attention and getting them to follow instructions. Great teachers know that all learners are not the same. They thus, address their needs by differential instruction. A great teacher believes that a teacher's control should be "an exercise in purpose, not in power."

A good teacher understands the needs of his students. He prepares his students not only to pass the exam, but also to lead an honest, successful and productive life. A good teacher understands the mind of the young, their confusions and ethical challenges. A good teacher tries to inculcate in his students beliefs and practices that are required to live a virtuous life. A good teacher does not preach, but practice virtue.

A good teacher believes that virtuous life has many practical benefits, and can be self-taught through practice. Equanimity is an essential virtue, and self-control is a habit that can be learned. He tells his students to be moderate in their actions and reactions. Humility and a limited narcissism are critical elements of his repertoire. He tries to imbibe in his students the ability to distinguish between material (perishable) and sublime (imperishable).

If I am asked – what the most flattering description of a teacher is, a hero or a role model - I would go for a hero. Role models impact our life for a shorter period. Once their roles are over, they disappear from the scene. Heroes with longer half-life remain with us for longer periods. The impact of their roles is never over. We don't say the role model of the century. We say the hero of the century. Amitabh Bachchan and Sachin Tendulkar are our role models. Mahatma Gandhi and Rabindranath Tagore are our heroes.

More than 2,500 years ago when Lao Tzu said that the wise are not academic and the academic are not wise, the expectations from an academic and a wise were quite different from what they are now. The challenge of the present-day teacher is to be both academic as well as wise.

I was not a great teacher. I was a successful teacher because I received more from my students than I could give them. I was most fortunate that I got the opportunity to interact with the brightest young minds. I understood that the knowledge of 'what is' is necessary but more important is to understand 'what it should be.' I learnt that aesthetic development of the senses is as important as the intellectual. In keeping with the spirit of the time I am happy that my students are now my guides.

The school I studied had special section for good students. My school perhaps thought, only 'good' students deserve the tutelage of 'better' teachers. Unfortunately, I was not a part of this special section. Fortunately, I became a teacher of a school that had no special section for good students. It worked on the premise that all students are good students.

I remember a young colleague of mine who was not very popular among his students. My colleague was an exceptional student; he never came second in the class. His students were not happy for the way he taught the course. My colleague felt that the course was too elementary, and failed to understand why the students should have any difficulty in following the course. My colleague, apparently, had no patience as a teacher. He moved faster than his students wanted him to move. His students were unable to keep track to his pace. I suggested my colleague to move a bit slowly. He gradually learnt to move with the class but my colleague still wonders why people take time to understand 'simple' theories.

"We must remember how children learn rather than how we teach" said Albert Cullum in a documentary. Learning should not be painful. Learning should be joyful. One of the main strengths of Steven Pinker as a teacher is "explaining difficult concepts in ways people can understand, breaking them down, systematising them." Too often, Pinker says, teaching is based on presenting and analysing flaws and contradictions. This, he says, "leaves the student in a state of confusion. Why spend all this time on flawed experiments and false theories? Why can't we think about true theories and why things do work?"

-82-

MIND OF A MOTHER

A little girl asks her mother,
Ma, how did you live for so long without me?
I lived in anticipation, says the mother;
In the anticipation of a bright tomorrow.
Ma, I know I am not the best.
Why then you say I am the best.
My child, I am not an exception.
For all mothers, her child is the best.
Mother's love is most natural.
Extreme emotions come naturally to a mother.
There is bias in mother's love.
Mothers can't be too critical.
Mother's love is like the love
A whole has for its parts.
Child was once part of a whole.
A mother is born
The day her child is born.

There can't be a caregiver better than a mother. Mother is the embodiment of care and love. Many things a mother does for her child, she would not do for anyone, including herself. A mother is born the day her child is born. For a woman, there is nothing quite like giving birth to a baby and becoming a mother.

Does a mother's love for her child depend upon birth pangs? Are adopting a child and giving birth to a child two different kinds of experiences? Is mother's love for her adopted child the same as her love for the child she gives birth to? Or is it a different kind of love? The adopter mother obviously would feel offended if she is asked these questions. What is on mother's mind?

Behavioural neuroscientist Alison Fleming (125) has been trying to find the answer to this question. Fleming wants to understand how mothers think, how hormonal changes regulate mood, how cognition changes. She wants to know what the long-term effects of mothering are. Working with rats, Fleming says that the mother's dendrites — thread-like extensions of neurons that receive electrochemical stimulation — become more complex when she is interacting with her babies. She says amygdala is very important for mothering. In rats that had never given birth, Fleming found that amygdala, which mediates emotion, was inhibited. In mothers, hormones worked to remove that inhibition.

Does one need to give birth to become a 'mother'? Fleming, based on her experiments with female rats, says that mothering doesn't necessarily have to come from a mother. Female rats that had never given birth were asked to take care of newborn rats. The rats did not like the idea initially. But slowly they started acting like mothers. One might rightly say that rats are not humans. What rats do, not necessarily humans would follow. But Fleming's studies showed that exposure to a baby over time can create the same mothering effect. Fleming says that any person who can raise a child is a mother. One needs to be sensitive and responsive.

Most adopters would be emphatic in saying that love is love, and it is not selective, and should not be because that is what good parenting means. But then there are many other views.

One view says that the love for a non-biological child is not the same as the love one has for the child born out of one's own flesh and blood. Some adopters find the essence of connectedness missing in their relationship with the adopted child. Some say it takes years to develop real connectedness. Nancy Verrier (126) says, "I wouldn't say that I love my adopted daughter or my biological daughter differently — I would do just about anything for either of them — but I would definitely say the bond is different, and I know now that is inevitable."

Why is the quality of love in the two cases different? Why is there an apparent delay in the formation of instant bond? If they are different, is it due to genes? "We are tuned in hormonally to what our natural children want," says an adopter. Does the adopted child need an additional measure of love to make up for the losses due to genes? One mother of three adopted and two natural children writes, "I think we were more overt with our love for them than we were with our own kids, certainly while they were growing up." Many adopters say they are not sure if their love is different, but they feel their feelings are different. While others feel the quality of love between parents and non-biological children has more chance of being better if the birth child arrives later than before.

Another view says that the parents who have already given birth are usually better placed to work at a relationship with a non-biological child because they have been through that. They say those who have their own baby and then decide to adopt a child, have different motivation for adopting a child. There is yet another view that thinks those parents who have not experienced adoption have missed so much; "You've missed the wonder of meeting a fully formed human being that is your child, complete with all the unspoken possibilities of that relationship."

Adoption of and giving birth to a child are two very different ways of building a relationship, just as establishing an organisation and acquiring an organisation are two different kinds of experiences. The reality of life is that there is a difference between 'creating' and 'acquiring'. One is more like nature and the other is more like nurture. And as one adoptee says, "But I'm OK with that difference, and see it as part of my life story that's made me who I am."

Mother's love for her child is self-love. Conflict between a mother and her child is quite likely. The intrusion in the mother-child space is natural. The mother-child conflict starts unconsciously long before the child is born. This 'parent-offspring conflict', according to behavioural scientists, is due to the fact that mother does not want to give everything the child wants. The child wants to maximise its chance of survival and expects the mother to meet all the demands. Nature has so beautifully resolved the unconscious mother-child conflict. It should not be difficult to resolve the conscious or unconscious conflict, if there is any, if there is understanding between the mother and the child, that this conflict is natural. The child may not need mother's safety net, but they know that to fulfill their emotional requirement there is no better place than the mother's lap.

The unborn child can see, hear, taste, and feel. Thomas Verny and John Kelly (127) say that the unborn child becomes sensitive to light from the 16th week of pregnancy and develops basic reflexes and facial expressions by the fourth month. From the sixth month on, the unborn child leads an active emotional life. The child becomes sensitive to touch at five or six months.

The child can listen to noises in the mother's body from the 24th week. The child responds to sound and melody from a source other than his mother. Agitated unborn children calm down when they listen to calming music. Yelling parents make them kick and move around more. An expectant mother who spends a few minutes each day listening to soothing music could make her child feel more relaxed and tranquil. Research also suggests important role the expectant fathers play during the gestation period. The attitudes of the parents impact the feelings of the unborn child, and their birth experience.

Communication between a mother and her unborn child takes place through hormones (such as adrenaline, noradrenaline, and oxytocin), child's behaviour (like child's kicking in the womb), and mother's love. The mother releases hormones when under stress. In moderation, these hormones stimulate child's neural and psychological systems beneficially, but in excess they can affect the child adversely (like low birth weight, reading difficulties, behaviour problems, and gastric disorders).

The mother's love, acceptance, and positive thoughts play a very important role in the development of the foetus. The unborn child appears to get affected strongly by the mother's negative or ambivalent attitude toward the pregnancy. Most traumatic experience the unborn child faces is when, due to some reason, the mother withdraws her love and support from the child. Withdrawal of love and affection for the child during pregnancy may lead to the birth of a depressed child.

A stressful relationship between the mother and the father also affects the child. A father who abuses or neglects his pregnant wife can affect a child, both emotionally and physically. An anxiety-ridden mother can leave a deep scar on the personality of the developing foetus. Likewise, a self-assured and confident mother instills in the child a deep sense of content and security.

For nurturing proper understanding between the two human beings, an open and inviting space is essential. This fundamental human understanding adequately explains the bond between a mother and her child. The mother-child bonding that begins prenatally is vital even after the birth. Empathy with the child and the ability to see things from a child's perspective are key factors that stimulate mother-child bond.

Mother knows the child much before the child is born. They have tools to make their child a happy child. The tools are her thoughts and feelings. During the gestation period, the foetus senses the comforting maternal heartbeat. It is the child's main source of life, safety, and love. Mother's steady heartbeat reassures the child that all is well.

Responsibilities of parenthood are immense. According to a study, supportive parents provide reassurance to their child, offer their child a strategy for coping with their distress, show affection, and encourage their child to wait patiently.

Scientists are now saying that mothers can be brain enhancers. Maternal support in early childhood predicted larger hippocampal volumes at school age, according to the studies. The hippocampus, a part of the brain, is strongly associated with forming, connecting, organizing, and storing memories. Hippocampus' size has been linked to the capacity to manage stress. A smaller hippocampus has been observed in people who have experienced a lot of stress. The researchers have found that preschool-age children whose mothers actively support them during a stressful incident later show greater volume in the hippocampus. The studies indicate that kids who receive warm, supportive parenting are better at coping with adversity and at completing cognitive tasks later in life. The positive effect of maternal support on hippocampal volumes was observed to be greater in non-depressed children.

Studies have demonstrated that poor-quality parenting is a risk factor for childhood major depressive disorder (MDD). The studies suggest that smaller hippocampal volumes in adolescents at risk for MDD are associated with increased susceptibility to the effects of psychosocial stress and subsequent risk for recurrence or development of MDD. These findings indicate that early maternal support exerts a positive influence on hippocampal development in children without depression, but not in depressed children, in whom the negative effects of this risk condition seem to impede the potential benefits of maternal support.

The message researchers have given us is that the healthy development of a key brain region impacts cognitive functioning and emotion regulation. This research opens an exciting opportunity to impact the development of the child in a powerful and positive fashion. These findings have profound public health implications, say the researchers, and suggest that greater public health emphasis on early parenting could be a very fruitful social investment. Although the studies were conducted primarily with mothers, researchers expect that this effect pertains to the primary caregiver (the provider of nurturance) whether it is a mother, a father, a grandparent, or others.

Mother-child bonding isn't just for brains, it is also an affair of the heart. Researchers say that heart cells not only contract and expand rhythmically to pump blood, they also communicate with fellow cells. Perhaps this is why most mothers instinctively place their babies close to their hearts. Scientific evidence indicates that a mother's heart stimulates a newborn's heart, thereby activating a dialogue between the infant's brain, mind, and heart. This heart-to-heart communication helps the mother too. It activates dormant intelligence in the mother. This is nature's way of keeping a mother's intelligence awake.

A growing body of scientific evidence shows that the way babies are cared for by their mothers will determine not only their emotional development, but the biological development of the child's central nervous system as well. Science says that mother's love acts as a template for love itself, and has far reaching effects on the child's ability to love throughout life. The developmental neuroscientists say that babies are born with a certain set of genetics, but they must be activated by early experience and interaction. Researchers believe the most crucial component of these earliest interactions is the primary caregiver - the mother.

Research in neuroscience has shown that touch is necessary for human development. During the critical period of development following birth, the infant brain undergoes a massive growth of neural connections. Synaptic connections in the cortex continue to proliferate. At about two years they peak. During this period, one of the most crucial things to survival and healthy development is touch. All mothers seem to know this instinctively. Newborns are born expecting to be held, handled, cuddled, rubbed, kissed, and maybe even licked! All mammals lick their newborns vigorously, off and on, during the first hours and days after birth in order to activate their sensory nerve endings, which are involved in motor movements, spatial, and visual orientation. Some researchers believe that sensory deprived mothers develop behavioural abnormalities such as depression, violence, substance abuse, and impaired immunological functioning. "In nature's nativity scene, mother's arms have always been baby's bed, breakfast, transportation, even entertainment."(128)

A mother's love is not only priceless, but can even prevent illness in middle age, scientists claim. Adults who grew up under the loving care of their mothers are found to be in better health overall than others who hadn't been as close to their mothers. This is because of the empathy, coping strategies and self-respect taught by loving mothers to their kids. Many of the health problems in midlife can be traced back to what happened in early childhood. The stresses of childhood can leave a biological residue that shows up in midlife.

The fundamental bond between mother and child is the result of an on-going conversation conducted on multiple levels, from the physiological to the emotional, cognitive, and social. The mother-child bonding is influenced by the smell, the skin-to-skin contact, the facial expressions, eye movements, body language, the kissing, the cooing, the cuddling, the tone of the mother's voice, the baby talk.

There is nothing like mother's milk. This watery thing is the mother's pride. It changes its composition to satisfy the needs of the child. The nutritious liquid that a mother produces for her newborn child is a source of all nutrition, emotional gratification, and sense of fulfillment. Mother's milk can't be replicated. As Oliver Wendell Holmes said, "A pair of substantial mammary glands has the advantage over the two hemispheres of the most learned professor's brain in the art of compounding a nutritious fluid for infants."

Breastfeeding leads to better mother-child interaction. According to one study, breastfeeding mothers bond better with their infants than formula-feeding mothers in the months after they are born. Oxytocin, the hormone that helps nurture emotional bonding between infants and mothers and is involved in breast milk let-down, is higher among breastfeeding mothers. Children who are breastfed for four months or more develop fewer behaviour problems, say the researchers. Researchers are, however, not sure whether it is because of the constituents in breast milk or the close interaction with the mother. Mothers who breastfeed also tend to interact with their children more, which could mean the babies learn more about acceptable ways of behaving. Mothers who breastfeed are less likely to abuse or neglect their babies, than either women who do not nurse, or those who nurse for fewer than four months. Breastfeeding helps the mother too. It is believed to assist the uterus in returning to its pre-pregnancy size and reduce post-partum bleeding, as well as assisting the mother in returning to her pre-pregnancy weight.

The Darwinian theory of evolution suggests that infant feeding should benefit both the mother and the child. In other words, "an infant should be breastfed as much as possible to maximise its chances of survival, whereas a mother must balance her current metabolic investment in milk production with her potential investment in future offspring". It means that maximum evolutionary gain is obtained when protein and energy levels in breast milk are just high enough to prevent prohibitive infant mortality rates, but low enough to spare the mother.

Many decades ago Donald Winnicott, the British pediatrician and psychoanalyst, said that there's no such thing as a baby. The point Winnicott wanted to convey was that there is never "just" a baby. There is a baby and her mother. And, more broadly, there is baby, her mother, her family, community, and a whole host of relationships that are critical to babies growing, learning, and realizing their potential.

-83-

MIND OF A BEAUTIFUL WOMAN

In order to sustain interest, even in oneself, one must find something interesting. How one looks is important to make one attractive, but good looks are not sufficient. The beauty also lies in the person's personality, intelligence and charm.

Beauty is as it appears to the eyes and the mind. Psychologists say attractiveness depends upon the beholder's mental processing ease. They say beauty is what comes easy to your mind. One finds things beautiful if these are easier for the brain to process. One's background and training also matters in deciding about attractiveness. One can even prepare the mind to make an arbitrary pattern look likeable, say the psychologists. The studies made at the University College London indicate that the orbito-frontal cortex (which is involved with emotion and reward) gets activated after seeing "beautiful" paintings. The "uglier" paintings, however, excited motor cortex activity; "As if the brain was preparing to escape" is how the researchers described the scenario.

Women are becoming more and more beautiful, evolutionary biologists believe. Thus writes The Sunday Times (129), "Evolution is driving women to become ever more beautiful, while men remain as aesthetically unappealing as their caveman ancestors."

Physical attractiveness is a heritable trait. One evolutionary biologist observes: "If more attractive parents have more daughters and if physical attractiveness is heritable, it logically follows that women over many generations gradually become more physically attractive on average than men." In terms of procreation abilities, this observation says that good looks don't matter so much in men as in women. It says, in other words, that there has been little pressure for men's appearance to evolve. Can we say that the evolutionary pressure on men and women were different? For women it was beauty, and for men, it was success. One would be little hesitant to accept the idea that we are DNA packets and therefore, the aesthetics of beauty could be understood only through our hardwired responses.

We are likely to find average faces attractive, but we also know that the faces we find most attractive are not average. Beauty is much more than what meets the eye. Our culture, learning, and experience influence our concept of beauty. Our conception of beauty is subjective. Our conception of beauty gets imprinted on our brains through experience.

As one computational biologist remarked, "People's preferences may be tied to the interplay between what and how long they see something and their cognitive conception of attractiveness". Maybe, as the computational biologist reasoned, "When you choose to buy something in a shop, you do not know why you choose it. The brain predetermines your choice and then the brain gives you the reason later." Perhaps attraction works on a similar guiding principle.

A beautiful person can see beauty in everything, even in herself. A person would not look at herself, unless she finds something attractive in her. She wants to get noticed and loved, and wants to look beautiful to others as well as to herself. She knows what that something is. Beauty lies in the body as well as in the mind. Beauty lies in the symmetry, complexion, youthfulness, health, personality, intelligence, grace, charm and elegance. Physical and intellectual beauty is complementary. We make efforts to keep ourselves outwardly beautiful, as it helps us to get noticed instantly and easily. The inner beauty, which requires intellect, is an essential part of the make-up of a complete woman. Abraham Maslow described the situation thus: "A husband's conviction that his wife is beautiful, or a wife's belief that her husband is courageous, to some extent, 'creates' that beauty or courage. This is not so much about a perception of something that already exists, but about bringing something into existence by sheer belief."

Perfection is often equated with beauty. Perfection need not be an obsession. About the annoyingly perfect people, it is said that they are, in fact, the most annoying. Accept natural limitations and learn to enjoy them. Natural imperfection can be beautiful. One need not be 'annoyingly perfect' to get noticed. To get noticed one needs to become different.

Time magazine posed a very interesting question to its readers more than 75 years ago - Must a woman be beautiful to be loved? The observations received were quite interesting. The observations were age stratified: In a girl of 16, it is 80% beauty and 20% mental coquetry that matters. In a woman of 30, it is 50% beauty and 15% mental coquetry, 15% intelligence, 10% physical coquetry and 10% generosity. In a female of 50, it is 40% generosity, 40% intelligence, 10% beauty, 10% physical coquetry and complete absence of mental coquetry. The survey suggested that charm vary according to the age. As women grow older, other charms evolve and outweigh beauty. What about today's women? Has the perception of 'beautiful' changed as the time moved?

Beauty comes in all sizes and specifications. And as we all know, one size doesn't fit all. Pythagoras saw a strong connection between the proportions of the human figure and beauty. His observations greatly influenced Greek art. Plato suggested 'golden proportion' — the width of an ideal face would be two-thirds its length, while a nose would be no longer than the distance between the eyes. We have known that beauty is symmetry. We have also known that too much of both symmetry and asymmetry creates chaos. Beauty, it is said, is asymmetry resting on symmetry.

In the glamour industry - fashion or films - size matters a lot. This industry is very competitive. The inmates of this industry want to achieve many things in a very short frame of time. In the competitive world, a person is eager to grab all the opportunities that come his/her way. One wants to know what others are up to, and tries to reach there. One learns to make quick calculations regarding one's affinities/distractions with acquaintances, friends, and enemies. Since the expectations of the industry are more than the inmates can deliver, one is forced to learn the tenacity of going to any length to achieve the goals.

The model-turned-sociologist Ashley Mears talks about arbitrariness behind the business of glamour. She says that the supply-demand imbalance in the glamour industry leads to unhealthy competition. The half-life of models is so short; at mid twenty they become ancient. The catch is that the lure of future possibilities is so enticing, and there simply isn't much time. Most wait for the big time to come, but that time reaches only to a few. Mears's research shows that success in high-fashion modeling has a lot more to do with marketing and chance than it does with the ineffable.

Good looks do matter. Catherine Hakim (130) says that not only good looks matter, they should matter a great deal more. She thinks one should legitimately get the best out of their "erotic capital." A woman's erotic capital, says Hakim, includes not only physical appearance and sex appeal, but also other skills such as charm and sociability. She says that a young woman's erotic capital is consistently greater than that of a young man, but it is also always undervalued.

What about size zero? Is it a reasonable expectation of glamour industry from its inmates to become one? Size zero is fancy thinking. If pressured, one should be bold enough, and refuse to become one. Where is the sanctity of glamourising a woman who has "to starve to feed herself"? An impoverished look can never be beautiful.

The most beautiful woman Maharani Gayatri Devi once said in an interview, "I never use make-up." She is right. Beautiful people don't need make-up.

-84-

MIND OF A COLOURBLIND

Colours reflect power, optimism, warmth, emotion, and balance. There is attention grabbing RED that symbolises courage, strength, warmth, energy, excitement, defiance, aggression, and strain. The soothing BLUE is symbolic of intelligence, communication, trust, efficiency, serenity, logic, reflection, and calm. It is also perceived as cold, unemotional and unfriendly. YELLOW, psychologically speaking, is a strong colour. "Yellow is capable of charming God", said Vincent Van Gogh. Yellow symbolises optimism, confidence, self-esteem, extraversion, emotional strength, friendliness, and creativity. It also represents irrationality, fear, depression, and anxiety. The right yellow hue lifts our spirits and our self-esteem. Too much of it, or the wrong tone in relation to the other tones in a colour scheme, can cause self-esteem to plummet. GREEN represents nature and symbolises harmony, balance, restoration, reassurance, environmental awareness. Green also represents boredom and stagnation. VIOLET symbolises spiritual awareness, containment, vision and also introversion, decadence, suppression. ORANGE is a 'fun' colour and it represents physical comfort, warmth, security, passion, abundance, and fun. PINK is the most romantic colour. It is symbolic of femininity, love, and sexuality. BLACK is the most 'absorbing' colour. It has sophistication, glamour, security, emotional safety, efficiency, and substance. Black signifies power and authority and oppression, coldness, menace. Black is uncompromising. WHITE reflects clarity, simplicity, sophistication, efficiency. White represents purity and innocence in some culture. White is also the colour of mourning in some cultures. Red, orange and yellow are warm colours. Blue, purple and green are cool colours.

Does the perception of colours affect our mind and body? Researchers say it does. Based on their studies with placebo pills, they say that red pills are more effective stimulants than blue pills; blue pills are more effective as sleeping tablets than orange tablets. Green, white or blue pills aren't as effective as red as painkillers. The work of researchers at the University of Rochester suggests that our perception of colour is controlled much more by our brains than by our eyes. They say that colour perception goes far beyond the hardware of the eye.

Our eyes contain photoreceptor cells, called rods and cones, so called because of their shapes. Rods sense light and dark. Cones are less sensitive to light and sense more colour. We have three different colour receptors in our eyes, each designed to pick up different wavelengths of light. Each of three cone types senses one of three primary colours: blue, green, or red. The information that these three cone types receive, when combined, is what our eyes perceive as colour. In people with a colour vision deficiency, one or more cone types malfunction or are missing. As a result, they cannot see as many colour hues as someone with normal colour vision can. Ordinary colorblindness, arising from a defect in the retinal cells, is almost always partial, and some forms are very common; red-green colorblindness occurs to some degree in one in twenty people. But total congenital colorblindness, or achromatopsia, is rare, affecting perhaps one person in thirty or forty thousand.

Ketaki Kushari Dyson's book Ronger Rabindranath/ Rabindranather Sahitye o Chitrakalay Ronger Byabahar (131) is, as the title suggests, about the world of colours of Rabindranath Tagore. Ketaki Kushari learnt from a paper that "Tagore had probably had a partial colour vision deficiency." (www. parabaas.com). This amazing fact prompted her to study Rabindra-rachanabali from a different perspective. She wanted to investigate the effects of colour vision on Tagore's literary language. In a passage in Chhinnapatrabali she found Tagore jocularly refers himself as "a celebrated colour-blind person".

A colour vision deficiency changes a person's colour perception and how he sees and describes the world. If the person is a writer and a painter his language, his paintings, his metaphors and his emotions would reveal explicitly his colour vision problems. Ketaki Kushari's research noticed that Tagore favoured certain 'colour-words' over others. "The most commonly used words for red and green in Bengali, lal and shobuj, are not common choices for him...... He uses the adjective shyamal to convey a wide range of shades, from the colour of leaves to the colour of the soil and of the human skin." Tagore's perception of green was thus different. Tagore used red in a roundabout and anomalous manner. In his poetry, he often connected red with pain. He preferred to describe sunsets and sunrises in golden colours. "In his prose he uses minor examples of red, such as the reddening of eyes or skin in anger, embarrassment or humiliation, routinely and obsessively to mark the stages of his fictional narration." Tagore doesn't describe the dazzling beauty of red flowers. Red is used by him regularly in negative associations and contexts (shame, anger, death, violence, disease). Red is often a-jana (unknown), a-dekha (unseen), often associated with dukkha (sorrow) and vyatha (pain). Blue was Tagore's favourite colour. For Tagore blue is roop (beauty), blue is lavanya (grace), blue is ananda (joy). Blue and yellow were Tagore's favourite colour contrast.

"Interestingly, while he sings hymns of praise to the colour blue in his writings, he does not use a great deal of blue in his paintings. One could explain this phenomenon in the following way. Blue was the most vivid hue in his field of vision. He celebrated it in his literary work, but he was not interested in experimenting with it in his visual art because he knew what it was all about. He was far more interested in understanding what the colour red was all about, that area of darkness about which others were so ecstatic, and in the range of the colour called green", writes Ketaki Kushari. She says that Tagore exhibited a "restricted colour space. Tagore used lots of brown. "Brown might well have been a dominant colour in his field of vision; there might have been an overlap between his perceptions of green and brown." Ketaki Kushari, however, observes the "evidence in favour of protanopia is more clinching in Tagore's literary works than in his paintings."

Ketaki Kushari asks some very relevant questions: Did his other senses tend to compensate for the loss in colour vision? Is that why his poetry is so exceptionally rich in references to fragrances? Is the emphatic musicality of his poetry or his genius as a musical composer a compensatory development? The mind of a colourblind perhaps always struggles to use a mental brush to paint the grey vision with all colours of the rainbow which he imagines but can't really perceive that way probably. Tagore could bring in extraordinary touch of sensitivity when he described the nature in colour of his own.

Ketaki Kushari thus concludes, "He has left us an ocean of words, melodies, and visual images. There could well be a connection between his colour vision problem and the exceptional fecundity of his genius. Perhaps the experience of a handicap, the condition of perceiving things differently from others, the consequent struggle with communication, hones a person's sensitivity, sharpens the edge of genius, encouraging intense self-expression in a million different ways."

"What it would be like to live in a completely colourless world, not just for a few minutes, but permanently", asks Oliver Sacks (132). Sacks gets partial answer to his question from one of his patients, a painter who had suddenly become totally colourblind following a car accident. His patient "had lost colour vision not through any damage to his eyes, it seemed, but through damage to parts of the brain which "construct" the sensation of colour." His patient not only lost the ability to see colour, but to imagine or remember it, even to dream of it. Do the colourblinds have a world less dense and vibrant than of those who are not colourblind? Writes Sacks, "Might they even have developed heightened perceptions of visual tone and texture and movement and depth, and live in a world in some ways more intense than our own, a world of heightened reality - one that we can only glimpse echoes of in the work of the great black-and-white photographers?" Sacks thinks it is possible for persons who are truly isolated and insulated to retain their humanity and dignity, and make a statement that he also can see the world in his own colours.

-85-

MANY MINDS OF MUSIC

Imagine the world without sound or with too much sound. Hearing seems an effortless process, but it is in fact a very complex process. From a limited number of sounds, isn't it fascinating to hear infinite varieties of music.

Sound is a pressure wave that propagates through the air. We can distinguish various kinds of sounds because we have auditory brain. The vibrations created by sound are sent to the brain via the auditory nerve. There are nearly 25,000 receptors in our ear that carry messages to our brain. Only then our brain makes sense of the messages and tells us what sounds we are hearing.

Is sound only a pressure wave? Can we all hear with the same subtlety the silence of the air, music of the sea, noise of the earth, vastness of the sky? It is only those who have sensitivity can hear them.

You can 'see' sound in Shabdo, a Bengali film made by Kaushik Ganguli. The film is about a foley artiste Tarak Dutta. Tarak creates a film's ambient sounds in the studio. His methods of creating sound are unique. For example, crushing a paper he creates the subtle noise of flickering flames. He is so obsessed with the sound that is used in movies, that he slowly loses grip of words and dialogues. For him, the whole interest lies in focussing on the ambience sound used in movies. He becomes the victim of his own obsession. This impacts his personal life too. There can't be more befitting tribute to 100 years of Indian cinema than this brilliant film.

Whenever we think of sound, the first thing comes to our mind is music. Music is so powerful. It has power to tap into brain circuits controlling our emotions and movement. Rhythmic sound synchronizes brain waves. That is the reason drums unite tribes and we dance. Rhythmic sound coordinates the behaviour of people in a group, writes R Douglas Fields in Scientific American. Fields describes the work of Annett Schirmer who says that rhythmic sound coordinates people's thinking—the mental processes of individuals in the group become synchronized. Fields write that our perception of the external world entering our mind through our eyes is affected by the rhythm of what we hear. Something seen at a point precisely in beat with an auditory rhythm is more likely to be perceived than if it appears out of synch with the rhythm. Schirmer feels "Rhythm facilitates our interpersonal interactions in term of not only how we move, but how we talk and think."

Music is much more than mere sound. We 'feel' music. We interact with music. We 'conduct', dance, and change facial expressions while listening to music. Experiments have suggested that the performer's body language makes a difference in our listening. Music improves our mood. "Music has got to be useful for survival, or we would have gotten rid of it years ago," says Daniel Levitin (133).

Music brings back so many fond memories. We love music but our affinity for music is different. For a singer music is altogether a different experience than for a listener. Our ancestors had far more music in their lives than we do. The difference between us and our ancestors is that then everyone joined in the music making. Now we love to sit quietly in passive listening mode. We believe in consuming (as listeners) as much music as possible.

Music is good for social bonding, coalition building, and generally for reducing interpersonal tensions. It has played crucial role in the evolution of the human mind. Music is both culturally biased and genetically determined. Even babies in the womb respond to music.

The right hemisphere of the human brain has been traditionally identified as the seat of music appreciation. But studies reveal that music perception emerges from the interplay of activity in both sides of the brain, and both left and right sides are necessary for complete perception of rhythm. Though there is connection, it is not clear which part of the brain predominantly 'feels' music and which part 'hears' it. Not one particular 'music centre' but the whole auditory system (consisting of tens of millions of neurons) is needed to make sense of the music.

We like to listen to our own kind of music in our own way. It is said that listening to music makes one smarter ("Mozart effect"). Oliver Sacks (134) is not sure if music makes one smarter, but he certainly feels "Mozart is sublime, and whenever I listen to his music, I feel something which only music, and only Mozart, can provide". Music making, says Sacks, engages much of our brains than simply listening. That was the reason Sacks re-started taking piano lessons (after a gap of 60 years) when he was 75. "I still have my iPod, but I also need to make music every day", he said.

Music is one of the most powerful means of communication, especially emotions. Studies have indicated that long years of musical training makes the brains of musicians better attuned to the emotional content, like anger, of vocal sounds; musicians' brain showed enhanced responses to the infant's cries.

Music is much more than entertainment. It has therapeutic value. Researchers say music reduces blood pressure and heart rate, lowers stress hormone levels, and reduces the need for sedatives. Investigators have found that music increases the efficiency of oxygen consumption by the heart. Another interesting observation made by the researchers is that music encourages relaxation and modulates immunity. Jessica Serretani writes in Harvard Medicine that in many operating rooms, surgical teams play recordings of everything from classical concertos to classic rock as a way to relax and focus.

Gottfried Schlaug of Music, Neuroimaging and Stroke Recovery Laboratories at Harvard Medical thinks of musicians "as auditory motor athletes whose long-term training has an effect on brain function and structure." Schlaug believes that professional musicians are not born with the natural advantage of an auditory-motor system that enables them to play a musical instrument. It is the brain plasticity, particularly at a young age, and continued musical practice that lead to brain changes. People with Alzheimer's or other dementias have often responded to music even when they were unable to respond to other things. In some individuals music can stop incessant seizure. Music, especially familiar music from one's early years, can help to orient and organise such people.

Oliver Sacks says music works because it engages so many parts of the brain. Rhythm, actual or imagined, activates areas of the motor cortex, crucial in synchronising and energising movement—whether for athletes or people with movement disorders. "By and large, though, there are few, if any, bad side effects of music, and music can often work where no medications can", says Sacks.

How did music evolve? Does the human brain have a dedicated space for music? Is music a biological adaptation or a cultural invention? Experts say that music was a cultural invention, like cave painting or writing, which we humans invented to make our lives easier and more pleasant. There are also some who believe that music has biological connection. Studies have indicated that long years of musical training makes brains better attuned to emotions. Steven Pinker says that "music is auditory cheesecake". Pinker believes music never contributed to the propagation of the species. He believes if music vanishes from our species the rest of our lifestyle would be virtually unchanged. He believes that music is something humans have invented and then cultivated because it gives pleasure to our senses.

Every culture has music. Choirs, symphonies, ensembles and bands suggest that it is a group activity. Music, it seems, could reveal deeper biological connections between people than characteristics, such as language, that change rapidly when one culture meets another, says Floyd Reed of the University of Maryland in College Park. The link between songs and genotypes, say researchers, are quite strong; "cultures next door aren't as likely to sing the same tunes as cultures with similar genotypes". Sandra Trehub of the University of Toronto says that every culture has lullabies, and one doesn't need to understand the language to know that it is a lullaby. People sing to their infants the same way: at a high pitch, in a slow tempo and in a distinctive tone.

Music is a cultural technology, says Gary Marcus (135). Marcus doesn't believe that some key brain areas are active when hearing or performing music. He argues that music is something that humans have crafted over the millennia, rather than something directly wired into our genomes. Marcus defends his argument, "Virtually every modern song revolves around harmony, but harmony is an invention that is only a thousand years old." Marcus compares talented musicians with Steve Jobs: grand cultural engineers who design entertainment technology that appeals to brains that evolved for millions of years before the technology was developed.

Geoffrey Miller (136) thinks that music has got some key features of an evolved adaptation, like it is universal across cultures, and children learn it early and spontaneously. The bone flute is at least 35,000 years old. Miller says, given the fossil evidence on humans and Neanderthal vocal tracts, vocal music might be a lot older. This is sufficient time for shaping a hard-to-learn cultural skill into a talent for music in some people. Miller refers to Darwin's argument to make his case.

Darwin said that more musically talented proto-humans attracted more sexual partners, or higher-quality sexual partners, than their less-musical rivals. Miller says that for music to work it needs to recruit a lot of different genes and gene-regulatory systems and biochemical pathways. It is not few music genes but thousands of contributing genes that are needed for appreciating and performing music.

Marcus says that the selection for music is perhaps possible in songbird but not in humans. No doubt these genes correlate with other things too, argues Marcus. "There are probably tons of genes that can help someone become musical, but that doesn't mean any of them was specifically selected because of their role in music." Miller counters saying, "And the songbirds never evolved language. If they had, we'd probably see overlapping brain areas for music and speech in their brains, just like ours."

Similar genes may promote human music or bird's songs, according to researchers at the University of Helsinki. According to the researchers, music draws on a system of brain wiring that more generally promotes attachment behaviours. "The results suggest that willingness to listen to music is related to neurobiological pathways affecting social affiliation and communication," they add.

Mark Bocko and Dave Headlam, professors at the University of Rochester's Music Research Lab, are musical engineers. They do musically-informed research. Bocko wants to understand, through computers, what musicians do to create sound. He wants to capture the essence of the physics of how the instrument works. He studies how the more subtle inputs and the changes of the blowing pressure over time, and how things are connected together. He tries to better understand what's critical, and what's not, in a music file.

Headlam wants to add another sense to music training. He wants music students to spend time not only with their ears, but also with their eyes. He wants them to better coordinate their ears with their eyes. Says Headlam, "So, you can imagine if you are playing something, you are looking at a screen, at some sort of oscilloscope display, and you see your line as you're playing, and then you see your teacher's line, and then those lines gradually come together as you are hearing what you want to do. Then, at a certain point, they come together. In that way you have accomplished your goal by combining your sight and your hearing."

Musically inclined neural scientists say that music stimulates right brain function, enhancing the ability to solve logical and mathematical problems. It could be due to the mathematical nature of music that engineers love music. Elain Chew says that music's imminently quantifiable attributes make it an ideal medium for studying human creativity and cognition. "The dynamics of musical ensemble offer models of human collaboration", thinks Chew.

Why music evokes emotion? A study, conducted by Nidhya Logeswaran and Joydeep Bhattacharya at the University of London, tells us that music can affect our visual images. After listening to happy or sad musical excerpts, the participants of the study were shown a photograph of a face. They were then asked to rate the emotional content of the face (1 meaning extremely sad and 7 extremely happy). Logeshwaran and Bhattacharya found that music powerfully influenced the emotional ratings of the faces. Happy music made happy faces seem even happier, while sad music exaggerated the melancholy of a frown.

Researchers have found deep connection between music and mathematics. Music has pitch and beat. It seems music also has mathematical shapes.

Pythagoras discovered that pleasing musical intervals could be described using simple ratios. Now, the researchers are trying to find mathematical sense of music. Music researchers Clifton Callender at Florida State University, Ian Quinn at Yale University, and Dmitri Tymoczko at Princeton University say that mathematics is a more fundamental language of nature than music. Their "geometrical music theory" turns music into shapes. For Tymoczko, the history of music represents "a long process of exploring different symmetries and different geometries". He says his method "might allow you to visualise some of the differences between John Lennon and Paul McCartney. McCartney's tunes tend to look more traditional, Lennon's tend to be a little more rock."

Music seems to me both nature and nurture. In the making of Rahul Dev Burman, can we ignore the contributions of enchanting musical environs of Kolkata, the musical support of Basu Chakravarti and Manohari Singh, and the assistance of his talented group of musicians? Can we ignore in RDB the music-talent genes of Sachin Dev Burman.

-86-

MIND OF A CITY

After more than three decades, a friend was returning to India for good. All these years, he was living in a city where the quality of life (in terms of safety, education, hygiene, political and economic stability, and public transportation) can be rated as one of the best. I asked him which city he would like to settle in after his return to India. I also asked him whether he would be comfortable living in any city in this country after living in a most 'livable' country. He said, "I am not returning to my country to lead a comfortable life. I wouldn't have left the country I am living in, if comfort was the only motive. I want to live in a live city."

A live city understands the fundamentals of a living organism. A live city believes in the proportionate growth of all its constituents. It knows that random growth of some organs is not good for the overall growth of the organism. To accommodate growth, a part of the organism dies. A live city knows which part should die and which should not, in the interest of its overall growth.

A live city has a brain and a nervous system to develop its vision and plan. Its neural network helps in connecting people. The city cares for the physical, social and personal development of its people. The heart of the city defines its essential identity. Also, the city has a special relationship with its people, streets, buildings, trees, celebrations, festivals and seasons. Such a city is proud of its roots as well as its posterity. A live city believes in improving the quality of life of its residents, but not at the expense of deteriorating the quality of its environment.

In a live city, hierarchy is respected, but is not everything. In this city, besides a specialised mould, a person has the opportunity to identify himself in various other moulds. A live city has zest for life, which is good for its health. Above all, it understands the need for balancing zest with accountability.

With time, the character of city changes, and live cities are no exception. Is it necessary to lose one's identity in order to be part of the mainstream? If a solute wants to be part of the solution, then it must make itself soluble; an insoluble solute can exist only as a precipitate. A live city knows appropriate chemistry to maintain a balance between solubility and insolubility; it knows when to retain identity and when to become part of the mainstream.

For my friend, a live city was more than "statistics" or a "green" or a "black" or a "white" city. This is how my friend concluded: "Rather than being invented by others, I would like to invent myself. I would like to return to the city I left many years ago. I have not forgotten it. I know my city has changed. I know it is chaotic, but I would love to live amid cheerful chaos. I would like to live with the hope that there is a better tomorrow."

Let us now talk about another friend of mine. This friend of mine spent most of his working life in big cities. After retirement, he returned to the town he grew up. Here he built a beautiful spacious house not far from the city, adjacent to his ancestral home. Within a year, he (more his wife) started missing the big city so much that he sold his town property at a throwaway price and moved back to the big city. There he rented a flat far away from the city.

My friend and his wife soon realised that they have made a mistake by returning to the big city. Now they were not getting the same warmth from their acquaintances as they got during their previous sojourn. Friendliness from the 'friends' was missing. His friends and acquaintances had no time to play with them in their second innings. They no longer wanted to live in the fictional world of big cities. They wanted to return again to the city they left merely a year ago. Simple life once again began to appeal them. They soon realized that small cities are not as boring as they are made out to be. His hurriedly taken decision made him a couple of lakhs poorer. Was it due to his childhood memories and sentiments or genuine friends or was it a practical move?

We think we can create our own as well as our family's future in big cities. We believe big cities give, not only to the affluent and the skilled, but also to middle class and poor better life opportunities. But the big cities are slowly losing their shine. They are transforming for the worse. There is more class conflict. The local's intolerance towards outsiders is growing rapidly. In big cities demographic structure is changing fast, number of poor is increasing and housing costs are escalating. These cities are in danger of permanently undermining the very thing that has made big cities so attractive. Small cities, on the other hand, are increasingly becoming more attractive.

My friend returned to the smaller city, because it is large hearted. The neural network of small city is not that extensive. So connecting with people is not as complex as in big cities. Jacob Vigil an evolutionary biologist at the University of New Mexico rightly pointed out the fact that the bigger the social network the lesser will be the time for interaction. Small cities provide an ambience for utilising time much more fruitfully. (In big cities commuting takes most of our limited time). Vigil says, "Under hardship, a smaller social circle is more protective. It allows more time to strengthen relationships with reliable social partners, and limits our interactions with risky folks. You can make the inverse argument for having a big social sphere when things are going really well."

My friend did not realise how much he valued intimacy with the city. His special bonding with the people, its streets, trees and celebrations resurfaced. He wanted to be known by his pet name, and not by his position and hierarchy. So far, he was invented by others. Now he wanted to invent himself. He no longer felt the need to 'grow'.

As the city grows its character changes; with growth, the consumption pattern and behaviour of the populace also change. A big city makes possible the economies of scale in infrastructure and facilitates and optimises delivery of social services. "An important result of urbanisation is the growth of occupations geared toward innovation and wealth creation," say Geoffrey West and Luis

Bettencourt of Santa Fe Institute. The character of the city changes when growth is driven by innovation and wealth creation. The continuous growth necessitates an "accelerating treadmill of dynamical cycles of innovation". Innovation is needed both for the organisms as well as cities, but their time scales are quite different. The innovation time scales of natural selection are very large. As the population increases and becomes more connected, time scale of innovation in cities become shorter.

The pace of biological life slows down with increasing size of the organism. This is, however, not true for urban life. The pace of urban life in cities above a certain population increase, as the size of the city increases. The growth of the cities as well as organism is constrained by the availability of resources and their rates of consumption. A system collapses when it runs out of resources. To avoid this crisis it becomes necessary for the organism or the cities to bring major qualitative changes. In case of cities, this includes innovation to ensure wealth and knowledge creation. "As we approach the collapse, a major innovation takes place, and we start all over again", West and Bettencourt explain.

In order to maintain livability, the cities are required to innovate at a faster rate. Innovation and wealth creation has the possibility of growing faster at places where better opportunities are available. Big cities provide such opportunities. As the size of the city increases, along with it increases income, wealth, number of creative people, number of patentable discoveries, number of criminals, number of sicknesses, the amount of waste, etc. West and Bettencourt argue that cities are mostly scaled-up, or scaled-down, versions of each other. Their model predicts that up to 85 per cent of the character of a city are determined simply by its size. Only about 15 per cent of a city's character is distinctive. It means city administrators, and the city's aesthetics can play with only 15 per cent.

The major character of a city is due to "social networks" that consist of human clusters and the social interactions and hierarchies that flow from them. The research of West says that if a city doubles in size, it needs only 85 per cent more infrastructure. The flipside of massive city growth, West says, is that some of the negative factors such as crime and disease increase by 15 per cent above the doubling rate. In spite of this, West and Bettencourt think bigger can be better for cities. About big cities, they say, "It may not be the feeling of many of us when we're in them, but it is very good and no doubt that is the reason so many people are attracted to them."

Let me describe a city for you that has its own mind and is live and livable.

This city is a city
of visionaries and revolutionaries,
a confluence of art and culture,
of litterateurs,
of Nobels and inventors.
A city
of contradictions and chaos,
of joys and sorrows,
of pride and despair,
of passions and provocations,
of refined intellect and fading charm,
of strikers and complainers,
of bhadraloks and addabaajs,
of bhojon rasiks and bhromon bilashis,
of tight rope walkers.
A city of undying hopes,
often unsure of itself,
difficult to live in,
but irresistible to live without.
Once the city of
Sahibs, Memsahibs, Babus
Ghotis, Bangals, Meros, Bhaiyyas.
Now the city of Amar, Tomar, Saubar.
A city that embraces all never dies.

-87-

HUMOUR AND THE MIND

Humour has always been a useful tool for communications and social interactions. The factors that influence our sense of humour includes where we grew up, the culture we grew up, our maturity and intelligence, and most importantly, the context. Humour is both universal and uniquely personal. It is often contagious. Each individual has his/her own mind, and own knowledge and belief system to understand the world. "When different minds bring different content to bear, they find different kinds of mirth."

What makes us laugh? Why things are funny? These questions have recently been addressed by Matthew Hurley, Daniel Dennett and Reginald Adams Jr (137). The authors present humour from an evolutionary and cognitive perspective. They say that humour has "cognitive cleanup mechanism" and is intimately linked to our thinking process. Brain scientists have shown that puns and other types of jokes are deciphered in different regions of the brain. They found activation in an area of the brain called the medial prefrontal cortex when jokes are processed. This area controls our reward-related behaviour.

We the human beings are blessed with the ability of pattern recognition. This ability of ours is unconscious and instant. We are unique because of this perceptual and intellectual ability. Humour encourages this ability. Brain scientists say that humour occurs when the brain recognises a pattern that surprises it and that recognition of this sort is rewarded with the experience of the humour response.

The theory of humour as proposed by Hurley, Dennett, and Adams begins with the notion that our brains daily observations are dependent on several assumptions and incomplete information. The brain has to complete the arduous task of anticipating the future in a world that is unfolding at a fast pace. Under the circumstances, mistakes are inevitable. As Hurley says, "We do a quick and dirty assessment and make a lot of best guesses. But this fills our mental spaces with junk, small mistakes that could trigger a cascade of errors if they go undetected, leading us to waste a lot of energy and resources and, in the worst case, inviting disaster".

Finding the errors and then disabling them is not easy. Our brain has to do this job, in addition to myriad other competing jobs. Hurley adds, "But it's a resource-hungry job that has to compete with everything else our brains are doing. We think the pleasure of humour, the emotion of mirth, is the brain's reward for discovering its mistaken inferences. Basically, the brain has to bribe itself to do this important work".

Humour, Dennett and his coauthors say, arose when our long-ago ancestors were furnished with open-ended thinking. The process of natural selection was not enough to order our brain to find and fix all our mistakes. The brain was needed to be 'bribed' with pleasure. This wired-in source of pleasure has made us addicted to humour.

Researchers say it is time we take humour little bit more seriously.

A joke or a cartoon can raise our spirits. We laugh from sudden feelings of superiority over other people. We laugh because laughter gives us relief by releasing pent-up psychic energy. Laugh during a stressful situation are often helpful in reducing the stress.

Our politicians are well aware of this fact. Writer and economist Kaushik Basu's comment about powerful people vis-à-vis humour is quite interesting. He says that the powerful have no way of knowing if they have a sense of humour because ordinary people will always laugh at their jokes.

Comedy is art. If we want to understand art the way science is understood, it gets ruined. If the genesis of humour is analysed too vigorously, it gets ruined. Jokes are ruined by taking too little time (for an active expectation to form) or too much time (so that the active belief is given up before the punch line).

"The most common kind of joke is that in which we expect one thing and another is said; here our own disappointed expectation makes us laugh," said Cicero. Humour is especially effective when people laugh at themselves. We often become fools in order to prove ourselves wise. Laughing at others gives one joy, but there is also joy at being laughed at.

We all have acoustically distinctive laughter. The context, frequency and intensity of laughter vary in different cultures. Laughter follows norms and customs of the society. Laughter does not imply only humour. Researchers say that laughter, in general, is more about communicating emotions than about humour. Laughter gives instant relief from hopeless situations.

Laughing is a ticklish matter. We don't laugh if someone slips on a banana peel and breaks his leg, but we laugh if he slips and gets up immediately. Charles Darwin referred to humour as "a tickling of the mind."

Jokes apart, laughter lightens up stressful, or psychologically overly demanding, circumstances. Humour reduces levels of stress hormones, such as cortisol, and is thought to enhance our immune, endocrine, and cardiovascular systems. It is common to use laughter as a friction dampener among warring factions. Laughter can likewise function to mitigate problems or social ambivalence within a group. Laughter has therapeutic properties. Laughing sessions can cure mysterious illnesses, believe some laughter associations. Laughter can be induced and there are 'qualified' laughter inducers. Laughter can also be induced chemically.

Our brains are hardwired for laughter. Richard Restak (138) often uses cartoons and jokes to measure a patient's neurologic and psychiatric well-being. It allows him to assess various things: abstraction ability, empathy, powers of observation and description, as well as sense of humour. "Over the years, I've learned that you can't fake an understanding of a cartoon; you either get it or you don't", he says. He asks, "Why am I interested in my patients' ability to appreciate humor? It is because "humour impairment may point to operational problems at various levels of brain functioning."

Why do people find cartoons funny? Restak says that humour has both a subjective component (exhilaration or mirth) and its physical expression (smiling or laughing). "One can exist without the other: we may find a risqué joke amusing but withhold a smile if we happen to be in polite company." We may take the help of laughter in situations when we are in uncomfortable situations. There is 'nervous laughter'.

Humour is our unique ability. Perhaps no other species has this sense. "Only we can do this because—thanks to the larger size of our frontal lobes compared with other species—we are the only creatures that possess a highly evolved working memory, which by creating and storing scripts allows us to appreciate sophisticated and subtle forms of humour," writes Restak.

Humour can be quite demanding to the brain. After entering through visual or auditory tracks humorous material triggers a precise repertoire of responses: the order, timing, and emphasis must be just right; irrelevant or distracting elements must be discounted or ignored. The job of a comedian is to entertain people. But it can take a personal toll on his or her mental health. Some comedians have described their act "very dangerous, like walking a tightrope, or like running across a lake of ice where the ice is breaking behind you and it is going to take an hour to get to the other side." Some comedians have suffered nervous breakdown during their performances. The worst thing for a comedian is to find no one laughing at his jokes. Also, jokes often are hierarchical in nature. One is expected to laugh at the boss's jokes, whether we find them funny or not.

Jokes also have some kind of gender bias. Psychologists say that, in general, women tend to favour men who make them laugh, while men favour women who laugh at their jokes. Men, in general, favour slapstick humour and hostile jokes, while women prefer self-deprecating humour and funny stories. The aggressive humour of men in times of turmoil often adversely affects bonding between partners, compared with the more soothing humour favoured by women. Male humour helps in establishing romantic relationships. Female humour, on the other hand, is more effective in maintaining romantic relationships. It is not easy to hold a laugh, and as Stephen King said, "You can't deny laughter; when it comes, it plops down in your favourite chair and stays as long as it wants." Humour has transformative power. Sense of humour is one of the most highly rated traits when people choose their friends, lovers or spouses.

Humour is generally at the cost of someone. There is a difference between "laughing at others" and "laughing at oneself". Laughing at oneself has therapeutic and pedagogical value, says Simon Critchley (139). Humour is especially effective when people laugh at themselves. We often become fools in order to prove ourselves wise. Laughing at others is generally based on malice. Spontaneous humour is more effective in eliciting laughter than deliberate humour.

All said and done, if a joke is explained, its humour is lost. Thus, the analysis of humour doesn't make much sense. As EB White said, "Analysing humour is like dissecting a frog. Few people are interested and the frog dies of it."

-88-

CREATIVE MIND

Is it a fact that highly creative people suffer from mental disorders? Are creative people at odds with the world and themselves? Is it true that creative people tend to see the world in unconventional ways? Is it true that touch of madness boosts creativity?

Creative people breathe work. Charles Dickens used to get extremely depressed when he stopped working. Tchaikovsky was chronically dysthmic having suicidal tendencies. He believed that only work can save him from the drudgery of life. "Without music I would go insane", he used to say. It is also said about creative people that they find themselves incapable of forming long-term personal relationships. One of the reasons for this discomfiture is the strong relationship they develop with their work. Many creative persons find numbers and abstracts more attractive than people and relationships.

Many gifted composers are potentially vulnerable individuals. In order to understand creativity vis-à-vis mental disorders, Richard Kogan a psychiatrist and a concert pianist, studied many gifted composers. In such individuals, Kogan believes, music provides temporary inner harmony, and that wards off the manifestations of mental illness. Kogan's studies on German composer Robert Schumann (140) revealed creative advantages as well as disadvantages of mental illness. Schumann's episodic depressive period was well compensated when he cycled into hypomanic state. During this state, Schumann felt more energetic, his imagination sharpened, and as a result he could produce musical masterpieces. Kogan, however, says that Schumann's disjointed and fragmented thought process was responsible to make his music incomprehensible to his contemporaries.

Composer Ludwig van Beethoven suffered from a variety of psychiatric symptoms, but he was also known for his exemplary mental health. He is still cited for his capacity to cope with adversity. Beethoven was deaf. But deafness could not deter him to fulfill his artistic destiny. He created outstanding music in his silent world of imagination.

Virginia Woolf is known as much for her writing as she is known for her periodic nervous breakdowns. Her mental illness profoundly influenced her writing. She complained about her illness, and at the same time acknowledged the strange utility of her illness. "Woolf's mental illness forced her to think about her mind, which fuelled her modernist writing style. But the illness itself was an obstacle: She wrote in spite of it, not because of it," Jonah Lehrer writes. Does that mean that the human brain actually becomes more creative during mild mania? Overgeneralisation is never good or desirable, and particularly when one talks about the compatibility of creativity with disorder.

It is said that creativity is born out of pain, and can't survive without it. This understanding is born from the case studies of some artists, who in spite of leading a chaotic life, have created masterpieces. One such artist was Edvard Munch. He underwent therapy. The therapy was 'unfortunately successful', and as a result of therapy his creativity was gone. Creativity is a mysterious process. Neuroscientists are striving to unlock the mystery and complexity of creativity. There are many creative individuals who don't wait for some kind of disorder to arrive to initiate their process of creativity. There are many creative people who are perfectly normal and have produced masterpieces.

-89-

ARTISTIC AND SCIENTIFIC MIND

Generally speaking, scientists are known to be serious types. Artists, on the other hand, are considered more playful. Does playful approach diminish seriousness? Creativity in science can influence creativity in art; cinema is the prime example. Science and art are not mechanical endeavours. Both are serious business. Both artists and scientists draw from their conscious and unconscious realms. Both need imagination. The source of imagination for both is their inner voice. Both get distracted by the blind alleys of complex social problems. Both want to come out of the blind alleys in their own way. In the hunches of a scientist, one can find the echoes of an artist.

We need to combine the bottom-up approach of science with the top-down approach of the arts to understand our deepest questions. Science gives us perfection. Art brings into the fold of science, the unexplainable world of magic. It doesn't matter if it also brings into the fold incoherence, imprecision, abstraction and contradiction. Because these are also the attributes we need to be equipped with.

Creativity is a chain reaction of many tiny sparks. The more ideas you have, the better. Sometimes you don't know which sparks are important. R Keith Sawyer (141) says that an idea may seem sudden, but in reality our minds have actually been working on it all along. Sawyer says that insight and execution are inextricably woven together. If the executioner is different from the one who first 'saw' the idea, chances of its success are lesser. One of the advices of Sawyer is to develop a network of colleagues and have freewheeling and unstructured discussions with them.

"Look at what others in your field are doing. Brainstorm with people in different fields. Research and anecdotal evidence suggest that distant analogies lead to new ideas," says Sawyer. There is nothing like "full-blown moment of inspiration". Ideas don't magically appear in a genius' head from nowhere. They always build on what came before. Creativity, like many other pursuits, is hard work. You have to work on it to achieve it.

Dean Keith Simonton (142) distinguishes creative scientists from creative artists on the basis of their training. According to Simonton, scientific creativity requires much more formal training than artistic creativity. "Indeed, some studies have found a curvilinear inverted-U relation between artistic creativity and formal education level so that those with higher degrees are at a relative disadvantage." Simonton says that scientists tend to be better students than artists. The third dimension of difference between an artist and a scientist is in the influence of mentors. Although the creative development is enhanced by working under notable creators in the same domain, artistic talent is best nurtured by studying under a diversity of artists, while scientific talent is better nourished by studying under just one.

The science behind creativity is little understood. Does anyone know why Mozart was Mozart? "Ten thousand hours may be a necessary, but not a sufficient condition" to make someone as creative as Mozart was, writes Bryan Appleyard. Can everything be explained by science? Is there something other than science that can explain why Mozart was Mozart? Some people are trying to understand the puzzle of creativity.

Solving puzzles is a way to assess one's creative insight. Cracking a puzzle requires "imagination, it's inference, it's guessing; and much of it is happening subconsciously," says Marcel Danesi (143). Researchers say that solving puzzles are easier when people are amused. A good joke, just before one attempts to solve a puzzle, can make the brain better prepared to solve it. The very idea of doing a puzzle typically shifts the brain into an open, playful state that is itself a pleasing escape, writes Benedict Carey. Problem solving usually requires both creative analysis and sudden out-of-the-box insight, but these are different brain states, brain imaging studies suggest. The positive mood engages both perceptual and visual states.

The minds of creative people are believed to be embedded with the ability to feel with great depth and passion. These special minds are wired for rapid and fluid thinking as they enjoy the ability to make quick associations. These minds can see things in new ways. They can make connections between old things. These minds are flooded with ideas like all other minds are, but they have the ability to control the flight of ideas that many minds don't have. These minds also get bad ideas but they possess the ability to purge the bad ones. These minds, like all other minds, suffer from mood swings of high and low, and are vulnerable and sensitive. But creative people know how to navigate the tides, write Jeff and Julie Crabtree (144).

Failure and learning from failure is part of creativity. The environment of anxiety doesn't help creativity. Fear inhibits the fluid nature of creative thinking. Creative people also lack confidence. They need encouragement, like us, to overcome their doubts. Collaboration and brainstorm can lead to distant analogies among various fields, and thus are often very useful for the emergence of creative ideas. It is therefore important to keep track of the surrounding, even though we know that if one keeps track of the surrounding it is not enough for creativity.

-90-

CURIOUS MIND

One wonders if curiosity is good or bad for us. It is generally believed that curiosity is the key to discovery. There are some who think that curiosity unnecessarily distracts us from our daily duties. Some think, "Curiosity is the unbridled desire of those who seek to know more than they should." They believe curious people are concerned about the things that don't concern them. We are generally curious by nature. I don't like someone if he is too curious about me. I also don't like the idea that no one is curious about me.

One can't get away so easily from curiosity. A curious mind is an active mind. To become curious, one needs to have interest in unfamiliar things. If you are not interested in things around you, there is little chance of you becoming curious. Todd Kashdan (145) says that curiosity is not about whether we pay attention, but how we pay attention to what is happening. Curiosity is one of the three traits that are needed to achieve success; the other two are intelligence and effort. The researchers Sophie Von Stumm, Benedikt Hell, and Tomas Chamorro-Premuzic say that the combined effects of curiosity and effort equals the impact of intellect on academic performance.

Curiosity is basically a hunger for exploration. A curious person likes to read books, likes to visit places to understand new culture, and likes to try different food to understand the place and the people. Curiosity makes one a better learner. It equips a person to deal with novel as well as problematic situations. It prepares one to protect oneself from unjust attacks. It helps one to defend his identity and reputation. Curiosity also leads us to dysfunctional extremes.

Curiosity is hard-wired into our psyche. Our brain drives us. It sets our goals and also helps us to prioritise them. Brain receives signals in various forms. Emotions influence these signals. Due to clashes in emotions, there is likelihood of clashes in our drives. Our brain sorts out the priority, based on our past experiences, skill sets, and cultural leanings. It sees what matters to us the most, and then it takes us there. It also takes us away from irrelevant goals.

Toxic curiosity, obviously, is not desirable. And as Francis Bacon writes, desire of learning and knowledge are sometimes based upon natural curiosity and inquisitive appetite, sometimes to entertain the minds, sometimes for ornament and reputation, most times for lucre and profession, and seldom sincerely to give a true account of the gift of reason, to the benefit and use of men. Bacon's advice to us is to separate and reject vain speculations and whatsoever is empty and void, and to preserve and augment whatsoever is solid and fruitful; that knowledge may not be for pleasure and vanity only.

-91-

INNOVATIVE MIND

Joichi Ito of MIT's media lab says that we try to make things more efficient, more effective on a local scale without looking at the system around it. Internet, according to Ito, is not only the triumph of chaos over control but also the triumph of distributed innovation over centralised innovation. Ito thinks innovation scenario needs to change. Earlier the chain was ideate — propose —raise money — plan — build. Now it should be completely the opposite, build and then figure out the business model. This is unstructured innovation. The older approach feels Ito, is 'incremental'. He says incremental research isn't going to be very disruptive. "Some of the most interesting innovations happen when the person doing it doesn't even know what's going on. True discovery, I think, happens in a very undirected way, when you figure it out as you go along".

"As you go along" is an important concept. Anything under control is not going to exhibit that behaviour. Ito follows the undirected approach in the lab he heads. He believes that if one wants to try something, one can bypass the explaining route. One can just go and do whatever one wants to do. When you focus your attention on something, you only see a very small fraction of your field of vision because your brain gets filled in with everything what you think is there. In doing so you may miss the disruptive things that are happening in the periphery.

Then what is the way of looking around? "You've got to be antidisciplinary because if you're in a discipline and you're worried about peer review and you're knowing more and more about less and less, that's by definition an incremental thing", Ito says. When you are anti-disciplinary, you have the "freedom to connect things together that aren't traditionally connected". It is practice before theory — build and then think about the business model. His logic is — if a thing works, theory can be sorted out later. Innovation at the edges is not for everyone and everybody should not be using it. You can't just give somebody a bunch of free time and then expect him or her to come up with brilliant ideas. Ito says, "So it's okay if most of society has plans". Ito believes in 'demo or die', rather than 'publish or perish'.

Some of Ito's prescriptions are: stop focusing on individuals and start focusing on communities; stop focusing on top-down and focus more on bottom-up; stop focusing on single experts and start focusing on the cloud. The world has a lot of misfits who believe in changing the nature of innovation, and in effect, changing the nature of society. This collection of misfits can really bring interesting capability. The togetherness need not be interdisciplinary. It need not be a conglomeration of, say, a physicist, an engineer and a designer working on the same project. "An anti-disciplinary project is when you can't tell who the designer is and who the engineer is, and the engineer knows designing, and the person who's dancing is going to be the one also doing the molecular biology." The other point Ito wants to convey is that you may have a first class degree, but it is better to know what really you are good at and what you are obsessed with.

We too have many 'misfits' in this country. We need to dig them out to steer the innovation boat of our country.

-92-

MIND OF AN ICONOCLAST

We, the Indians discovered such a complex thing called ZERO. Why can't we discover or invent simple things? The man who deliberated for quite some time "Imagining India", Nandan Nilekani, possibly has the answer; "A big reason for our struggle lies in our ability to push through and implement critical ideas."

If one wants to become world-class one must have the ambition to become world-class. One doesn't become world-class simply by putting just hard work. Talent is necessary, but not sufficient to make one world-class. The world class mindsets are ruthlessly self-critical, but boundlessly self-confident. Such mindsets have identified goals that surpass mundane considerations.

The 'magic moments' come when one frees oneself from structured thinking. Critical thinking is divergent. Such thinking is open to alternate perspectives, so essential for 'out-of-the-box' mindset. It identifies goals, examines assumptions, accomplishes actions, and assesses conclusions. Critical thinkers can see the big picture. Their neural pathways are also operative in unconventional networks.

To become world-class one needs a creative ecosystem. An improper ecosystem can jeopardise the entire innovation process. It is well-known that intellectual capital is an extremely important component of the creative ecosystem. It is also known that intellectual capital, like any other form of capital, appreciates and depreciates, becomes obsolete, requires maintenance, repair, replacement and modification.

Nobel laureate Venkat Ramakrishnan, when asked what was lacking here in India, said, "While it (India) has many good scientists, it has too few who are considered real international leaders in their field. To do that sort of science, you have to know the delicate balance between taking the risks to work on important but difficult problems and knowing what is actually feasible over the long term." He then added, "It is hard for young scientists to develop a feel for doing this sort of science in the absence of appropriate mentors and role models."

It is always helpful to understand that democratic principles are not applicable everywhere and on all occasions. It simply means that everything is not meant for everyone, and more importantly, few things are only meant for the brightest and the best. We need to recognise the necessity of sufficient inputs for commensurate outputs. We need to understand the value of incentives for furthering a purpose. We need to respect the essence of time and speed.

Innovation has become a highly perishable commodity. We need to recognise the opportunities as well as the risks involved with innovation. The challenge before the innovator is to anticipate or evaluate the correct status of his discovery.

Neurobiologists say creative drive results from an interaction of the frontal lobes (for idea generation), the temporal lobes (for idea evaluation), and dopamine (for general arousal and goal-directed behaviour) from the limbic system. Creativity may require co-activation and communication between regions of the brain that ordinarily are not strongly connected.

The brains of iconoclasts are wired differently, writes Gregory Berns (146). What we see through the retina is not the real picture. The real picture depends upon how the brain interprets these signals. The roadblock that stands in the way of truly innovative thinking is perception. Iconoclasts don't see things differently, but perceive things differently. Iconoclasts can conquer the fear of failure, of the unknown, and of ridicule. Our fear system is largely unconscious or subconscious, and it is triggered by very primitive aversions relating to survival.

Our social brains are deeply hardwired to care what other people think about us. The fear of being humiliated, or of being shunned from the group, for the majority of us, becomes a powerful impediment to do something differently. The iconoclasts understand that to create something new you may have to tear down conventional ways of thinking. Since it is relatively difficult for others to accept uncommon ways of thinking or things, an iconoclast needs to be equipped with a fair amount of social intelligence to overcome such difficulties.

Our brain is responsible for our lack of imagination. It doesn't want to waste energy in visualisation. The iconic brain knows how to take the least path of resistance and reactivate neurons that have been optimised to process this sort of scene. Berns says that visual perception is the brain's way of explaining ambiguous visual signals in the most likely way. The networks that govern both perception and imagination can be re-programmed. By deploying your attention differently, the frontal cortex, which governs decision-making, can reconfigure neural networks so that you can see things that you didn't see before.

One needs a novel stimulus (like a new piece of information or an unfamiliar environment) to fully awaken the attention systems; the more radical the change, the greater the likelihood of fresh insights. Novel experiences are so effective at unleashing the imagination. They force the perceptual system out of categorisation and allow the brains to take shortcuts.

Is creativity the preserve of a few geniuses or can be found, in some form, in all individuals? Rex Jung, a neuropsychologist, studied the interaction between creativity and intelligence. He monitored divergent thinking among his subjects, mainly college students. Jung says, "Creativity and intelligence are linked at lower levels of IQ, but above a certain threshold, they don't necessarily go hand in hand." He claims that people with high and low IQs appear to use their brains differently to achieve creativity.

Among the ways suggested to foster creativity, besides purpose and intention, are building motivation, developing self-management, and leading a fulfilling life. These qualities come under the purview of "No Man's Land". Bertrand Russell said that definite knowledge belongs to science, what surpasses definite knowledge belongs to theology. Between theology and science lies "No Man's Land" and this space belongs to philosophy.

One needs to visit "No Man's Land" for innovation nourishment. This land of Plato and Kant is quite useful for achieving excellence as it gives one the ability to see things from various perspectives and with an open mind. It is good but, as one Cambridge philosophy professor said, "Wittgensteinian air about philosophy" is changing.

Peter Drucker once said that the most successful innovators are the creative imitators. How about imitating the wonder that was India? We, the people of India, that is Bharat, once believed that there was no country like ours, no king like ours, and no science like ours. Can't we regain that spirit and that confidence? Can't we, a country of 1.2 billion people, get back, literally, to ZERO?

-93-

MIND OF A WINNER

In a race between two straight, equal and parallel lines, winner is the one that can become longer than the other. To become the longer line, the lines can adopt different strategies. Line 1 can use an eraser to cut short Line 2. Line 2 can use a pencil to draw a line longer than line 1. Line 1 resort to bad practice to win the race. Line 2 uses fair practice to win the race. Can there be a fair way when one knows that one can't please his rival as well as win? It is a simple logic that one has to be better than the other to win a race. To win a race one has to make necessary efforts. What needs more effort, a pencil or an eraser? Perhaps carrying a pencil with an eraser is the appropriate way.

Be fitter than the other is the usual mantra of winning. Does that mean only the fittest win? This question needs to be asked more appropriately. Along with the question, one must specify trait and environment where one has to prove her/his fitness. One person could be fitter in one trait or one environment. The other person could be fitter in another trait or another environment. The trait and environment are not always interchangeable. One becomes the fittest in his own trait, and in his own environment. Each winner knows the ways of winning. It also has to be her/his day.

Who decides the winner in an electoral battle? Obviously, people decide people's representatives. There are many among us who possess the attributes to become neocorticle politicians; larger the neocortex a person has, better is his or her capacity to handle intricacies.

How can we ascertain that a person possesses the qualities that are required to become an effective mass leader? We want 'smart' people to be our representatives. We expect our representatives to understand and act on the needs of an open system in society. We expect the winners to appreciate the value of their time as well as ours. We expect them to be mass leaders so that they can handle the complexities and expectations of large social groups. We also expect them not to bring politics in every walk of our life.

Another thing that we need to remember is that followers are as vital as leaders. We need to remember that "good leaders have good followers" and "vulnerable leaders have susceptible followers." If we follow and tolerate a bad leader, we will get the leadership we deserve. In fact, a manipulative follower intensifies a leader's vulnerability. There are people who are good followers, but not necessarily good leaders. Some don't even want to be one. But it is rare to find a good leader who was not efficient learner and a good follower. Being a follower must not stop one from thinking critically and impartially. A good follower tells palatable as well as bitter truths to the leader candidly and sensitively. The dynamics between leaders and followers is changing, and this change is changing the levels of expectations and sense of empowerment. Unless we prove to be good followers, good leaders would seem unlikely to emerge.

Drew Westen (147) says that political brain is an emotional brain. He says that the people make decisions with their feelings, not their brains, and that more than the ideas, emotions matter. If that is true, can then heredity and caste be neglected in electoral battles? Perhaps they can be.

Winners understand that responsibility is as important as freedom. Freedom is a necessity but we need to couple it with responsibility to forge a symbiotic relationship between them. More the freedom winners enjoy, greater the responsibility winners must bear. Unlimited freedom is as undesirable as imposed social responsibility is. Freedom is needed to grow, but it may cause an increase in social disorder. Responsibility tends to decrease this disorder, and thus is essential for maintaining stability in society. Responsibility is not a 'detachable burden', nor is it a 'popularity contest'. The responsibilities of the winners and the losers do not end with the end of electoral battle. In fact, responsibility starts the day battle is over or taken up.

Often, a person is assigned or takes up responsibilities disproportionate to his capabilities. There is a need to restrain this enthusiasm, while assigning and accepting responsibilities. It is easier to propagate a principle than to practice it. In order to follow the principles, particularly in matters related to public issues, courage is needed more than vigilance.

While rights of choice relate more to freedom, obligations are associated with responsibility. If we have the right to freedom, we must have the obligation to respect others' freedom. If we have the right to security, we must feel obliged to create conditions for every human being to enjoy that security. If we have a right to be educated, then we have the obligation to learn as much as our capabilities would allow us to and where possible, share our knowledge with others. If we have a right to participate in our country's political process and elect leaders, then we have the obligation to ensure that the best leaders are chosen.

Choosing the right political winners is our collective responsibility. It is our responsibility to periodically monitor the conduct and commitment of our leaders. One of the big problems our society faces is collective blindness. The collective blindness is when we all lose the ability to see, when the visible disappears in front of our eyes, when the society itself becomes blind. Jose Saramago writes, "I don't think we go blind, I think we are blind, blind, but seeing, blind people who can see, but do not see." Our leaders may have the freedom to act the way they choose to meet their ends, but it is our responsibility to remind them that we are neither invisible, even if they refuse to see us, nor can we be made invisible, even if they turn a blind eye to us. Let the power not blind our leaders.

Almost everything can be an asset as well as a liability. Virtually any positive trait when taken to extremes, or misapplied, can become a liability. Power is an asset as well as a liability. The powerful possess freedom to exercise many choices. As Kaushik Basu said, "If you lack talent, cultivate power. This will attract fawners around you and you will never again know you don't have talent." Power is generally seen as evil or unjust, but it is not always the case. The 'influence' of the powerful can have positive connotations. Michel

Foucault's concept of power involves both constraint and enablement. The powerful control their environment. They often forget that power is also a form of responsibility. But those who possess real power understand that responsibility is not a burden. They understand the value of restraint.

We all would agree that the opinion of the powerful matters a lot. We expect them to be extra careful when they deal with important public issues. We expect them to be vigilant, prudent and courageous when confronted with those issues. The powerful can't afford or pretend to be sleeping when time comes for action. We, the people, can't afford the luxury of such pretentious sleepers in responsible positions. Some of our leaders, after attaining power, attain the sense of responsibility. Accepting responsibilities disproportionately is not a good idea. One should not bear the burden of responsibilities more than her/his capacity allows.

Psychologists say power makes one less sympathetic to the concerns and emotions of others. Studies indicate that people in positions of authority rely more on stereotypes and generalisations when judging other people. Often the sense of power makes it easier for them to rationalise away the ethical lapse. Often the powerful become so powerful that they begin to think that they only have the right to do wrong things. They easily indulge in the misuse of power. They think rules are meant only for the commoners and not the privileged ones like them. They take it as an insult when they are treated as commoners. Power is not poison if one is not attached to it. The powerful need to understand that the power they are entrusted is to empower others.

The powerful often forget that the world is made of glass. The powerful should remember that they are occupying an important and responsible chair. They should respect the responsibility of the chair, as the decision of the person on the chair can affect so many other lives. Once a wise man told me that one should worship the chair one occupies. He should say to the chair, give me the strength and the balance so that I don't misuse the power bestowed on me. He believed this is the ethics of power in true sense.

We live in a world where we need to have large amount of optimism. We surely want to live more productive, more effective and more meaningful lives.

We want to live in a far more peaceful, stable, secure and loving environment. Some questions bother us — should we aspire to live in a perfect world when we are not perfect? Is it enough to blame our public figures for all our ills? Why should we value civility?

Civility simply means to be proper. It enables us to see 'what is right'. We like to follow standard civil behaviour because it helps to build community. As civility honours diversity, and accepts different perspectives, it offers an opportunity to open an active communication between people in an age of diversity, change and difference. We expect the virtues of civility be present in our citizens, and more so in our 'first citizens'.

It is possible to remain civil even in the 'me-first' world. Our world might have begun with 'me', but it need not end there. Cassandra Dahnke and Tomas Spath (148) say that "civility is claiming and caring for one's identity, needs and beliefs without degrading someone else's in the process". Civility is collective self-consciousness. If we recognise the concept of collective, we automatically value the concepts of diversity and difference. The concepts of diversity and difference are also the most powerful adversaries of civility. Diversity and difference may also imply openness to illiberal and uncivil modes of conduct, writes Clifford Orwin.

We can't overlook the role of leadership in maintaining civility. Ethical leadership needs ethical followers, and vice versa. Blaming the leadership for all our ills is not enough. We need leaders, as well as followers, who can combine passion and moral values. The problem is that we have "a horizonless mind of pragmatic and radical self-interest". We forget that our true self is found inside as well as outside, and as David Brooks notes, we are embedded creatures who find meaning and purpose in the context of living and working with others.

Civility promotes shared values. Communities break down and become crowd if there is loss of shared values among its constituents. We all like to be moral. We all have moral capacity. This capacity unfortunately is time, place, and circumstance dependent. The problem is that we find it hard to put the community or the organisation above ourselves. What we need to do is our periodic self-assessment.

Uncivil behaviour can be quite disturbing and depressing for many. There are many people who are concerned about the lack of civility in our society. The difficult part is to deal with it. More disturbing and depressing is the fact that incivility prevails the most of those places that are supposedly the guardians of civility.

This brings us to face another question — what kind of a world would we wish to live in? I don't know the answer. Let me present to you the imaginary world of Armory Lovins. In this world, "the war against the earth is over; where we've stopped treating soil like dirt, forests are expanding, farms emulate natural ecosystems, rivers run clean, oceans are starting to recover, fish and wildlife are returning, and a stabilising, radically resource-efficient human population needs ever less of the world's land and metabolism, leaving more for all the relatives who give us life." I find it difficult even to imagine such a world. Would we like to live in a world that is even difficult to imagine? I think we should. It will need infinite positivism to think of living in such a world.

Trustworthy and competent leadership is part of infinite positivism. We expect our politicians to be trustworthy. It is not a unique Indian phenomenon but a universal one. We expect from our representatives not to create problems for us. It is fine if they can't solve our problems. One who does not create problem is as good as the one who provides solutions.

Trust matters to practically every aspect of our daily life. We like to live in a social group. We have evolved to depend upon others. We are still evolving to resolve the dilemmas of group living. We need trustworthy companions and try to be trustworthy to others. A trustful mind is always in search of new methods to succeed in life. To become trustworthy, we need to cooperate with the self that is both selfish and selfless. We need to grapple with the conscious and unconscious minds. Trust has inherent risk, but then everything involves risk. The greatest risk is not to take risks. We hope to achieve more when we take risks. We take risks because benefits from potential risks often outweigh losses.

We try to gauge the trustworthiness of others. Similarly, others try to gauge our trustworthiness. In order to be trustworthy to others, we often suitably fine tune our conduct. Becoming trustworthy is the cumulative effect of our behaviour, and the conduct for our behaviour fluctuates. Our responsibility is to see that it fluctuates within limits and in a balanced manner. The quantum of trust depends upon how trust was built. Trust is context-specific. A person can be trusted in some contexts, but not necessarily in all the contexts. Trustworthiness, more often than not, is a function of ability, integrity, and benevolence of other person and that is why one person is more trustworthy than the other in a particular context. Trust also needs periodic check-ups. We must remember that excessive trust can be as dysfunctional as distrust is. Relationship experts say "trust is valuable insofar as it is appropriate to the context, and that a healthy amount of distrust can protect against the risk of exploitation".

Both trustworthiness and competence are needed to get noticed, or to gain favour. Competence is often overlooked because of its capacity to overshadow. So what matters more — competence or trust? Evolutionary psychologist Jacob Vigil says that it depends upon how much ability the other person has either to harm or help. A competent person needs opportunity and he must also have intention. In the absence of these, a competent person is of zero value. Vigil contends that the people having gone through life's various facets and phases without serious obstacles are more competency-oriented. On the other hand, for people who have faced setbacks of various kinds (such as illness and an unstable home environment, among others) trusting and caring is the route of choice to reach others. We need to carefully understand that, as Vigil said, "A demonstration of trust and a demonstration of capacity are equally plausible ways of manipulating other folks." It is our responsibility to see that our leaders don't get enough opportunity to manipulate us. We need not only competent but also trustworthy leadership.

We need fair performers for a society to function. We admire fairness and we try to be fair because we suffer from a "fairness instinct". Many times, we are fair even in situations that we know are going to cost us for being fair. But we also suffer from an "inequity aversion". We are acutely sensitive to "who is getting how much." Many of us pretend to be fair, while secretly hoping for a fair deal for the self. Real winners, however, know that one way of maximising one's payoff is to judiciously monitor the payoff of others. Real winners understand the necessity of providing a level playing field to all. They also know that all can't be winners. Equality of opportunity is not enough. It is also the efficiency that decides the winner.

The victors understand the real meaning of victory. Some of the worthy perceptions of victors are a good nose for talent and low tolerance of nonsense. A real victor cares for the struggles and dreams of ordinary people. They understand the difference between hope and hype; just a matter of one alphabet and how different the meaning is. Hope reaffirms optimism. The unrealistic expansion of hope results in hype. In some situations, particularly those where nothing works, hope works; it works like a drug. But we also know that drug overdose is generally dangerous. Let the victors promise only what they can deliver.

It will be good to the victors if they remember that in the victory of the people lies the secret of their success. Power makes one so self-centred that one becomes less concerned about others. The consequence of too much self-absorption is that one's concern slowly shifts away from the common welfare and public service to self-serving benefits. The victors need to balance the self-need with the concerns for others.

It feels good to believe that majority of the people are good and want to do the right things. It gives a good feeling to think that in a democratic setup, disagreement is not always a bad word, and every opponent is not a malevolent. It is good to remember that complex behaviours, such as politics, when tied to emotions can't be ruled out, nor can be predetermined. It is good to believe that the winners know that the ability to survive is not enough; a real winner has the capability to perform. The winners of the real world are made of "global genome, innovative mind and democratic spirit." The genome of the winners contain the genes of tolerance. The real winners have the ability to restore faith of the people in the nobility of politics and public service.

The real winners know that graceful entry is as essential. It is also good to know the meaning of graceful exit. Those who know what graceful exit means know that it means "leaving what's over without denying its value." We have also heard that every exit is an entry somewhere else. "Somewhere else" makes the winner as well as the loser hopeful as well as fearful.

It is said that hope, and fear can't occupy the same space, but the fact is that they do. We do certainly need a mind without fear to keep our head high. But we also need to be fearful. Evolution says that only those species survived who feared the right thing at the right time. As it is said, where there is no hope, there is no fear.

The winners win because they can instil hope in common man. Winners know that man can't live without hope. "Man can live about 40 days without food, about three days without water, about eight minutes without air, but only for one second without hope", said Andre Gide. Benjamin Franklin offered a different view: "He that lives upon hope will die fasting." Hope is a mix of emotion and illusion. Reasonable hope is constructive. Unreasonable hope is destructive. We must act without hope, is what Jean-Paul Sartre said. Sartre's hope is hope without any illusions; "One need not hope in order to undertake one's work."

Hope is finite. Optimism grows out of hope. Euphoria kills it. Daniel Kahneman says that most of us think ourselves to be smarter, more attractive, and more talented than the average, and that is one of the reasons we commonly overestimate our future successes. Once in a while, therefore, we need to wash our eyes by our tears so that we can see life with a clearer view again. Our shattered hopes sometimes work like our tears. Often, they help us to see life more clearly.

We commonly observe sharp differences in the ideologies of the winner and the loser. This clash of ideologies results in animosity and acrimonious debates between them. Can't we all disagree more constructively, asks Jonathan Haidt (149). Getting along despite differences seems to be a difficult proposition. It is because our morality binds and blinds us, writes Haidt. Our morality binds us to our group's ideologies. We tend to believe that our group follows the best ideology. We tend to reject alternate ideologies. Our morality "blinds us to the fact that each team is composed of good people who have something important to say." The two b's – bind and blind – lead us to 'groupish righteousness'.

Because of groupish righteousness, our moral foundations have different configurations and we 'agree to disagree'. The compatibility between two temperamentally different personalities is therefore, difficult.

A balanced mind is needed to overcome this difficulty. In a balanced mind, both empathising and systemising are equally strong. A balanced mind is disciplined, creative, ethical and respectful. Balanced minds can get along despite differences. A balanced mind respects the views of the other. A balanced mind is not so blind to the anomalies that exist in the group. A balanced mind is both a mirror and a window. It can see the self as well as others.

Do winners need special qualification? Does 'qualification' for a job only mean academic qualification?

If I have to get hired for a specific job, what would I look for myself in it? How would I know that I deserve the job or the job deserves me? Just as a lock should meet the requirement of the key and vice-versa, I would like to know if my credentials meet the requirements of the job. I would also like to know if I am aware of the short and long-term demands of the job.

Would I be dissatisfied if I'm unable to deliver what I promised? Or would I be happy with the perks that come along? I would make a list of the possible exit routes for me if I were not satisfied with my performance. The work culture of the place where I would be employed is extremely important, and I must know if I would fit in or not. How would I react in an inherently hostile atmosphere? Do I have the authority to change it, or I would change myself for the same? Will I have the freedom to establish the philosophy that the environment can be changed to suit one's requirement?

I must also know if I have the capability to 'control' uneasy situations. Can I take the blame when I am wrong? If I find someone is wrong, can I say so? This is a common situation we face at our workplace. We don't want to hurt someone because she, or he is our friend, but we fail to realise that by doing so, we are harming our friend even more.

Our world is rapidly changing. Our perception and expectation from people are also varying. It is a common phenomenon today that an individual is trained in one area but works in an entirely different field. Not only is she working in a different area, but also excelling in the chosen profession. We expect certain things from a particular person. If he does the task differently from our perception, we feel uncomfortable.

Should one be conversant or ignorant about the job one is getting into? Orson Welles said, "It's only when you know something about a profession, I think, that you're timid or careful." Charles Darwin believed that men who are very clever never originate anything.

Is there an age band when one's potential peaks? Some people think that some jobs are meant only for the 'young'. Some people, think after a person crosses a certain age, their capacity to work efficiently decreases. They think that the old are stereotyped, orthodox and rigid. I am not sure if Nirad Choudhury, who wrote Three Horsemen of the New Apocalypse shortly before his 100th birthday, was stereotyped, orthodox and rigid. Sculptor Louise Bourgeois produced her best when she was 84, who said, before that, she was not sophisticated enough to do so. For many, greatness blooms late. Perhaps late bloomers are exceptions.

To summarize, winners can shift attention to the right point at the right time and have the ability to capture collective attention and understand collective emotions. Winners know 'what is not important' is as important as 'what is important'. Winners have gut sense. Winners can disengage focus from comfort zones. Winners are alert to emerging patterns. Winners are self-aware, and can inspire and empathize. Winners know that system awareness is important but more important is self-awareness. Winners are attentive listeners. Winners can say 'no' when they are required to say so. Winners are not afraid to fail. Winners can anticipate people's reactions. Winners know that cognitive abilities are not enough. Non-cognitive competencies often outweigh purely cognitive talents. Winners know that having a good time is not a waste of time but a way to build emotional capital (150).

The winners are in a very precarious situation when there is no opposition for them. Ayn Rand thus described the predicament: "The question isn't who is going to let me; it's who is going to stop me." If no one is there to stop me, it should be my bounden duty to stop myself. If I must lead I must also follow.

NOTES

(1) John Tierney, Discovering the Virtues of a Wandering Mind, The New York Times, June 28, 2010.

(2) Mathew Killingworth, Daniel Gilbert, A Wandering Mind is an Unhappy Mind, Science, Nov 12, 2010.

(3) Jonathan Schooler, The Restless Mind, Psychological Bulletin, 132, 946, 2006.

(4) Brain Basics: Know Your Brain, Prepared by US National Institutes of Health.

(5) Janelle Weaver, Amygdala at the Centre of Your Social Network, Nature, December 26 2010.

(6) K O'Craven, N Kanwisher, Mental Imagery of Faces and Places Activates Corresponding Stimulus-Specific Brain Regions, Journal of Cognitive Neuroscience, Nov 1, 2000.

(7) David Eagleman, The Brain on Trial, The Atlantic, June 7, 2011.

(8) Derek Dean, Caroline Webb, Recovering from Information Overload, McKinsey Quarterly, January 2011.

(9) Nicholas Carr, IT Doesn't Matter, Harvard Business Review, May 2003.

(10) EDGE Annual Question, Has the Internet Changed the Way we Think, www.edge.org.

(11) Betsy Sparrow, Jenny Liu, DM Wegner, Google Effects on Memory: Cognitive Consequences of Having Information at our Fingertips, Science, August 5, 2011.

(12) Viktor Frankl, Man's Search for Meaning, Pocket Books, 1997.

(13)   Simon Baron-Cohen, Essential Difference: Men, Women and the Extreme Male Brain, Allen Lane, 2003.

(14)   Semir Zeki, JP Romaya, Neural Correlates of Hate, PLOS One, October 29, 2008.

(15)   Paul Zak, The Moral Molecule, Dutton Adult, 2012.

(16)   The Dark Side of Oxytocin, Association for Psychological Science.

(17)   Nicholas Wade, Depth of the Kindness Hormone Appears to Know Some Bounds, The New York Times, January 10, 2011.

(18)   CKW De Dreu, LL Greer, GA Van Kleef, S Shalvi, MJJ Handgraaf, Oxytocin Promotes Human Ethnocentrism, Proceedings National Academy of Sciences (US), 108(4), 1262, 2010.

(19)   Sonja Lyubomirsky, The How of Happiness, Penguin Books, 2008

(20)   JP Shonkoff, DA Phillips, Editors, From Neurons to Neighbourhoods, The Science of Early Childhood Development, National Academy Press, Washington.

(21)   Sarah-Jayne Blakemore, What should we be worried about, www. edge.org.

(22)   Richard Nisbett, The Geography of Thought, Free Press, 2004.

(23)   Bipin Chandra Pal, The Soul of India, Rupa Publications.

(24)   Steven Johnson, Mind Wide Open, Scribner, 2005.

(25)   Anne Marie Menting, The Chill of Fear, Harvard Medicine.

(26)   David Robson, Chaos and Brain, New Scientist, June 27, 2009.

(27)   Roy Baumeister, John Tierney, Willpower: Rediscovering the Greatest Human Strength, Penguin Books, 2011.

(28)   James Surowiecki, The Wisdom of Crowds, Abacus, 2005.

(29)   Gustave Le Bon, The Crowd: A study of the Popular Mind, Dover Publications, 2002.

(30)   John Armstrong, How to Worry Less About Money, Macmillan, 2012.

(31)   Daniel Ariely, Predictably Irrational, Harper Perennial, 2010.

(32)   George Lowenstein, S Rick, JD Cohen, Neuroeconomics, Ann. Rev. Psychol. 59, 647, 2008.

(33)   Daniel Gilbert, Stumbling on Happiness, Vintage, 2007

(34) M Pessiglione, L Schmidt, B Draganski, R Kalisch, H Lau, RJ Dolan, CD Faith, How the Brain Translates Money into Force, Science, May 11, 2007.

(35) Gerd Gigerenzer, Gut feelings: The intelligence of the unconscious, Penguin Books, 2008.

(36) Daniel Simons, Christopher Chabris, The Invisible Gorilla and Other Ways Our Intuitions deceive Us, HarperCollins, 2010.

(37) Dan Sperber, Hugo Mercier, Why do Humans Reason? Arguments for an Argumentative Theory, Behavioural and Brain Sciences, 2010.

(38) Gary Klein, Sources of Power and Intuition, Crown Business, 2004.

(39) Richard Wrangham, Catching Fire: How Cooking Made Us Human, Basic Books, 30 September 2010.

(40) Dan Hurley, A New Suspect in the Obesity Epidemic: Our Brains, Discovery, August 23, 2011.

(41) Michael Gazzaniga, The Ethical Brain, Harper Collins, 2006.

(42) Marc Hauser, Moral Minds: The Nature of Right and Wrong, Harper Perrenial, 2007.

(43) David Dobbs, The Science of Success, The Atlantic, Dec 1, 2009.

(44) L Fredholm, Pavlov's Dog, Nobleprize.org, May 15, 2001.

(45) Simon Keller, Limits of Loyalty, Cambridge University Press, 2007.

(46) Emory Westacott, Does Surveillance Make us Morally Better? Philosophy Now.org.

(47) Ian Leslie, Born liars: Why We Can't Live Without Deceit, Quercus, 2012.

(48) Julian Baggini, The Whole Truth, Prospect Magazine, April 20, 2011.

(49) Michael Shermer, The Believing Brain, Robinson, 2012.

(50) Jesse Bering, We are Programmed to Believe in a God, The Guardian, January 4, 2011.

(51) George Herbert Mead, Stanford Encyclopedia.

(52) Fritjof Capra, The Web of Life, Flamingo, 1997.

(53) Albert-László Barabási, Linked: The New Science of Networks.

(54) William Hirstein, Brain Fiction, MIT Press, 2006.

(55)   Yann Martel, Life of Pi, Mariner Books, 2003.

(56)   David Novitz, Knowledge, Fiction, and Imagination, Temple University Press, 1987.

(57)   Tilottama Rajan, The Supplement of Reading.

(58)   Daeyeol Lee, Daniel Salzman, Xiao- Jing Wang, The Neuroscience of Decision Making, The Kavli Foundation.

(59)   David DeSteno, The Truth About Trust: How It Determines Success in Life, Love, Learning, and More, Hudson Street Press, an imprint of Penguin Group, 2014.

(60)   John T. Cacioppo, Loneliness: Human Nature and the Need for Social Connection, W. W. Norton & Company.

(61)   Ellen Goldbaum, New Form of Brain Plasticity: Study Shows How Social Isolation Disrupts Myelin Production, University at Buffalo, November 12, 2012.

(62)   Mario Dalmaso, Giulia Pavan, Luigi Castelli and Giovanni Galfano, Social Status Gates Social Attention in Humans, Biology Letters, November 16, 2011.

(63)   Beatrice de Gelder, Uncanny sight in the blind, Scientific American, May 2010.

(64)   Jacques Lusseyran, And There Was Light, Floris Books, 1985.

(65)   Zoltan Torey, Out of Darkness: a Memoir, Picador, 2003.

(66)   Ralph Ellison, The invisible man, Penguin Classics, 2001.

(67)   Jose Saramago, Blindness, Vintage Classics, 2013.

(68)   Fritjof Capra, The Hidden Connections, Flamingo, 2010.

(69)   Keith Payne, Your Hidden Censor: What Your Mind Will Not Let You See, Scientific American Jun 11, 2013.

(70)   Vilanayur Ramachandran, The Tell-Tale Brain, Windmill Books, 2012.

(71)   Jared Diamond, Collapse: How Societies Choose to Fail or Succeed, Penguin, 30 Jun 2011.

(72)   Monika Ardelt, Wisdom as Expert Knowledge System: A Critical Review of a Contemporary Operationalization of an Ancient Concept, Human Development, 47, 257, 2004.

(73) Steven Pinker, The Better Angels of Our Nature: Why Violence Has Declined, Penguin, 2012.

(74) Debra Niehoff, The Biology of Violence, Free Press, 1999.

(75) Michael Dirda, Classics of Pleasure, Harcourt Trade, 2007.

(76) Kenneth MacLeish, Longman Guide to Shakespeare's Characters, Longman Trade/Caroline House, 1985.

(77) Edward Hoagland, On Friendship, American Scholar, Winter, 2013.

(78) John Mac-Murray, Reason and Emotion, Humanity Books, 1999.

(79) Stephen Covey, 7 Habits of Highly Effective People, Simon & Schuster, 2013.

(80) Roy Baumeister, Can Virtuous Habits Be Cultivated, Big Question Online, July 24, 2012.

(81) Joe Moran, The Crystalline Wall, aeon Magazine, July 17, 2013.

(82) Ad Vingerhoets, Why Only Humans Weep, Oxford University Press, 2013.

(83) Thomas Dixon, The Waterworks, aeon Magazine, February 22, 2013.

(84) Sandor Feldman, Crying at the Happy Ending.

(85) Jonathan Rottenberg, Lauren M. Bylsma, Ad J.J.M. Vingerhoets, Is Crying Beneficial, Current Directions in Psychological Science, 17, 400. 2008.

(86) Charles Darwin, In the Expression of Emotions in Man and Animals, Create Space Independent Publishing Platform, 2012.

(87) Paul Lawrence, Nitin Nohria, Driven, Jossey-Bass, 2002

(88) Arnold Modell, Imagination and the Meaningful Brain, A Bradford Book, 2006.

(89) Friedrich Schiller, On the Aesthetic Education of Man, Dover Publications, 2004.

(90) Arthur Martine, Hand-book of Etiquette and Guide to True Politeness.

(91) Sherry Turkle, Alone Together: Why We Expect More from Technology and Less from Each Other, Basic Books, 2012.

(92) Phil McKinney, Beyond the Obvious, Hyperion, 2012.

(93)   Tony Wagner, The Global Achievement Gap: Why Even Our Best Schools Don't Teach The New Survival Skills Our Children Need, Basic Books, 2010.

(94)   Gemma Elwin Harris, Big Questions from Little People, Ecco, 2012.

(95)   Ernst Schumacher, A Guide for the Perplexed, Harper Perennial, 1978.

(96)   Nathaniel Hawthorne, The Birth-Mark.

(97)   Howard Gardner, Five Minds for the Future, Harvard Business Review Press, 2009.

(98)   David M Eagleman, Brain Time, Edge, June 23, 2009.

(99)   Claudia Hammond, Time Warped: Unlocking the Mysteries of Time Perception, Harper Perennial, 2013.

(100) Biman Basu, Astrology: Sense or Nonsense, National Book Trust, 2008.

(101) Robert Thouless, Straight and Crooked Thinking, Hodder & Stoughton, 2011.

(102) Arthur Schopenhauer, The Art of Controversy.

(103) Emrys Westacott, Does Surveillance Make Us Morally Better? Philosophy Now, 2010.

(104) Joseph Hallinan, How We Look Without Seeing, Forget Things In Seconds. Why We Make Mistakes: How We Look Without Seeing, Forget Things in Seconds, and Are All Pretty Sure We Are Way Above Average, Broadway Books, 2010.

(105) Peter Toohey, Boredom: A Lively History, Yale University Press, 2012.

(106) Simon Baron-Cohen, Testosterone on my Mind ans in my Brain, Edge, April 30, 2012.

(107) Henry Tajfel, John Turner, An integrative theory of intergroup conflict, The Social Psychology of Intergroup Relations, 33, 47, 1979.

(108) Jennifer Kubota, Mahzarin Banaji, Elizabeth Phelps, The Neuroscience of Race, Nat Neurosci. Jun 26, 2012.

(109) Melissa McDonald, Carlos Navarrete, Mark Van Vugt, Evolution and the Psychology of Intergroup Conflict: The Male Warrior Hypothesis, Philosophical Transactions of the Royal Society B, January 23, 2012.

(110) Aneesha Dharwadekar, The Nature of Truth and Time, www.arts. cornell.edu.

(111) Samuel Arbesman, The Half-Life of Facts.

(112) Joseph Hallinan, Why We Make Mistakes: How We Look Without Seeing, Forget Things in Seconds and Are All Pretty Sure We Are Way Above Average, Broadway Books, 2010.

(113) Stephen Hall, Wisdom: From Philosophy to Neuroscience, Knopf, 2010.

(114) Daniel Schacter, The Seven Sins of Memory: How the Mind Forgets and Remembers, Mariner Books, 2002.

(115) Daniela Schiller, Marie-H. Monfils, Candace M. Raio, David C. Johnson, Joseph E. LeDoux, Elizabeth A. Phelps, Preventing the Return of Fear in Humans Using Reconsolidation Update Mechanisms, Nature 463, 49, 2010.

(116) Stephen S Hall, Repairing Bad Memories, MIT Technology Review, June 17, 2013.

(117) Michael Sandel, What Money Can't Buy: The Moral Limits of Markets, Farrar, 2013.

(118) Nina Mazar, On Amir, Dan Ariely, The Dishonesty of Honest People: A Theory of Self-Concept Maintenance, Journal of Marketing Research, Dec 2008.

(119) Donald Hoffman, Visual Intelligence, W. W. Norton & Company, 2000.

(120) Robert Provine, Curious Behaviour, Belknap Press, 2012.

(121) Mary Catherine Bateson, Composing a Further Life, Vintage, 2011.

(122) Michio Kaku, The Future of Mind, Doubleday, 2014.

(123) Sri Aurobindo, On Education. Sir Aurobindo Education Society, Pondicherry.

(124) Budhadev Bose, The Bokok of Yudhisthir (Translated from Bengali by Sujit Mukherjee), Parabas.com.

(125) Alison Fleming, The Mind of a Mother, Edge (University of Toronto), Winter 2013.

(126) Nancy Verrier, The Primal Wound: Understanding the Adopted Child, Verrier Publishing, 1993.

(127) Thomas Verny, John Kelly, The Secret Life of the Unborn Child, Dell, 1982.

(128) Sharon Heller, The Vital Touch, Holt Paperbacks, 1997.

(129) Jonathan Leake, Women are Getting More Beautiful, The Sunday Times, July 26, 2009.

(130) Catherine Hakim, Honey Money: The Power of Erotic Capital, Penguin, 2011.

(131) Ketaki Kushari Dyson, Sushobhan Adhikary, Adrian Hill, Robert Dyson, Tagore of Colours/ A Study of the Use of Colour in the Writings and Art of Rabindranath Tagore.

(132) Oliver Sacks, The Island of the Colourblind and Cycad Island, Picador, 2011.

(133) Daniel Levitin, This is Your Brain on Music, Plume, 2007.

(134) Oliver Sacks, Musicophilia, Vintage, 2008.

(135) Gary Marcus, Guitar Zero: The New Musician.

(136) Geoffrey Miller, The Mating Mind: How Sexual Choice Shaped the Evolution of Human Nature, Anchor, 2001.

(137) Matthew Hurley, Daniel Dennett, Reginald Adams Jr, Inside Jokes: Using Humour to Reverse-Engineer the Mind, The MIT Press, 2011.

(138) Richard Restak, Playful Brain, Riverhead Trade, 2011.

(139) Simon Critchley, On Humour, Routledge, 2002.

(140) A Conversation with Dr Richard Kogan, Psychiatric Times, November 29, 2010.

(141) R Keith Sawyer, Explaining Creativity: The Science of Human Innovation, Oxford University Press, 2012.

(142) Dean Keith Simonton, Creativity in Science, Cambridge University Press, 2004.

(143) Marcel Danesi, The Puzzle Instinct: The Meaning of Puzzles in Human Life, Indiana University Press, 2004.

(144) Jeff and Julie Crabtree, Living With a Creative Mind, Zebra Collective, 2011.

(145) Todd Kashdan, Curious, Harper Perennial, 2010.

(146) Gregory Berns, Iconoclasts, Harvard Business Review Press, 2010.

(147) Drew Westen, The Political Brain, PublicAffairs, 2008.

(148) Cassandra Dahnke and Tomas Spath, Reclaiming Civility in the Public Square – 10 Rules That Work.

(149) Jonathan Haidt, The Righteous Mind, Vintage, 2013.

(150) Daniel Golman, Focus, The Hidden Driver of Excellence, Bloomsbury India, 2014.